Bodies
of
Life

Bodies
of
Life

Shaker Literature
and Literacies

ETTA M. MADDEN

Contributions to the Study of Religion, Number 52
Henry Warner Bowden, Series Editor

GREENWOOD PRESS
Westport, Connecticut • London

PS
153
.S54
M33
1998

Library of Congress Cataloging-in-Publication Data

Madden, Etta M., 1962–
     Bodies of life : Shaker literature and literacies / Etta M.
Madden.
          p.   cm.—(Contributions to the study of religion, ISSN
0196–7053 ; no. 52)
     Includes bibliographical references and index.
     ISBN 0–313–30303–7 (alk. paper)
     1. American literature—Shaker authors—History and criticism.
2. Christian literature, American—History and criticism.
3. Christianity and literature—United States.   4. Shakers—United
States—Intellectual life.   5. Shakers—United States—Books and
reading.   6. Christian communities in literature.   7. Christian life
in literature.   8. Shakers—In literature.   9. Sects in literature.
I. Title.   II. Series.
PS153.S54M33   1998
289′.8—dc21   97–30110

British Library Cataloguing in Publication Data is available.

Library of Congress Catalog Card Number: 97–30110
ISBN: 0–313–30303–7
ISSN: 0196–7053

First published in 1998

Greenwood Press, 88 Post Road West, Westport, CT 06881
An imprint of Greenwood Publishing Group, Inc.

Printed in the United States of America

The paper used in this book complies with the
Permanent Paper Standard issued by the National
Information Standards Organization (Z39.48–1984).

10 9 8 7 6 5 4 3 2 1

09109 8 - 11

To my mother's father and to my father, for believing in their daughters

Contents

Preface

Memories of my childhood days in Arkansas reverberate with phrases I heard repeatedly in the church services and Bible classes I attended three times weekly: "We speak where the Bible speaks, and we are silent where the Bible is silent"; "we let the Bible interpret itself." Long before I questioned those phrases, I wondered about the interpretations of Scripture handed to me by church leaders and teachers. Like bittersweet pills, the interpretations promised to provide an antidote to the spiritual ills caused by ignorance of proper Bible reading. Those powerful pills penetrated my blood, making me the person who, many years later, chose to explore religious communities whose attitudes toward literacy and whose daily practices seemed so different from those of religious communities I had experienced. A portion of that exploration appears here.

Though my understanding of the relationship between reading, writing, and spirituality is incomplete, I believe that these published pages provide insights to literacies and spirituality that should enrich the visions of those perusing them.

As with any book, the numerous teachers, friends, and mentors who influenced this work are beyond acknowledgment here. Nonetheless I note those who assisted directly with the formation of the questions, research in the archives, and shaping of the text before you.

Most recently, during the final phases of the book's completion, the faculty of the Department of English and the administration at Southwest Missouri State University have supported me intellectually, emotionally, and financially. I especially appreciate the Graduate College's Summer Faculty Fellowship, Rosemary Curb's graciousness with my teaching schedule, and Jane Hoogestraat's sensitive and always open ears and eyes. As a quick and eager to learn graduate student, Joe Goeke has more than ably assisted in the book's production.

The University of New Hampshire also provided, during my many years of graduate work, financial support that enabled me to begin and move through most of this project. A Summer Fellowship for Teaching Assistants and a Dissertation Year Fellowship from the Graduate School of Arts and Sciences allowed me to begin and then to fully immerse myself in a study of the Shakers. Several at the University deserve thanks for their intellectual insights: the dissertation writers group in the Department of English persistently muddled through early chapter drafts. Professor Susan Scibanoff, Michael Pugh, Anne Downey, Bill Sayres, and Lisa Sisco consistently puzzled together my fragmented analyses. Professors Tom Newkirk, John Ernest, and Sarah Sherman, also at the University of New Hampshire, provoked refinements in my thinking after reading an early version of the full manuscript.

Many Shaker scholars offered suggestions that provoked the research and writing to varying degrees; in addition to offering specific advice, Jean Humez, Jerry Grant, Jane Crosthwaite, Diane Sasson, and Stephen Stein served as exemplars of those who had "been there." Jean Humez, in particular, willingly responded to my ideas and my writing at several stages; her insights, I believe, have made this book more rigorous and readable. Suzanne Thurman's collegiality was like cool water in a dry land during the last year of writing. Archivists at libraries holding Shaker materials not only handed me necessary sources but also, sometimes serendepitously, provided information beyond my requests that extended and enriched my work: Paige Lilly and Anne Gilbert at Sabbathday Lake, Maine; Renee Fox at Canterbury, New Hampshire; and numerous staff members in Media Services and the Special Collections of the University of New Hampshire's Dimond Library.

I owe many thanks to the University of New Hampshire's Professor David Watters, who, perceiving my questions and research interests long before I could articulate them clearly, supported my fascination with religious communities and introduced me to Shaker literature. His patience in reading my writing and his professional counsel exceeded that of anyone else.

Finally, two others have influenced my life in ways that made this book possible: By his example my father, Joe Madden, encouraged not only my reading and critical thinking but also my faith, hope, and vision; and Neil Guion's daily patience and companionship during the past ten years have sustained my mind, body, and spirit.

Abbreviations

The following abbreviations refer to archives that hold Shaker manuscripts and to bibliographies of Shaker materials.

MPB   Berkshire Athenaeum, Pittsfield, Massachusetts
DeWint   Henry Francis du Pont Winterthur Museum, Winterthur, Delaware
R   Richmond, Mary L., ed. *Shaker Literature: A Bibliography.*
MeSl   United Society of Shakers, Sabbathday Lake, Maine
NhCa   Shaker Village, Canterbury, New Hampshire
OClWHi   Western Reserve Historical Society, Cleveland, Ohio

Introduction

According to Shaker histories, in 1780 an illiterate woman from England named Ann Lee, who had journeyed to America with a handful of kindred souls, opened her testimony against the flesh. Emerging from her mystical, visionary experiences, Lee's testimony became best known as a message of celibacy, motivated by the second appearance of Christ within her and adhered to by her followers. Derisively called the Shakers by skeptical outsiders who labeled them such due to the dancing and ecstatic gestures of their gatherings, members of the sect later referred to themselves as the United Society of Believers in Christ's Second Appearing, or Believers.

Believers have continually looked at the story of Ann Lee as a cornerstone of the theological architecture that has distinguished their church from other American religious groups. In addition to celibacy and communal living in rural, supposedly "simple" villages, the Shakers have come to be known for their institutionally sanctioned male and female leaders, dually gendered godhead, and belief in continual divine revelation. Shaker theology, its manifestations in material artifacts such as furniture and oval boxes, and the Ann Lee story have continually drawn the attention of outsiders either fascinated with or repulsed by them. Lee's controversial testimony based on mystical experiences, her lack of a single domestic site or "home," and her eventual lack of a husband contributed to both her power and her persecution.

Growing from a persecuted band of seven individuals in Revolutionary America to some 4,000 members in sixteen communities in the 1820s, the Shakers peaked numerically near 6,000 at mid-century, before steadily declining in number.[1] A community of fewer than a dozen lives today at Sabbathday Lake, Maine. This numerical history also has captured the attention of outsiders—referred to by Shakers as "the world"—and invited speculation about the growth and demise of religious institutions. One proposed reason for the decline is celibacy, since many institutions depend on members' offspring to provide growth and sustenance. Another possible factor is the increase in literacy among Believers.

During the periods of numerical growth and the first fifty years of decline, the religious group's literary practices shifted from Bible reading in a culture dominated by oral modes of communication to reading and writing in a variety of genres. Following Ann Lee's biblically based but orally conveyed teachings of the 1770s and 1780s, with the publication of *A Concise Statement of the Principles of the Only True Church* ([Meacham] 1790), Shaker leaders initiated a phase of writing and reading practices dominated by the inscription and interpretation of doctrinal works and personal testimonies—genres meant to further the cause of the church. From 1827 onward, the varieties of texts written and read within Shaker communities increased to include, in addition to an abundance of records of daily affairs, "spirit messages" inscribed during the revival known as the Era of Manifestations; sentimental, occasional verse, quite typical of American culture at large; newspapers and periodicals; and even fiction from the world. Today the Shakers' doctrinal works, testimonies, letters, journals, poetry, hymns, recipes, scrapbooks, and the like comprise several collections that contain more than 12,000 imprints and manuscripts.[2] Thus the Shakers' increasing literacy and literary practices suggest some association with their numerical growth and decline.

These records indicate that from the early days of Lee, Shaker leaders have, to a degree, controlled the *kinds* of texts Believers have written and read, the *situations* in which the writing and reading acts have occurred, and the *ways* in which Believers have written and read. Although some left the sect because the leadership did not assuage their desires to read and write freely, some remained, content with practices that drove others away and that they were able to digest as spiritual nourishment. Ann Lee's influence upon these later Shakers and the historically and geographically specific story of the illiterate woman's leadership evoked in me a transhistorical question: What are the relationships among reading, writing, and religious life? Deprivation theories that have asserted that people turn to religious beliefs to fulfill some type of need or lack—psychological, economic, physical, educational, and so forth—suggest that less educated or less literate individuals tend to be more religious or more spiritually inclined. At least, these educationally deprived people choose less reasonable religious practices than those who are more educated or more literate.[3] Yet hasty assertions such as these, which fail "to discern the meaning of literacy" and "preempt criticism and investigation" with assumptions (3), contribute to what Harvey J. Graff calls "the literacy myth." According to Graff, whose study of nineteenth-century culture demonstrates the myth's inconsistencies, it is the belief that literacy is a major contributing factor to societal and individual "progress"—"a basic human right and a tool for productive citizenship and fulfilling lives" (3). Applied to the Shakers, for example, the myth implies that illiterate Believers neither were productive American citizens nor led fulfilling lives; additionally, it suggests that increasing literacy led to the sect's "progress," which corresponded with its numerical decline.

This second implication, especially, is a paradox that I sought to untangle, for the Shakers themselves have claimed to believe in progress and to see their own history as reflecting the continual unfolding of spiritual truth. Their lesser numbers of the twentieth century demonstrate, as Anna White and Leila Taylor wrote in

1904, a new age of Shakerism, in which the church would appear as spiritually strong as ever, though in new form. This prophecy continues to be heard today by those who listen to the voices of the texts the Society publishes, sounding forth with ecumenical notes. Yet is the dissolution and disappearance of Believers' bodies from their communal villages a reflection of progress?

My purpose here is neither to determine whether the Shakers have "progressed" nor to prove or disprove the literacy myth. Rather, I want readers of this work, whom I envision as not only those interested in the Shakers and religious life but also those interested in literacy and American culture, to come to a better understanding of the ways in which literacies enrich people's lives. I discovered, first, that the increase in literary acts, especially after 1850, which appears to contribute to an emphasis on individualism and the fragmentation of the Shaker church, also actually allows them to revise their theology so that they see Shakerism as continuing to grow rather than as in numerical decline. Second, I discovered that multiple kinds of reading and writing acts reinforce the beliefs of these individual Shakers and the church as a whole.

The method of exploration I employed that led to these conclusions about Shaker literacies emerged from Graff's work as well as from other literacy studies that have appeared during the past two decades.[4] Only detailed and qualitative rather than merely quantitative analysis of any social group—and individuals comprising it—during a given historical period may enrich our understanding of the role of literacy within it. As Graff writes, "To consider any of the ways in which literacy intersects with social, political, economic, cultural, or psychological life . . . requires excursions into . . . records" other than ones easily quantified (16–17). Since I began this project, two other brief analyses of the Shakers and their literacies have appeared, employing Graff's call to interdisciplinary approaches. Both John E. Murray's and Kathryn M. Olson's works deserve mention here because their projects more nearly correspond to the purposes of this project than any other published works on the Shakers to date. Murray argues in his study of the Shaker villages of North Union, Ohio, and South Union, Kentucky, that after 1820 the "new entrants [to Shakerism] tended to be less literate than both established Shakers and people in nearby areas" ("Human Capital in Religious Communes," 217). He argues that illiterate or less literate converts to the church in these communities and in this period were drawn to the institution's economic shelter; they sought a "free ride" because literacy was becoming more prevalent and necessary for survival in the world of the West. As Murray points out, "Religious beliefs and economic incentives each affect choices made by individuals" (217). He concludes, "One hitherto neglected source of Shaker decline may have been the *changing quality* of members" (232, emphasis mine). Thus he associates literacy levels with conversion as well as with apostasy and the sect's numerical decline. Olson, in contrast, considers epistemological attributes rather than economic ones. Olson provides a close reading of the *Manifesto,* the monthly periodical published from 1871 to 1899, to argue that through "dissociation"—"an ingenious rhetorical move" or, in other words, a particular way of reading and writing, the Shakers resist reading their numerical decline as empirical evidence of their spiritual failure.

As different as these two works appear in methodology and historical scope, their concerns dovetail with mine by centering upon literacies and their relationship to numerical decline and spiritual fervor.

As this book's subtitle suggests, my approach to answering questions of the relationships between the Shakers' literacies and their spirituality follows more closely the path of Olson's work than Murray's. Rather than counting signatures and comparing them to membership records, for example, I explore records I call the Shakers' literature—not literature simply in the traditional sense of *belles lettres,* but works of prose and poetry that provide insights to the sect's literacies. Cathy N. Davidson forged such a link between a culture's literature and its literacies in *Revolution and the Word* by defining literature as "not simply words upon a page but a complex social, political, and material process of cultural production" (viii). She suggested to me by her example that readers and writers and their interpretive and expressive acts are objects worthy of inclusion in the analysis of the material artifacts referred to as literature.

Such an historically grounded analysis of Shaker reading and writing practices and Shaker texts posed some difficulties. First was the problem of the sheer number and diversity of texts that exist. Since my question was not as narrow as Davidson's question about novel reading in revolutionary America, I did not limit myself to reading one genre nor to the texts of one historical moment. As I absorbed from these numerous and diverse texts shifts in Shaker theology and lifestyles from the late eighteenth through the early twentieth century and details about individual writers and Shaker genres, my initial question of the role of writing and reading in religious life splintered into sharper ones. I came to ask, for example, how do gendered ways of writing, reading, and knowing influence spiritual life? How do particular genres function in religious communities? What impact does a religious leader's literacy have upon her followers? And what role does Shaker theology of the spirit and its relationship to the body play in writing and reading?[5]

This final question deserves added explanation. Recent literacy studies and my own experiences have emphasized people's bodies as integral to reading and writing processes. These encompass more than the psychoanalytic emphases of sexuality and parent-child bonding, often prescribed as overarching, universal keys that allow readers to decode the reasons for human behavior. Rather, recent emphases upon the roles of culturally constructed codes upon gendered, sexual, and class relations have produced insightful semiotic readings of such material signs as dress and body language in a variety of settings; the performances of elementary school reading circles and the multiple, interactive audiences of college composition classrooms have been the subjects of recent literacy studies, for example. The ethnographic methodology—the Geertzian "thick description" (5–30) of some such exemplary studies, impossible to duplicate in explorations of communities of the past, presented the problem of reconstructing bodily involvement in the Shakers' reading and writing. The varied pictures of Shaker literacies I sketch in the chapters that follow emerge primarily from the sect's surviving literature: the genres or kinds of texts they wrote and read at particular historical moments; information about the lives of the authors of these texts; and statements Shakers made about the ways in which their writing and reading practices occurred—the social and physical settings as well as the manners and methods of interpretation, vocalization, and inscription they used. The examples discussed demonstrate that not only one-time bodily events such as the loss of loved ones but also recurring bodily rituals and sustained physical suffering due to spiritual beliefs empowered writing and reading subjects in Shaker communities.

The Shakers' bodily involvement in their literacies is important not merely because recent literacy studies have dictated that we need consider this element of reading and writing but, more importantly, because the sect's belief system points to it. The Shakers' theology, from their early days, suggested the body's significance to a person's spirituality; a Believer's body was also involved in his or her literacy. Kathleen Deignan and Robley Whitson have argued that this sect-specific theology of the embodied Holy Spirit, the belief in the *paraousia,* or the "being present" of the Deity and the divine spirit, distinguishes the Shakers from other sects and gives them continuity and power today. Extending their forceful arguments, I assert that this theology contributes to the Shakers' acceptance of many kinds of reading and writing, all of which depend upon the spirit's active and embodied presence.[6]

This intertwining of body and spirit with many kinds of literacies was manifested and exemplified in the story of Ann Lee's life. I use the plural "literacies" to underscore variety, interpretive acts involving more than inscribed texts. As I illuminate in Chapter 2, "Letter, Spirits, and Bodies," Lee's example of rational, traditional, emotional, and innovative interpretive acts, which blur boundaries often gendered masculine and feminine, recur throughout the Shaker texts I examine. As recorded in the biographical 1816 *Testimonies,* Lee "reads" uninscribed texts such as visions, people's minds, and their bodies; through her speech she "publishes" mini-sermons. All these actions exhibit a blend of reason and emotion that depend upon people's minds as well as their bodies. The literacies Lee exhibits involve her own body and mind, the bodies and minds of the human "texts" she reads, and the bodies and minds of those in her audiences. Further, they illustrate the interplay of orality and literacy. My analysis of these literacies as they appear in inscribed texts demonstrates varieties of literary experiences over time, from Believer to Believer, and even within individual Believers' lives.

Although the Shakers' literary endeavors have shifted, as I describe in the chronological survey of Chapter 1, "Varieties of Literary Experiences," two consistent elements of Shaker literacies emerge. The first is a willingness to submit to communal control, however indirectly exerted or subtly experienced, because of a belief in the idea of the community—of idealized images of the institution and individuals within it. Chief among these is Ann Lee. The second, in a symbiotic relationship with the first, is the belief in the presence of an embodied spirit. These beliefs, I explain with the historical, theological, and epistemological perspectives of the first two chapters, give the Shakers' hermeneutic a unique shape.

The case studies of the remaining chapters, informed but not restricted by this introductory material, illustrate the most important points of this study. The varied Shaker literacies and literature depend not only upon a belief in the presence of the

Christ Spirit as initially exemplified in Lee but also upon the religious imagination as it draws from memories—memories of idealized images of individuals and of the institution. These images become communal constructs as Believers hand them down orally, in writing, and through bodily performance. The spiritual power of the literature and literacies of the present—for individuals and their communities—I argue, comes from remembering and reinscribing the past. Thus in Chapters 3 through 7 I analyze the writing and reading of texts that explicitly reconstruct aspects of the lives of particular Shakers and the collective body of Believers: doctrinal treatises, histories, biographies, autobiographies, and elegies. Influenced partially because the Shakers wrote no "fiction," this selection of "nonfictional" genres assists us more aptly in exploring the role of writing and reading in individuals' spiritual lives; no explicit "veil of fiction" between writer and perceived or invoked audience exists to complicate an already difficult analysis. The selected "authors" or writing and reading subjects, faithful for lengthy periods in spite of what many outsiders and apostates saw as repressive literary practices, help us to understand how the writing and reading of idealized images of individuals and the institution enhanced their Shaker travels.

Richard McNemar's narrative history and John Dunlavy's dense and lengthy theological treatise, for example, present the sect's sanctioned hermeneutic as "reasoned" from Scripture and imply that many, if not all, Shakers use such reasoning and have such literary skills. Yet these examples vary greatly from the pictures other Shaker works present. Although Ann Lee does not appear explicitly within the texts, the controversial female figure emerges as the "absent presence" that controls and shapes McNemar's and Dunlavy's faith-strengthening defenses of the Shaker church. Additionally, the works suggest the significance of personal experience for each writer. They strengthen themselves as well as the church by delineating the doctrinal differences of those within from those without.

Though published in the same period and compiled by other male writers, the generically amphibious 1816 *Testimonies* elicits analysis of leaders' and readers' reasoning and their responses to the stories of Ann Lee. In Chapter 4, subtitled "Writing and Readings of the 1816 *Testimonies*," I suggest that the editors' construction of the narrative depends upon their own literacies and those they imagined other Believers possessed: an awareness of such popular spiritual and sentimental narratives as John Bunyan's *Pilgrim's Progress*, Mary Rowlandson's *Narrative of Captivity and Restauration*, and Susanna Rowson's *Charlotte Temple*. They selected and arranged images of female piety, such as physical suffering, to counter accusations of sexual sin and unfeminine behavior the world levied against Lee and the Shakers. They omitted references to these accusations because of their awareness of the ability of even verbal depictions of sexuality to disrupt the narrative. Complementing these pious images of Lee, other images depict her as transgressing the sacred and secular boundaries of "woman's sphere," marking her as a woman of difference.

Both kinds of imagery—"canonized" in print after 1816 but continually handed down orally—inform the spiritual literacies of Shakers such as African-American Rebecca Cox Jackson and her white editor, Alonzo Giles Hollister. Jackson's and

Hollister's physical experiences differed radically not only because of their genders and races but also because of the time periods in which they were involved with the Shakers. Jackson's personal testimony exemplifies the genre used at mid-century primarily for internal strengthening; Hollister's writing, more heavily saturated than Jackson's with the world's literary discourses, reflects the Shakers' employment of the world's devices to preserve spiritual literacies around the end of the nineteenth century. He continues the "masculine" tradition of apologetic writing leaders such as McNemar and Dunlavy established, but he self-consciously creates an archive for researchers rather than an evangelical library for possible converts. Yet in spite of their radically different experiences and literacies, both Jackson and Hollister, discussed in Chapter 5, underscore the impact of Lee's androgynous spiritual literacy upon Believers throughout the second half of the nineteenth century. Even while the writers work within the constraints of Shakerism, their literacies blur gender boundaries, provide freedom for creativity, and offer spiritual sustenance.

Like Alonzo Hollister in some ways, Emeline Kimball created a repository of the Canterbury, New Hampshire, community that exhibits literacies that blur gender boundaries. Known as physician and nurse at Canterbury, Kimball blended scientific and sentimental elements of spirituality as the primary compositor of the three-volume *Obituary Journal,* a manuscript record that contains more than 400 elegies to deceased Shakers. These poems demonstrate the Shakers' paradoxical attitudes toward physical bodies and their roles in spirituality, as they use images of physical bodies and the physicality of pen and paper to embody the spirits of deceased Shakers. The *Journal* also reflects the increasing sense of individualism, fragmentation, and loss within Shaker communities after the mid-nineteenth century. By binding these poems into volumes, the compositors of the *Obituary Journal* demonstrate the Shakers' strategy and ability to unify and strengthen individuals within the community through reading and writing rituals. Yet while these poems preserve Believers, they also demonstrate Shaker awareness of the world's literacies and funerary literature as they mimic popular nineteenth century elegies. Thus they illuminate how the Shakers reach out to the world even as they attempt to strengthen their own circle.

Anna White and Leila Taylor illustrate this simultaneous double vision in *Shakerism: Its Meaning and Message* (1904) as they reach back into the sect's past and look forward to its future. In my concluding chapter, "Private Acts and Possible Worlds: Shaker Literacies at the Turn of the Century," I argue that these well-educated women retell the stories of Ann Lee's literacies, Shaker reading and writing practices, and Shaker spirituality in a way that sketches the sect as progressive, rational, and scientific. White and Taylor, like many Believers prior to them, point to the importance of ecstatic gifts and uninscribed "reading" and "publishing" while they illustrate the importance of reason, education, and alphabetic literacy. Their belief in an active, living spirit both grounds and energizes the prophetic and evangelical text.

Analyses of the lives of Shakers such as Leila Taylor, Emeline Kimball, Alonzo Hollister, John Dunlavy, Rebecca Jackson, Richard McNemar, and Ann Lee, and the inscribed texts that construct and reflect these lives, demonstrate the complexity of individuals' literacies; simultaneously, they show that the Shakers' multiple kinds of writing and reading practices problematize dichotomies often associated with reading and writing acts. Among works on reading, for example, Davidson refers to reading as an act of "production" as opposed to "consumption"; Roland Barthes uses the term "writerly" to describe the kind of text in which a reader actively creates or produces meaning; Graff explains that critics of literacy distinguish between "critical" reading and "functional" reading, the former being the more "productive" type.[7] Such "productive" writing and reading acts occur within Shakerism, but equally empowering "passive" and "mechanical" writing and reading acts accompany them. The Shakers' literacies—what I call their "spiritual literacies"—ask us to view these apparently oppositional realms as symbiotic and to see the boundaries between them as permeable. Thus this book should contribute to the field of literacy studies not only pictures of Shaker literacies but also reminders of the many dimensions of reading and writing as it asserts the role of readers' and writers' bodies in their interpretive and expressive acts. These emphases emerge from the Shakers' association of the spirit with neither side of the oppositional mind-body dichotomy but as a unifying third term—Shakers associate spirits and spirituality with both minds and bodies.

My emphasis on the spirit's role in this study of Shaker literacies and literature contributes to the growing field of Shaker scholarship in two areas. With its focus on spirituality in addition to the material artifacts of textual production, my work joins those studies that have emphasized the Shakers' theology and lived experiences as at least equal in importance to the physical manifestations such as furniture and architecture that the world has admired since the early twentieth century. By examining Shaker texts, I contribute to the analysis of Shaker literature begun by Jean Humez and Diane Sasson.[8] I, as have they, assert the importance of linguistic acts in spiritual development and sustenance and in cultural studies.

My study demonstrates that Shaker writing, like the Puritan texts that for so long have undergirded studies of American literature and culture, not only reflects the thinking of individuals but also provides information about the culture in which they live. By being both separate from and a part of discourses of American culture, Shaker literature and literacies remind us of the ongoing dialectic between individual writers and readers and their supportive communities and of the continual conversations between their communities and the larger culture. The Shakers' literature and their literacies are necessary complements to the studies of the religious "mainstream" and *belles lettres* that have dominated studies of American literature and culture. I attempt to give voice here to people and texts who have been undervalued primarily because they have been unheard.

Though the readers and writers I discuss primarily were Shakers of nineteenth-century America, and though I recognize the intellectual pitfalls of transposing too rapidly examples from past cultural settings upon contemporary situations, these Shaker voices speak here in ways that enhance the lives of readers on the cusps of two centuries. The relationships between the Shakers' literacies and their spiritual fervor helps us understand the plight of people participating in religious groups today, some of whom are motivated to political actions incongruent with our own.

And not completely separate from the spaces of politics and religion, cyberspace calls us—especially those of us who love the materiality of turning a text's pages—to rethink our visions of literacy. We must continually revise our understandings of readers and writers in our own culture and the ways in which their literacies and literature enrich them.

NOTES

1. These numbers are based on the reports by Shakers Calvin Green and Seth Y. Wells in *A Summary View of the Millennial Church* (1823). In addition there are two demographic studies of the sect by non-Shakers William Sims Bainbridge ("Shaker Demographics, 1840–1900") and Priscilla Brewer (*Shaker Communities*). For comments on the discrepancies among the figures of these three works see Stephen Stein (*Shaker Experience*, 87–90).

2. The most comprehensive bibliography of these Shaker texts is Mary L. Richmond's *Shaker Literature*. See also John P. MacLean's *Bibliography of Shaker Literature*. Often a particular collection has a published or unpublished bibliography of works within it, such as Richard E. McKinstry's *Edward Deming Andrews Memorial Shaker Collection*.

3. Stephen Stein and Stephen Marini have also argued against "deprivation theory" as an infallible explanation for why individuals became or remained Shakers. Stein writes, "According to deprivation theory, the Shakers and other enthusiastic religious groups on the frontier offered refuge and solace to individuals experiencing difficulty in times of social dislocation and cultural transition" (*Letters*, 5). Citing Marini's *Radical Sects of Revolutionary New England*, he argues that "Believers came from all classes" (*Letters*, 5).

4. The numerous studies of literacy and literature that have influenced my thinking are almost impossible to list here. Among literacy studies, Andrea Fishman's ethnographic study, *Amish Literacy*, provided an example of analyzing a religious community as well as thought-provoking insights to the community's performative readings at home, at church and in the schoolroom. James Gee's *Social Linguistics and Literacies* also emphasized the performative elements of reading in the classroom. Sylvia Scribner and Michael Cole's *The Psychology of Literacy* provided me examples of framing questions and categorizing types of literacy. Walter J. Ong's *Orality and Literacy* first caused me to consider the differences between orally dominated cultures and those ruled by inscribed texts.

Among the historical studies of reading and writing in particular communities, those that emphasize the interplay between literacy and orality have been particularly helpful: Richard Bauman's study of seventeenth-century Quakers, *Let Your Words Be Few;* David D. Hall's *World's of Wonder, Days of Judgment,* on Puritan writing and reading; Robert St. George's "'Heated' Speech and Literacy in Seventeenth-Century New England"; Richard H. Brodhead's *Cultures of Letters;* and Robert Darnton's *Great Cat Massacre.*

My analysis has also been influenced by numerous studies of Puritan and Protestant hermeneutics, such as Perry Miller's *New England Mind,* Mason I. Lowance's *Language of Canaan,* and Chapter 1 of Larzer Ziff's *Writing in the New Nation,* as well as by studies specific to New England communities, such as Lawrence Buell's *New England Literary Culture* and William J. Gilmore's *Reading Becomes a Necessity of Life.*

5. The earliest and perhaps most significant Shaker theological works are Joseph Meacham's *Concise Statement of the Principles of the Only True Church,* Benjamin Seth Youngs's *Testimony of Christ's Second Appearing,* and John Dunlavy's *Manifesto.* The most helpful secondary works that draw from these to explain Shaker theology are Kathleen Deignan's *Christ Spirit,* Robley Whitson's *Two Centuries of Spiritual Reflection,* and Marini's *Radical Sects.* The most recent comprehensive history of the Shakers is Stein's

Shaker Experience in America. In addition to details about the sect's theology and their reading, writing, and publishing, Stein's work provides information about individual writers I analyze in this study. Other histories include Edward Deming Andrews's *People Called Shakers* and Henri Desroche's *American Shakers.* The foremost works on the Shaker doctrine of celibacy are Louis J. Kern's *Ordered Love,* Lawrence Foster's *Religion and Sexuality,* and Sally Kitch's *Chaste Liberation.* Studies of women's roles in Shakerism, in addition to these three works on celibacy, include Marjorie Proctor-Smith's *Women in Shaker Community and Worship,* Priscilla Brewer's "'Tho' of the Weaker Sex,'" and Jean Humez's *Mother's First-Born Daughters.*

These questions have also been instigated by several works on women's epistemology, literacy, and spirituality, such as Mary Field Belenky's *Women's Ways of Knowing,* Elaine Pagels's *Gnostic Gospels,* and Nellie McKay's "Nineteenth Century Black Women's Spiritual Autobiographies."

6. Deignan and Whitson describe the Shakers' theological perspectives as millennialists concerned with pneumatology. Marini also describes Shaker theology within the context of millennialism in revolutionary New England (*Radical Sects*).

7. Barthes explains the terms "writerly" and "readerly" in the opening of *S/Z* (4). Graff describes the categorizing work of critics of literacy as an admirable beginning to the oversimplification of early literacy studies (4). Ong argues that literacy contributes to such higher order thinking skills in *Orality and Literacy* (36–57).

In addition to Davidson's study of the literature of the early Republic, in which she argues that reading contributed to women's empowerment, Jane Tompkins's *Sensational Designs* and Nina Baym's *Woman's Fiction* argue that previously underrated literature by women rewrites the authoritative discourse of mid-nineteenth-century American culture. Tompkin's and Baym's works illustrate that even if a writer believes she freely expresses herself, the "product" may appear to be a stereotype of other pieces of the same genre. With texts that appear to be individualized acts of self-expression, analysts have a difficult time determining the degree to which a writer freely expresses herself. This ideal to which apostates and other "outsiders" aspired held little attraction for those within Shakerism. I argue in Chapter 4, for example, that Rebecca Jackson's spiritual literacy allows her to write and read innovatively both the symbol of Ann Lee and the genre called "spiritual narrative," thus giving herself agency even within the confines of the institution. Yet under the influence of what she already knew, she was in many ways "already written" by the discourse communities in which she lived. She did not necessarily desire to create unique, personal-ized, self-expression. Thus it is difficult to measure the "progress" of her literacy and her personal development.

8. Sally Promey's *Spiritual Spectacles,* on the gift-drawings of the mid-nineteenth century, and Daniel W. Patterson's study of hymns, *The Shaker Spiritual,* are two examples of recent works that bring together the sect's spiritual impetus with its material manifesta-tions. Diane Sasson's *Shaker Spiritual Narrative,* which also emphasizes spirituality, was the first study of Shaker literature. More recently she has analyzed Shaker writings of the Era of Manifestations ("Individual Experience"). Jean Humez initially added to Sasson's pattern of literary study with her edition and analysis of Rebecca Cox Jackson's autobiographical writings (*Gifts of Power*). Since then she has analyzed the 1816 *Testimonies* ("'Ye Are My Epistles'"), the writings of early Shaker women (*Mother's First-Born Daughters*), and the publications of apostate Mary Marshal Dyer ("'A Woman Mighty'"). Deignan's theological study is also a literary one, providing an analysis of several theological works.

Chapter 1

Varieties of Literary Experiences: An Overview of Shaker Writing and Reading

Not many years back "God hates grammar" was a common expression.
—Nicholas Briggs, "Forty Years a Shaker," 1920

In revolutionary New England, members of the sect known as the Shakers exhibited varied literary skills. According to their records, the exemplary female leader Ann Lee was "illiterate" and "unlettered." However, her male counterparts, Joseph Meacham and James Whitaker, read the Bible and exhibited a knowledge of ecclesiastical histories and religious tracts.[1] By the mid-nineteenth century, when the Shakers had published numerous theological works such as John Dunlavy's *Manifesto, or A Declaration of the Doctrines and Practice of the Church of Christ* (1818), some adult Believers and children exhibited only minimal literary skills or interest in literary endeavors. In journals they kept as adults, John and Lucy Holmes of the Sabbathday Lake community record with very rough verbal skills only minimal sketches of their daily tasks, illnesses, and meetings for worship.[2] Lucy recorded in 1843, "16 of January i begun to take the Medson of of [*sic*] Cloverheds toothcake root Raspberry leaves" and in 1844 "13 April very worm wether." Lucy's numerous entries about her health are not surprising, since she was near and in her sixties when keeping the journal; she recorded the daily impressions most important to her life. Similarly, John's sketchy journal notes his labor in the fields and the woodshop. In spring 1804 he records, "John Holmes he was workin in the gardin the 24th and the 25th of May . . . and I was work a plowing the 6th day and from the 6th to the 10th I was holding the plow. May the 18th in the afternoon and I was work plantin potatoes."

This young man well fit for labor and this older woman, members of the same community, were not unexposed to schooling. Shaker community schools, first supported by taxes in Connecticut in 1792, enrolled as many as 200 young people by 1811 in Union Village, Ohio, and were well established by 1830 (Stein, *Shaker*

Experience, 100–101). By 1856 the New Lebanon, New York, community awarded such books as *Life of Washington* and John Milton's *Paradise Lost* as incentives for learning. However, not all students were excited by the potential of additional literary endeavors. Of the books, for example, the community record states, "'The prizes were eagerly received, although sometimes there was reported grumblings of disappointment'" (qtd. in Taylor, F., 219). And not all Shakers who wished to do so were allowed to develop their literary skills. Nicholas Briggs's apostate account, published in 1920, woefully describes the limitations he felt during the mid-nineteenth century at the Canterbury, New Hampshire, community:

My school life closed when I was fifteen. I was greatly disappointed at not being permitted one more term as the boys usually were, but they seemed to think my education was sufficient for a Shaker. As a little condescension I was allowed to study morning and evening through the winter, instead of making leather mittens as otherwise I should have done. Even at this late date in the Society's history, erudition was not strongly favored. Not many years back "God hates grammar" was a common expression, and their reading was pretty much limited to the Bible and Almanacs and the Society publications, which were quite voluminous. The only newspaper taken to serve this body of 160 people was the *Boston Weekly Journal,* and very few enjoyed the separate personal reading of this. If I recall it correctly, this arrived Friday noon. Until supper time it was retained by the Elders, and then given to a brother who read it to the brethren in the evening assembled in one of the shops. Next morning it was given to the Eldress who read it in the afternoon to the sisters convened in the dining hall. (59)

These variations among individual Shakers, due to their historical moments, interests, educational levels, geographical locales, and roles in their communities, reflect in part the "varieties of literary experiences" to which this chapter's title points. Reading and writing practices of particular individuals, whose habits and skills shift from moment to moment as occasions demand, illustrate not only the multiple ways individuals read but also the individuality of Shakers, who are sometimes viewed by outsiders as a group of cardboard characters with no unique personalities or interests. Apostate David Lamson writes in an 1848 publication, for example, "There is almost perfect uniformity among them, of dress, language, manners, forms of worship, government, etc." (18). Yet individual Shakers, whose reading and writing skills and practices varied, saw themselves as part of a whole; their literacies, explored in the following chapters, come to light when considered against the backdrop of beliefs and practices they share with others in the sect. Thus this chapter also describes the varieties in writing and reading practices of the sect as a whole, from the opening of Ann Lee's "testimony against the flesh" in 1780 to the early twentieth century, when Anna White and Leila Taylor's *Shakerism: Its Meaning and Message* (1904) appeared.

Other scholars of Shakerism have traced or mentioned the sect's literary endeavors and educational practices, noting, for example, the sect's move from orally conveyed teachings to inscribed theology, the educational and literary differences among Shakers of the east and the west, and the influences of the world's genres, such as spiritual autobiography and polemical pamphlets, upon

Shaker writers. For example, Diane Sasson, analyzing Shaker spiritual narratives and their relationships to those of the world, describes eastern communities of New York, Massachusetts, Maine, and New Hampshire as more grounded in literature than those in the West (*Shaker Spiritual,* xii). Stephen Stein, in contrast, describes the Shakers in the western communities of Ohio and Kentucky in the early nineteenth century as more intellectual and as more advanced in their educational practices than their counterparts in the East (*Shaker Experience,* 75–76).[3] These analyses, seemingly at odds about Shaker literacies and literature, merely discuss different kinds of texts and literary practices. Stein points to the rise of polemical writing in the West, due to the training and background in Scottish "new light" epistemology western leaders possessed; Sasson's study considers the role of spiritual autobiographies among the traditions of *belles lettres* read and composed in New England.

Yet neither Sasson, Stein, nor the others have discussed the relationship between the world's reading and writing practices and those within the sect at any great length, and none has considered in any detail the relationship between Shaker beliefs about the spirit and reading and writing acts.[4] These two forces—the world's attitudes toward literacies and literature and the sect's pneumatology—shaped the shifts in Shaker writing and reading practices up through the early twentieth century.

These shifts demonstrate both the leaders' willingness and their need to listen and respond to pressures of the larger culture brought into the sect by new converts and by the world's literature and discourses. "Shaker communitarianism has," as Jean Humez has recently written, "held a mirror up to developing U.S. Anglo-American culture, from a position at once 'outside' and 'inside' that culture" ("'A Woman Mighty,'" 90). The sect's reading and writing practices cannot be analyzed accurately without attention to these forces of the larger American culture shaping them.

The Shakers' literary experiences from the late-eighteenth century through the early twentieth century coincide in many ways with those of their middle-class evangelical counterparts, whose reading and writing practices have been described by literary historians.[5] Initially the Shakers read only the Bible and religious literature because they retained a belief in the connections between imaginative literature and sexual license in the years of the early Republic. As Cathy Davidson argues, women in this period began to turn fiction to uses of social and pietistic improvement. When evangelical and popular authors, as Jane Tompkins explains, built sentimental fiction on popular religious narratives in the 1830s and 1840s, the Shakers continued to be resistant to "fiction" but employed similar narrative strategies in their testimonial writing; they both echoed and revised what Harvey Graff calls the "literacy myth" (1–19). In Graff's view, many people since the nineteenth century have believed reading and writing allows individuals to think independently and reasonably. As a result the literate individuals will make choices about matters such as religion that will contribute to their success either in this world or in the next and to the "progress" of the society in which they live.

Based upon their own understandings of literacy, which emerged from their beliefs as millennial eschatologists, the Shakers revised the "literacy myth" slightly to construct their own: Reading and writing were always put to the purposes of *spiritual* progress. The embodied presence of the Christ Spirit allowed a variety of literary practices among Believers from the sect's earliest days. Thus the Shakers moved from a skepticism of writing and reading other than the Bible (including fiction) to appropriation of the world's fictional and lyrical techniques; as they observed these techniques in texts they read, they incorporated them within the genres they wrote.[6]

Shifts in Shaker writing and reading practices are illuminated not only by analyses of American literary culture but also by visions of Shaker history. In her analysis of the Shakers' systematic theology and their pneumatic eschatology, Kathleen Deignan offers a useful chronological framework as she explores the sect's shifting conceptions of the eschaton, or the "being present" of the spirit, during three periods. She argues that from the opening of Ann Lee's testimony until the first publication in 1790, Lee herself was viewed as the eschaton; in a second period, from 1790 up through 1850, doctrinal writers began to refer to the millennial church or body of Believers, each containing the spirit, as the eschaton; and from 1850 to the present, Shakers have viewed the eschaton as the universal Christ Spirit, immanent outside as well as within Shaker communities. I modify Deignan's lengthy second period, breaking the sixty-year span emphasizing the millennial church (1790–1850) at 1827, the publication year of the second edition of the *Testimonies Concerning the Character and Ministry of Mother Ann Lee and the First Witnesses of the Gospel of Christ's Second Appearing.* The period from 1790 to 1827 is, as Stein labels it, a period of "Gathering and Building," partially through writing and publication by the leaders and by the establishment of Shaker schools.[7] In the years prior to 1827, when leaders limited Believers' alphabetic literacies to the basest competencies, "progress" by the world's standards was not one of the goals they sought. Because they sought spiritual progression, they used alphabetic literacy only to assist Believers in their "travels" down the roads of progressive spiritual perfection. In the early years spiritual achievement did not necessitate much interpretation or inscription of texts but only the competence needed for the communities' functions. Thus they began writing and publishing theological works, used letters for communication, and instructed children in writing and reading.

In the period 1827–1850 communal publications continued to be important, but the leadership encouraged individual manuscript writing. The second edition of the *Testimonies,* as Sasson has explained, differs from the first edition by putting in print free-standing recollections of early Believers' conversions and Lee's influence upon them, whereas individualized accounts in the first edition had been merged into one lengthy narrative (*Shaker Spiritual*). Believers were given blank books for composing daily records of their "production" in communal labors and of their spiritual progress. They were also encouraged to write hymns for sharing publically in worship. During this period of revival known as the Era of Manifestations, the Shakers also produced numerous "spirit" writings. Although writers, moved by the powers of spiritual "instruments" within them, embodied characteristics similar to those Lee had manifested fifty years prior, leaders were troubled by their inability to determine the authenticity of these works. As Sasson has explained, drawing from an analysis of the spirit writings of the Harvard, Massachusetts, community, some young women such as Minerva Hill received gifts that threatened leadership because they suggested changes in communal rituals and structure and increased the gifted person's status in the village. Thus leaders formed new laws about literary practices; they attempted to channel rather than dam the spiritual gifts ("Individual Experience"). The acceptable writings reinforced the belief in the eschaton as the millennial church, more than merely in Ann Lee or in individualized Believers.

Shaker leaders' shifting attitudes toward writing and reading and their communal results echo assertions about private, individualized readings in the early Republic and public attempts to channel the independent thought into a unified whole. Davidson argues that the private reading of fiction, which provides readers with personal authority and agency, led to anti-fiction campaigns by Noah Webster and others concerned with unifying the new nation, culminating in the patriotic, rhetorical readings of the common school movement. Private acts of interpreting nonfictional genres could have similar effects, threatening those in positions of communal or cultural authority. Thus Shaker leaders validated public, oral readings over private ones. They "feminized" Shaker readers and writers, in the sense Richard Brodhead describes, by emphasizing internal rather than external discipline. The Shakers' supervisor of schools, Seth Young Wells, for example, "trained his teachers to be flexible and loving, [and] stressed mild and minimal discipline" (Taylor, F., 3). Yet the sect more importantly provided a kind of internal discipline through personal writing and public reading, which complemented and gradually replaced the corporal discipline of Shaker dances as the century progressed.[8]

By 1850 the Shakers also had increased their involvement in the world's economics by depending financially upon such profitable industries as chairs, baskets, seeds, and extracts (Stein, *Shaker Experience,* 135–42); consequently, because progress by the world's standards was more acceptable, alphabetic literacy and the reading and writing of the world's genres increased as well. When the Shakers began reading some fiction and allowing more private reading, they contributed unwittingly not only to the increasing fragmentation of the communities but also to the concern for the loss of a Shaker identity. Ironically, the leaders' beliefs in the spiritual reception and production of texts allowed them to make the shifts that significantly contributed to changes in the communities. Kathryn M. Olson describes this flexibility as the result of "dissociation," "an ingenious rhetorical move through which multiple elements of a single concept are differentiated and arranged hierarchically. . . . One aspect is endorsed while its devalued partner is given new coherence within the particular system of thought" (45). She contends, "When evidence meeting one's knowledge criteria discredits a highly valued knowledge claim, one may use dissociation to revise one's knowledge criteria, or rules of evidence, rather than reject the knowledge claim.

The advantage of such a practice is that it protects the knowledge claim by moving to a higher level of abstraction than the level of evidence" (46). In this case, the knowledge claim is that of the embodied and ever-present spirit that influences reading and writing acts (Olson refers to the belief in progressive divine revelation, which of course is a manifestation of the active and living spirit); the incompatible evidence is the concrete description of what texts were written and read during Shaker history. As Olson describes, the beauty of this dissociation is that it "not only renders irrelevant the immediate complication, but also immunizes the thought system from similar future incompatibilities" (46). Thus the increased reading and writing of the latter-nineteenth century allowed Believers to see Shakerism and the Christ Spirit as reaching beyond the confines of physical communities; reading and writing provided them visions of larger and continuing worlds of Shakerism. The reading and writing of the world's genres and texts allowed Shaker readers and writers to discover the universal Christ Spirit.

These sources of change both inside and outside Shaker communities, in composite, provide glimmers of the heated elements that burned some Believers' faiths and kept others fermenting. Accounts by apostates and other outsiders reiterate the shifts noted by insider accounts, but in the process they voice a few consistent complaints, ranging from the lack of education the institution provided (compared to that offered in the world) to the inability of Believers to read fiction. Mary Marshall Dyer expresses in her *Portraiture of Shakerism* (1822) the "folk" attitude common in the years of the early Republic—that the Shakers, vessels of Satan, used writing as a tool to deceive and control others. (Dyer herself cleverly constructs arguments against the Shakers with the purpose of manipulating her readers). Later accounts, such as Lamson's *Two Years' Experience among the People Called Shakers* (1848), complain about the unreasonableness of the Shaker belief in "inspired" writings, the censorship of popular periodicals and fiction, and the limited physical settings of writing and reading acts. The most frequently and consistently voiced complaints are about the lack of freedom to reason from and about inscribed texts and to express opinions, either orally or in writing, as a result of using this reason. Although some left the sect because leaders did not assuage their desires to write and read "freely," many remained, content with or willing to endure practices they saw as essential to their personal spirituality and to the Shaker way.

Apostates' complaints about writing and reading practices, rarely the only complaints being voiced, are intertwined with other irritations. The writer usually turns from the initial problem and gropes for additional reasons to complain about the Shakers and their lifestyle. Nevertheless, these apostates' complaints about writing and reading, in juxtaposition with those of Believers, highlight varying perspectives of the same topic and the same practices. These varied responses are a result of diverse experiences influenced by gender, race, literacy, and family life prior to meeting the Shakers, by the historical moments within which each lived, and by the influences of Shakerism within particular moments and particular communities.

THE PRIMACY OF ORALITY: SHAKER WRITING AND READING PRIOR TO 1790

Stein explains that "the early hostility of the society toward written creeds, statements of belief, and even written testimonies" emerged "in part from Ann Lee's illiteracy, a limitation that fueled her rejection of all writing" (9). Yet according to the most lengthy biography of Lee, the *Testimonies Concerning the Life, Character, Revelations, and Doctrines of Our Ever Blessed Mother Ann Lee, and the Elders with Her* (1816), she quotes Scripture readily, even directing her colleague James Whitaker to read a specific passage from the book of James on one occasion (XXX, 26–27). The Scripture Lee suggests, as I explain more fully in Chapter 2, supports the orally conveyed message she preaches. Because texts, like the bread and the wine of Protestant communion, served in the absence of God and the Christ as signs pointing the way to divine truth, they were not necessary when the Christ Spirit was present. With the presence of the Christ Spirit embodied in the physically living "Mother" Ann, written texts such as the Bible, when used, were in subordination to the primacy of orally conveyed teachings. Thus, Stein aptly recognizes, "for Ann Lee and her followers, the written word paled in veracity as well as efficacy when compared with the spoken word" (*Shaker Experience,* 9). This "affirmation of the value they perceived in verbal [oral] testimonies offered by 'eye and ear witnesses'" such as Lee also "reflect[ed] their view of revelation as dynamic and changing" (*Shaker Experience,* 9). By accepting revelation as dynamic and changing, and by believing Lee's teachings to be "authentically divine," the Shakers paved the way for later innovative reading and writing and shifts in literary practices.[9]

After Lee's physical death in 1784, written texts that had been subordinated to her physical and spiritual presence began to be used in her absence, as the Church began to be "gathered into order" by Joseph Meacham and James Whitaker. The first Shaker publication, the *Concise Statement of the Principles of the Only True Church According to the Gospel of the Present Appearance of Christ* (1790), generally attributed to Meacham (Richmond, I, 145), illustrates the leadership's continued attempt to emphasize the body as Lee had. The body is an organizing image for the theological tract; the writer uses the image to refer to the church as a whole as well as to the literal house of the spirit for individual believers (Deignan, 79–82). Additionally, the tract contains traces of the oral culture in which Meacham taught; it reads as though it were meant to be heard. The first paragraph, initiating a discourse on God's dispensations of history, contains only four lengthy sentences consisting of numerous phrases linked by semi-colons and colons rather than verbal conjunctions indicating logical relations. Rather, the writer attempts to sweep his audience along by a swiftly moving current of Biblical allusions and repeated words:

And altho' they could not receive regeneration or the fulness of salvation, from the fleshly or fallen nature in this life; because the fulness of time was not yet come, that they should receive the baptism of the Holy Ghost and fire; for the destruction of the body of sin, and purification of the soul; but Abram being called, and chosen of God as the father of the faithful; was received into covenant relation with God by promise; that in him (and his seed which was Christ) all the families of the earth should be blessed, and these earthly blessings, which were promised to Abram, were a shadow of gospel or spiritual blessings to come: and circumcision, though it was a seal of Abram's faith, yet it was but a sign of the mortification and destruction of the flesh by the gospel in a future day. (qtd. in Whitson, 62)[10]

Prior to this initial reference to the bodily act of circumcision in Abraham's day as "a sign of the mortification and destruction of the flesh . . . in a future day," the passage reads almost like a seventeenth-century Puritan tract. Yet as the writer explains outward acts of the body as signs of the inner state—the presence of the indwelling spirit, "which does indeed destroy the body of sin, or fleshly nature, and purify the man from all sin both soul and body" (qtd. in Whitson, 62)—he begins to distinguish the "true church of Christ," the Shakers, from other millennialists. The indwelling spirit, according to the *Concise Statement,* is "manifested in divers operations and gifts" (qtd. in Whitson, 62). Thus Shaker theologians such as Meacham defended, explained, and built upon Lee's foundational testimony. They emphasized the innovative gifts of the indwelling spirit and the body's role in spirituality, yet they used Scripture (especially Joel, Daniel, and Revelation) and employed the polemical writing styles of their enemies to explain God's dispensations of history, ending in the present "last days" of the millennial church. They attempted to maintain the immediate power of oral culture, yet they recognized the importance of print to gather, strengthen, and sustain the sect.

After 1790 writing and reading of texts began to take on added significance. Leaders wrote letters on behalf of the Society, kept communal journals and records, composed tracts for the world and read enough popular periodical literature to be familiar with the world's events.[11] This pragmatic move into more literate practices served two purposes: "instructing members" and providing "defense" against "the sting of repeated attacks" by the world (Stein, *Shaker Experience*, 9).

EXTERNAL FORCES AND EDUCATING FOR THE PROGRESS OF THE SECT: 1790–1827

Among the accounts that stung the Shakers with accusations of limited education and reading and writing activities, Thomas Brown's *Account of the People Called Shakers* (1812) and Mary Marshall Dyer's *Portraiture of Shakerism* (1822) merit attention because of their length and relatively wide circulation.[12] In addition, the two provide glimpses of the arguments of earlier accounts, in part by embedding references to and quotations from them, and in part by employing similar arguments.

In his *Account,* discussed further in Chapter 4, Brown asserts that he was told by "Elder Ebenezer," "'Ah, Thomas must put away his books, if he intends to become a good believer'" (227). The books he was allowed to read, since he responded that he *needed* to read, were "Almanacks and spellingbooks" (227). He was also told, "We have no objection against geographical, and some historical books; but respecting our salvation, nothing is necessary, but to keep in the gift, and in obedience to what we are taught" (236). "Keep[ing] in the gift" here refers to abiding in the spirit, a Shaker belief that had appealed to Brown. Of Quaker heritage, Brown had a strong belief in the significance of personal divine revelation as a means of knowing God and receiving the light of Truth before his contact with the Shakers, who claimed a similar belief. However, Brown explains, his ideas about the value of other books conflicted with that of Shaker leaders.

Brown's primary complaints about the Shakers are the apparent contradictions between what they claim and what they practice—a failure to see the inconsistencies and flaws in their reasoning. For example, "the gift" of the spirit arrives not merely through individual, personal experience as they claim, but also by way of the Elders. The Church's control over reading material is but one example. Another example of lack of reason is their dependence upon Lee as the cornerstone of their faith. Based upon personal investigation of accurate sources, Brown believes that Lee was a fraud. Drunkenness, prostitution, and deceitfulness—characteristics of which she was accused—cannot be of a woman of God, he explains. The Shakers fail to see the unreasonableness of their claims because they have been too personally involved with the woman.

Unlike Brown's situation, Dyer's problems have not so much to do with Lee's religious life and views of reason as with Dyer's physical and emotional needs as a woman and mother in the early Republic. According to Dyer's account, her husband "went to the Shakers" at Enfield, New Hampshire, with a promise to leave her set up with a house. He reneged because he and his property, including his children, are under the order of the Elders. Initially provoked by the loss of child custody and her own financial support, she develops an extensive argument including accusations about Shaker writing and reading practices. In the 446-page work, she compiles testimonies against the Shakers, written or given orally by many other than herself. [13] These testimonies—in sum an excellent example of literacy's entanglement in cultural and economic politics associated with family life—argue that the Shakers use the Bible and other written documents deceitfully to accomplish their tasks, and that they deny children education and thus repress their use of reasoning, which would allow them to make the right choices about religion.

Before voicing her own complaints, Dyer lets others speak of their knowledge of the Shakers, building a case against them with a community of voices and setting the stage for her own testimony. For example, Clement Beck, who as a child lived with the Shakers in New Hampshire, testifies:

My education is poor; when I was a child and a youth, the Shakers did not allow their subjects to have learning—what I have, I obtained by stealth, contrary to orders—since then the authority [of the State] has compelled them to give their children some learning. . . . I have known them when people were coming to inspect their schools, make some write composition—then another copy it off better, and show the copy, saying it was the former one's writing. I have known others make a mark on paper, then another write composition on the same paper, and call it the persons [sic] writing which made the mark. (186–87)

Beck's testimony centers on relationships between truth and the written word in two ways. First, the Shakers' practices force him to become immoral and dishonest, since he must acquire learning by "stealth," much as Frederick Douglass did as a slave. Second, the Shakers themselves exhibit dishonesty by using writing to deceive.

Ebenezer Kimball's testimony against the Shakers focuses neither on deceit nor stealth but exhibits the literacy myth by linking education with the early Republic's ideal of freedom, including the freedom to discover "true" religion. He raises several rhetorical questions: "I wish to know why Shaker children should be deprived of useful knowledge and intelligence, more than other children? I call on the public mind. Is it not undermining the foundation of society and good government, civil and religious liberty, to permit their being thus enslaved?" (203). Kimball then provides, by hearsay evidence, his understanding of the literary and educational deprivations of New Hampshire Shakers: "I am informed that there are in Canterbury and Enfield, about 200 children, and some adults nearly 40 years old, who never heard a christian [sic] sermon: there is no liberty for them to attend any other denomination, but they must be in subjection to their elder, and he approves of no information in religion but their own" (203).[14]

Dyer reinforces these accusations that the Shakers use writing to repress freedom and to deceive by quoting extensively from other apostate and outsider accounts. A Colonel Smith of Kentucky, for example, has written that the Latin and Greek within the voluminous *Testimony of Christ's Second Appearing* (1808) indicate that it could not have been written by David Darrow, John Meacham, and Benjamin Youngs; the volume must have been "dressed up" by someone else in an attempt to make the Shakers appear learned (115–16). Dyer includes an excerpt from Daniel Rathbun's *Letter*, printed initially in 1785, in which Rathbun accuses the Shakers of using the Bible as a prop to entice prospective converts: "You say it is a new dispensation, where God, Christ, nor Bible are of any use, only what is in the Mother. Then leave the Bible, and not impose on people with it. You make use of it, to persuade people into a belief with you; then they must renounce it or be chastised" (53). Dyer's accusations about the Shakers' use of writing and reading to deceive culminate in her own testimony of her treatment while living in the community. In the description Dyer cleverly draws from sentimental and popular discourse of the period to present herself as a victim incapable of decoding the legal document the Elders extend to her and her husband.[15] She writes that she learns only *ipso facto* the power of her signature upon this incomprehensible text she refers to as "a writing":

This writing did not oblige the Shakers to educate our children, nor to provide for them in sickness, or to give them any thing when of age; in case of inability they were liable to become paupers. The writing bound us to give them up entirely to the disposal of the Elders—and in no case however cruel, we should be treated to interfere. My husband said he was willing to put this confidence in the elders, he signed the writing and compelled me to also. I had no relief only to weep. (347–48)

In contrast to these accusations, the accounts by Shakers during this early period present positively what the apostates describe as repression and deceit, echoing the world's emphasis on "use" and "improvement" as the goals of literacy and education. According to Calvin Green's biographical account of Joseph Meacham (1827), Meacham emphasized necessity, usefulness, and personal capacity as determining factors in a child's education:

Father established it as a rule for believers, that children brot up among them should have suitable education for all necessary purposes, according to the proper order & calling of the true church of Christ, but not be taught unnecessary arts & sciences which naturally draw back to the world.

He expressly said in meeting that, if any had obtained more than common learning, if they thot they were the better for it, in a gospel or virtuous sense, it was a loss to them. Of these words I was an ear witness, & they made a lasting impression on my mind. (65)

Even as Green's written testimony upholds a "useful" education for children within Shaker communities, it underscores the continued importance of orality—Meacham's thoughts were orally conveyed ("said in meeting") and Green testifies that he "was an ear witness."[16] According to records of the West family of Canterbury, New Hampshire, in 1802 the teachers Hannah Bronson and Hannah Beedee used Webster's *Spelling Book,* the New Testament, and secular primers to teach two subjects deemed useful—reading and spelling (Taylor, F., 146). Yet by the time of Green's writing in 1827, leaders such as he had been compelled (due to the accusations from without) to articulate and explain prior educational practices.

They also sought to improve them. "Mother" Lucy Wright, who had gained prominence as a female leader after Lee's death, "tried to bring the Believers' behavior up-to-date, particularly in the area of language" (Brewer, *Shaker Communities*, 36). A member of the mercantile class prior to conversion (Stein, *Shaker Experience,* 53) and in many ways an exemplar of Republican motherhood, Mother Lucy was partially responsible for the publication of the sect's theological works and for continued "progression" in literary practices (Stein, *Shaker Experience,* 66–76).[17] One result of Wright's efforts was an educational system that was, according to one critic, "beyond those of the world" up through the Civil War (Taylor, F., 4).[18] In 1821 she appointed Seth Young Wells "General Superintendent of Believers' Literature, Schools, etc. in the First Bishopric," which consisted of the Watervliet, Hancock, and Mount Lebanon communities. Wells had been a teacher in the Albany, New York, public schools and the Academy in Hudson prior to becoming a Shaker. He soon evidenced a "special ability in legal and literary matters" and edited, "after careful revision, the early publications of the societies" (White and Taylor, 132–33). By 1823, when Wells visited Canterbury to examine the school, in addition to Webster's *Spelling Book* and the New Testament, the texts included Jackson's *Arithmetic,* Seavill's *Small Arithmetic,* Gould's *Penmanship and Arithmetic Tables,* Ingersoll's *Grammar, Easy Lessons,* and *The New York Reader.* Shaker teachers also used one of the most accessible doctrinal works, *A Summary View of the Millennial Church* (Taylor, F., 153). Although the incomplete records, the sheer numbers of texts, and the variations from community to community prevent the creation of a comprehensive list of the "useful" texts Shakers wrote and read at particular historical moments, the list of books used at the Canterbury school suggests that the sect was little different from the world in the subjects taught at the end of this second period in 1827. In spite of what Frank Taylor sees as the Shakers' "advanced" methods of education, the leadership still controlled writing and reading practices.[19] And the general attitude expressed by the leadership about education had not changed much from Meacham's voiced remarks before the turn of the century.

RITUALIZED LITERACIES AND INTERNAL REVIVAL: 1828–1850

In his 1836 manuscript "Remarks on Learning and the Use of Books," Wells describes "classical learning as purposelessness or . . . 'mere lumber of the brain.'" He writes, "'This life is short at the longest, and ought not to be spent in acquiring any kind of knowledge which cannot be put to a good use'" (qtd. in Taylor, F., 161). In his "Letter to the Elders, Deacons, Brethren & Sisters of the Society in Watervliet" (1832) he reiterates the same two points: that reading materials should be selected for their "usefulness" in a reader's "improvement" and that "undirected knowledge" or "self-government" could be "detrimental to society" (qtd. in Taylor, F., 160–62). In sum, these works show that Shaker literary practices at the beginning of the third period still emphasized usefulness and a distinction between "directed and undirected knowledge" (Taylor, F., 142).[20] Yet the literary practices of this period changed in at least three ways: an increase in writing as a means of private and public expression by Believers other than leaders; the appearance of writings inspired by spirits and inscribed by mediums; and an increase in the ritualization of writing and reading practices. These changes both reflect and emerge from practices of the world and the internal revival referred to as the Era of Manifestations or the period of "Mother's Work."

Records of Wells's second visit to Canterbury, in 1832, suggest these changes. The community gave him "2 *Parkers Rhetorical Readers*" (Blinn, *Historical Record,* 763). The *Readers,* which addressed patriotism and contemporary politics as well as fostering sentiment, reveal that during this period the Shakers continued to read some of the world's literature. (They also continued to write and publish for the world. In 1834, for example, Richard McNemar initiated a periodical, *The Western Review,* and the Union Village, Ohio, community published the semi-monthly *Day-Star* from 1846 to 1849, which circulated within and outside of Shaker communities.[21]) The *Readers* provide a sense of the *polis* of the community. They demonstrate that the teaching of reading was more than using primers to teach a mere interpretation of alphabetic symbols; it emphasized audience awareness and oral interpretation—performative reading that unifies in ritualized fashion. Except for their ritualization, these practices echo Lee's spiritually embodied performances.

In echoing Lee's teachings, the revival period demonstrates both a conservative backlash or remembering of the past among those few that had known the founder during her physical life; it also indicates an innovative thrust among younger Believers who never experienced her physical presence. Several kinds of ecstatic behavior, instigated by spirit possession, were manifested during the period. Some Believers spun like tops during meetings; others received prophetic utterances in English or in "tongues" they shared orally or in writing with other Believers. In addition, numerous spirits visited the Shakers during this period. Among them, Shakers no longer living in the flesh, national political heroes such as George Washington and Benjamin Franklin, and ethnic minorities such as Indians, Arabs, Africans, and Asians made appearances in living Shaker mediums or "instruments." Famous and "exotic" spirits alike usually described their conversions to Shakerism while in the spirit world.[22]

During these years Shaker leaders encouraged writing as a means of spiritual expression among Believers, who recorded "testimonies" and spiritual autobiographies and jotted hymns, poems, and at times messages instigated by the spirits of departed Believers. Alonzo Hollister refers to this type of writing in his "Reminiscenses" of his childhood at Mount Lebanon in the 1830s (163–64). Accounts by apostates Nicholas Briggs and Hervey Elkins attest to the institution's support of manuscript records prior to 1850. Elkins records, "The elders once requested that all the youth should write their faith" (66). Similarly Briggs recalls, "The Trustees always remembered us on Christmas in their own way. Every one received a diary for the New Year. Those for the little folks were of course very small, but sufficient to teach them the importance of keeping a record of their daily doings" (23).

The significance of this "keeping a record" we may extrapolate from another comment Briggs makes about year-end reviews, which had "the intent of correcting all errors and to be ready to begin the new year with clean hands and pure heart" (23). The diary was a key instrument in maintaining spirituality through this review of the past year. Thus these little books may also be seen as a means of control, since they were to contribute to each Believer's spiritual progression and life as an ideal Shaker.[23]

Even though writing and reading had taken on added significance and increased in quantity, the embodiment of the spirit in physically deceased and living Believers continued to be a crucial complement to inscribed texts. The Shakers' ways of writing and reading continued to be highly controlled. David Lamson's *Two Years' Experience among the People Called Shakers* (1848), exemplary of the apostate accusations of these years, continues earlier arguments against the repression of freedoms. But in Lamson's work the connections between writing, reading, and deceitfulness have disappeared; he highlights the control of individualized writing and reading and complains about Shaker attitudes toward the use of reason and the nature of divine revelation.[24]

As early as his preface, Lamson skeptically remarks, "Doubtless the 'Lead' will do as they have done in regard to other works on this subject: viz. use the means in their power to prevent their subjects from reading it. Such is the policy of their government, and is necessary for their continuance as a people." "The arts and sciences," he later explains, "are considered as entirely unworthy the notice of a Shaker" (46).[25] He also complains that common members are not allowed to read newspapers, nor to read anything on Saturday and Sunday except the Bible (42). With regard to writing, Lamson explains that "it is forbidden to write any thing [*sic*] without the knowledge and approval of the elders. Every letter sent, or received, must be read to the elders" (44). Lamson further describes the control exerted through communal reading of the written "regulations" that appear in two books he refers to as the "holy Laws" (given by "inspiration" in 1840) and the "Order Book." Of these he writes: "Every family has a written copy of them; and they are read to the members of the family by the elders, once or twice in every year. . . . It is a divine order that these and other inspired writings should be kept by the elders under lock and key; and by them they are read to the family at stated seasons. None others are permitted to peruse them" (31–32). Two of the reading days, he later explains, are Ann Lee's birthday and Christmas. Particularly bothered that leaders omit some chapters of these texts during the ritualized public readings, Lamson guesses that the omissions contain more "regulations"—on education, books, newspapers, and the arts and sciences. The regularity of these occasions and the oral reading mark the situations as rituals, which contribute to the institutional control of the material and its reception.[26]

Skeptical of the supposedly inspired writings of Philemon Stewart and others, Lamson writes, "The instrument through whom it is pretended they are revealed, is most plainly the author. The revelation is the production of his own mind" (74). The Shakers draw too heavily from "feel[ings]" rather than reasoned "discussion" when determining "inspiration," he explains: "But ask them why they believe in these things, and their only answer is, 'I *feel* that it is a reality.' But what evidence is there that there is any reality in these things. 'I *feel* that it is a reality. I know it is true.' This is the beginning and ending of the discussion with them" (emphasis mine, 96). He admits that he believes like the Shakers "in modern as well as ancient revelation," but his approach to revelation is more similar to Emersonian transcendentalism than to Shaker teachings of the period. He explained to Shaker leaders before he seceded from the sect: "Everyone who strove aright for communion with God, was more or less inspired. But it is to be considered, that a revelation to me, is not necessarily a revelation to others" (82).

Lamson's complaints, especially the discrepancies over inspired writings, were not uncommon during the period. Sasson describes the Harvard leadership's selection and appointment of mediums, including men who did not appear to have the spiritual gifts that younger women such as Minerva Hill had. These examples indicate the tensions between tradition and innovation, personal freedom and communal authority, which also have emerged through analysis of the period's gift-drawings (Promey).

Although many left or lost their inspiration after leaders began exerting control over medium-channeled messages, many others remained, sustained by the spirit. Hervey Elkins, for example, thrived on the spiritualism but seceded for other reasons related to literary practices. In *Fifteen Years in the Senior Order of*

Shakers: A Narration of Facts, Concerning that Singular People (1853), which appeared only five years after Lamson's work, Elkins uses his writing while a Shaker as an example of the sect's approval of reason and education and to counter the stereotype that the community allows no individualized expression. He makes no negative comments about literary self-expression; instead he includes several letters he wrote during a period of convalescence, claiming they were his first compositions and reveal the increases in his education (60–70). Praising the Shakers for the "rationalism" of their religion, Elkins gives as an example their belief in a spiritual rather than physical afterlife, a teaching that set them apart from most nineteenth-century Christians. Explaining the Era of Manifestations, for example, he quotes from a secular "scientist" who wrote on the phenomenon of "spiritualism." From these examples and others he argues that all Shaker teachings run parallel to or in keeping with the "natural" laws of science (36–37). Yet Elkins also describes the limited texts and conversations about literature as among the flaws of Shakerism. He writes of union meetings, which Shakers held three nights a week during this period to allow members of both sexes within a particular "family" to converse: "To talk of literary matters, would be termed bombastic pedantry, and small display, and would serve to exhibit accomplishments which might be enticingly dangerous" (26). Of reading, he writes that each dwelling room might contain "two or three bibles and all the religious works edited by the Society, a concordance, grammar, dictionary, etc. These are all the books they tolerate in the mansion where they retire from labor and worldly pursuits" (25–26).

Elkins's complaints about control of reading suggest why he left the sect, but do so only partially. He explains that his apostasy emerged from the teachings that Believers were not to develop strong friendship with individuals nor to express emotions of love in this regard. Elkins was influenced, as he states, by what he read—largely romances. He includes a list of texts that contributed to his self-education and explains how they also lead first to the "fall" of his dear friend, who seceded, and then to his own apostasy.

The experiences of Elkins, Briggs, Lamson, Stewart, and Hill during the Era of Manifestations illustrate the problems of categorizing varieties of writing and reading within Shaker communities according to dichotomies such as active-passive and production-consumption. Believers inscribed spirit messages through what appear to be acts of "mechanical" writing akin to romantic or mid-nineteenth-century notions of poetic inspiration. Is this writing "active" or "passive"? Are these acts of "production" or acts of "consumption"? Even when such writing acts appear to be functional or passive, material "products" still result. An inscribed text that may be handled, saved, reread, and/or passed on to someone else, such as Stewart's "Holy Laws of Zion," contains as much force within a community as a piece of writing produced by critical or innovative work. The power depends upon the communities' and individuals' perceptions of the texts. Rather than viewing these acts as pejorative, passive, and functional, the Believers saw them as contributing to the progress of individuals and the Society, primarily because of their belief in the embodied spirit.

READING AND WRITING THE WORLD'S GENRES AFTER 1850: PRIVATE ACTS AND POSSIBLE WORLDS[27]

Shaker attitudes about the usefulness of literary activities in their contribution to spiritual progression continued to hold through the early twentieth century. Though the attitudes remained the same, the kinds of texts considered useful had changed from earlier years. Records of the New Lebanon, New York, community reveal that by 1856 students there were given books as awards. These included Norton's *Agriculture Improved, An American Reader, Travels in the North of Europe, The Life of Washington,* and *Paradise Lost* (Taylor, F., 219). This list, representing generically science, literature, travel narrative, biography, and epic, also demonstrates that the Shakers were not too much unlike their neighbors in the world. In light of this list, it may not be surprising, then, to learn that the Shakers in at least one community later in the century enjoyed the works of Mark Twain and Brett Harte.[28]

Nicholas Briggs, noting a change in the reading practices at Canterbury after 1850, associates the shift with changes in leadership in the village, which had become the publishing headquarters for the Society during the revival.

About this time Elder Henry C. Blinn and Eldress Dorothy A. Durgin became the Elders of the Family. Both of them had been teachers of the school, were highly progressive in their ideas, and they stimulated reading and study, and we now began to have *The Scientific American, Phrenological Journal* and *Life Illustrated.* A small library had been formed a little while before, of all books belonging to the members, and this library was enlarged gradually until we had, as nearly as I can remember, about 3000 volumes. There was little or no fiction. I do not recall a single book of this kind; it was and always had been banished absolutely from the Society. Yet naughtily we boys and young men now and then allowed ourselves to read the stories in the magazines to which we occasionally had access. (59)

The lack of fiction, a major concern of Briggs, contributes to his dishonesty as the lack of education had contributed to Clement Beck's "stealth" in earlier years. It becomes a point of his later judgment of Blinn and Durgin. Of Blinn, Briggs writes: "He was a beautiful penman and general good teacher, and would have attained high proficiency in a theological school, as that seemed to be his literary preference. He did hold Bible School at the Village, and he delved in Mosheim and other ecclesiastical scholars. A familiarity with the classics and best fiction would have rounded out his character and made him more able as a leader" (60).[29] Familiar with "classics" and the "best fiction," Dorothy Durgin receives more adulation from Briggs than Blinn does: "Very different from Elder Henry, she imposed no restriction upon herself in reading. She managed to get most of the leading novels of the times. She had quite a library of fiction, and sometimes loaned the books to those with whom in her opinion it was safe" (61). Although this loaning of books probably included Briggs, since he knew of it and received extra study time, he believes the Shakers restricted reading and alphabetic texts even after mid-century. Briggs's comments about Durgin, as well as the award of books to individuals in 1856, demonstrate a change—a move toward privatization of the reading act. Although oral, performative readings continued to be an important part of Shaker spiritual and communal life—readings of the Twain and Harte works, for example, were not individualized, private ones but orally conveyed ones in public settings—there were more opportunities for individualized, private readings and writings.

The Shakers were *reading* fiction after 1850; their *writing* of the period, however, did not include fiction. As White and Taylor expressed in 1904, because of "the religious sense of separation from the world and worldly interests, Shaker literary genius has not revealed itself in the world's markets." That is, they were not writing the sentimental "fiction" that had provided women such as Harriet Beecher Stowe and Susan Warner with economic sustenance; probably this was so because (as I discuss in Chapter 4) the plots of sentimental novels were not in conjunction with the spiritual direction the celibate Shakers advocated. Although not writing the type of marketable literature they were sometimes reading, Shaker women and men were writing other popular genres. In 1871 the sect reinstituted publication of a religious periodical with *The Shaker,* which circulated within and outside Shaker communities. The periodical served as a means of expression for individuals who submitted letters, articles, poems, and the like. The publication continued through 1899 under several titles (*Shaker and Shakeress, The Shaker Manifesto,* and *The Manifesto*). The Shakers had written verse to be used as hymns and as memorials to deceased Shakers since before mid-century (a topic I consider in Chapter 6), but these pieces of "art" had remained in manuscript form or were published in hymnals to be used within the sect. In 1895 one of the sect's first forays into publishing popular "artistic" genres for a wider audience appeared—a collection of occasional, sentimental verse, *Mount Lebanon Cedar Boughs,* not unlike Lydia Sigourney's verse collections. In the latter part of the century they also published several tracts dedicated to deceased Shakers; these writings served as both memorials and evangelical tools. Accompanying these officially published works, Shakers continued to write and "publish" numerous manuscripts within their communities.

Reading the world's genres and about the world's events and writing for the world became more prominent after 1850.[30] In this period of numerical decline and theological shifts, inscribed texts achieved primacy as they replaced physical bodies. The acts of private reading and the multiplicity of texts and genres contributed to the increasingly felt individualization and fragmentation that, ironically, contributed to the need to preserve the past nostalgically. Reading and writing continued to be used to preserve and revise the past and to evangelize, unifying and strengthening the sect in the process. However, reading and writing increasingly manifested a new purpose—discovery. Lee remained an important figure in Shaker writing, but she became auxillary to new understandings of the "presence" of the spirit. Reading inscribed texts took on added significance as a means of discovering the Christ Spirit at large, contributing to the belief in the universal spirit. Reading about Buddhism, for example, allowed Shakers to construct an understanding of the universal spirit of the deity, seen as existing in spaces apart from the physical communities of the Church (in Russia and in

England, for example). Many Shaker publications after 1850 attempted to spread this understanding elsewhere.

White and Taylor's comments in *Shakerism: Its Meaning and Message* (1904) summarize the attitudes that had influenced the sect's writing and reading practices for the previous century: "In seeking the highest possible spiritual development, Shakers have left behind much in art and literature commonly regarded as of value, yet, in this very renunciation, in attaining purity of life and thought, they have developed a pure, refined, spiritual taste, eminently fitting them for the appreciation of the highest in art and literature" (319). The texts they had "left behind" had been omitted conscientiously in hopes of "attaining purity of life and thought" and "in seeking the highest possible spiritual development." These writing and reading practices, which reinforced the faiths of many, sometimes frustrated them nonetheless. Some Shakers complained about the same problems the apostates did. For example, the letters of the young William Byrd of Kentucky, who corresponded with his family during the years he lived in the Pleasant Hill community, indicate that his writing was overseen. To achieve some freedom of expression in his journal writing, Isaac Newton Youngs created a coded language.[31] Alonzo Hollister, when expressing his struggles with his Shaker brothers and sisters and what appear to be struggles with "the flesh," lapses into extremely vague language ("Reminiscenses," 175–77). Although these Shaker documents correspond with apostate accounts that refer to a lack of privacy and freedom of self-expression, many Believers were either not bothered by the lack of privacy, found ways of achieving privacy anyway, or endured personal repression because they believed in the spirit.

During all these periods Shaker reading and writing was in subjection to the greater purpose of spiritual achievement. The Shakers' belief in the spiritual reception and production of texts allowed them to write and read the world's genres and to believe that in spite of numerical decline, a new form of Shakerism would emerge. As Chapter 2 describes, the possession of the spirit allowed readers to perceive and apply texts appropriately. In a kind of circularity, this spiritual reading reinforced the life of the spirit within them. Understanding Shaker writing and reading as informed by the interplay of body and spirit depends upon first understanding Shaker attitudes toward spirits and spirituality and beliefs about physical bodies. The symbiotic relationship between spirit and body is not a new concept in Christianity introduced by the Shakers. Yet the sect's daily emphasis on the interplay between body and spirit informed their reading and writing practices, influencing their views of literacies in ways that distinguished them from the world. For the group that interacted verbally and visually with visitors from the "spirit world," what was the spirit and how did it manifest itself? For the celibate sect often viewed as ascetic in its attempts to achieve a "simple" life of "spiritual perfection," what roles did bodies play? And what were the relationships between spirituality, literacies, and bodily behavior? The answers to these questions emerge from the stories of Ann Lee's spiritually informed reading and writing acts.

NOTES

1. For Whitaker's and Lee's literacies, discussed in Chapter 2, see the 1816 *Testimonies* (XXX, 26–27). Meacham's reliance on Scripture and religious texts is evident in his *Concise Statement.*

2. Rebecca Jackson's testimonial writings, for example, the subject of Chapter 5, demonstrate her interest in reading and writing, but the works simultaneously reflect her lack of knowledge of grammatical correctness.

3. John E. Murray's essay on the relationship between economics, literacy, conversion, and retention in Shaker communities of Ohio at mid-century provides an excellent example of the highly specialized concerns of other scholars ("Human Capital"). See also Frank Taylor's "An Analysis of Shaker Education," not only for comments on differences between east and west but also diversity among communities (147). Clarke Garrett provides a thorough discussion of the move from orally conveyed teachings to inscribed theology in *Spirit Possession and Popular Religion* (195–213). Linda Mercadante analyzes the testimonies of the mid-nineteenth century in *Gender, Doctrine, and God.* Jean Humez analyzes Shaker letters, autobiographies, and biographies with attention to the world's genres and Shaker influences in *Gifts of Power*, "'Ye Are My Epistles,'" and "'A Woman Mighty.'" Each focuses on specific individuals and moments within Shaker history.

4. Henri Desroche briefly discusses Shaker hermeneutics within the context of the sect's literary and sexual practices (*American Shakers,* 79–81, 148–62). Katherine Clay Bassard picks up on this "spiritual" reading in her analysis of Rebecca Cox Jackson's literacy, "Spiritual Interrogations."

5. See William Gilmore's *Reading Becomes a Necessity of Life,* Nancy Cott's *Bonds of Womanhood,* Ann Douglas's *Feminization of American Culture,* Jane Tompkins's *Sensational Designs,* and Lawrence Buell's *New England Literary Culture.* Gilmore argues that between 1780 and 1835 in rural New England, print culture began to infiltrate all areas of daily life, even among common farm folk. During this period the Shakers also realized that reading was a necessity for their continuance. Cott describes reading the "right" kinds of literature as an element of female piety, one of the characteristics of "true womanhood." On the interplay of "secular" fictional and "sacred" nonfictional narrative strategies, see Tompkins (149–53). Douglas was among the first literary critics to describe the similar work of Protestant ministers and female writers in the nineteenth century. Buell's argument for the image of the New England town as a nineteenth-century social construct, an icon representing the American ideals "smallness, isolation, cohesiveness, innocence, and unchangingness," also describes the way in which, by the mid-nineteenth century, the Shakers viewed themselves (304–18). Their images of their villages and their "church" were microcosms of these ideals, and their literature and literacies sustained these images.

6. One of the earliest American teachings on the spiritual and civil purposes of reading, which foreshadows the Shaker teachings, appears in Cotton Mather's *Bonifacius, or To Do Good* (1710). In his advice on achieving a "better kingdom, spiritual or temporal," he includes these words on teaching children: "I will then assign them such *Books* to *Read,* as I may judge most agreeable and profitable; obliging them to give me some Account of what they *Read;* but keep a strict eye upon them, that they don't stumble on the Devils Library and poison themselves with foolish *Romances,* or *Novels,* or *Playes,* or *Songs,* or *Jests that are not convenient.* I will set them also, to *Write* out such things, as may be of the greatest Benefit unto them" (58). Davidson discusses Benjamin Franklin's and Noah Webster's slight revisions of this attitude in the early Republic (63–64).

7. Stein divides the sect's history into five periods: 1747–1787, "The Age of the Founders"; 1787–1826, "The Gathering and Building"; 1827–1875, "The Maturation and Revitalization"; 1876–1947, "The Transformation"; and 1948–present, "The Rebirth." Both Stein and Deignan recognize the move into publication as an important date. After that, their divisions do not correspond.

8. Susan McCully's "Oh I Love Mother, I Love Her Power: Shaker Spirit Possession and the Performance of Desire" discusses the ecstatic dances of mid-century, provides an overview of the controlled and disciplined motions of earlier years, and describes the leadership's desires to repress and channel "sexualized, somewhat homoerotic, performances by the girls, the most disenfranchised of an already marginalized and sexually deviant society" (89).

9. As Garrett writes, "When a religious community incorporates spirit possession into its ritual, the potential extent of innovation is limited only by the capacity of the believers to accept the revelations as authentically divine" (195).

10. The first seventeen pages of the tract appear in Whitson's *Two Centuries of Spiritual Reflection*, 61–66.

11. Stein summarizes: "The Believers also, ironically, inaugurated a program of systematic record keeping that eventually covered all aspects of the society's activities. As a result, the problem of scarce documentary resources is confined to the Age of Founders" (*Shaker Experience*, 9).

12. Garrett refers in some detail to several apostate accounts and accusations, such as those by Daniel and Valentine Rathbun (195–213). He is "persuaded that" their story "is the truer one" (197). Lawrence Foster also sees the merits of these accounts (*Religion and Sexuality*, 51–54).

13. Mary was engaged in a pamphlet war with her husband, Joseph, and the Shakers. The wife's first pamphlet appeared in 1818; the husband's response, the same year. Joseph countered with *A compendious Narrative, elucidating the Character, Disposition, and conduct of Mary Dyer, from the Time of her Marriage, in 1799, Till She Left the Society Called Shakers, in 1815* (1818). Next, Mary produced her lengthy book *A Portraiture of Shakerism* (1822). Joseph's "Compendious Narrative" saw two editions (Richmond, I, 74). All these texts had overt political and juridical purposes, as Joseph's subtitle acknowledges. For example, the second edition of his book (1826) includes "a remonstrance Against the Testimony and application of the said Mary, for Legislative Interference." Humez, "'A Woman Mighty,'" and Elizabeth DeWolfe, "'Erroneous Principles, Base Deceptions, and Pious Frauds,'" provide discussions of the Dyers' writings within the historical context. In its compendious nature Dyer's *Portraiture* is not unlike Stephen Burroughs's *Memoirs*, first published in 1798 and republished several times in the early nineteenth century. Burroughs was also involved in New Hampshire courts.

14. Another passage links literacy and the freedom of the individual to find "true" religion: "Children are kept as ignorant as possible of literary knowledge, or the true doctrines of the gospel" (279).

15. Blythe Forcey, for example, accurately ascribes Charlotte's victimization in Susanna Rowson's *Charlotte Temple* to her poor reading skills. Humez also calls attention to Dyer's depiction of herself as a "suffering victim" ("'A Woman Mighty,'" 92).

16. See Meacham's *Notes,* copied by Rufus Bishop in 1850, for the earliest written philosophy of learning and teaching within the sect.

17. In spite of her concern with education of children and other Believers, Wright wanted to maintain Lee's emphasis on orality; she resisted the initial codification in writing of the Millennial Laws, whose relationship to literacy I discuss in Chapter 2. For a description of "Republican motherhood," see Nancy F. Cott's *Bonds of Womanhood*.

4

18. Wright's reputation for giving guidelines for education appears to have been well known and sustained even after her death in 1821. In 1841 an unnamed Shaker "instrument" received from Wright instructions she had been given by Mother Ann. The published work is *The Gospel Monitor. A Little Book of Mother Ann's Word to Those Who are Placed as Instructors & Care-takers of Children; Written by Mother Lucy Wright, and Brought by Her to the Elders of the First Order, on the Holy Mount, March 1, 1841.*

19. Drawing from sources at Canterbury, New Hampshire, and published works by and about the Shakers, Taylor argues that Shaker "dedication, innovation and community served as an early model for modern alternative education programs both public and private" (4). To make his case he lists such attributes as "team teaching, flexible scheduling, the all-year school, student published texts, activity periods during the day, infant education and interdisciplinary studies . . . the use of concrete objects to reinforce learning, the practical application of theory and the creation of unique teaching tools" (3).

20. The circulation of these pieces within the sect may be extrapolated not only from evidence of the Shaker practice of circulating letters within communities but also from a copy of "Remarks on Learning" in the *Copy Book (ca.* 1833) of John Coffin, a teacher at the Sabbathday Lake community.

21. John MacLean traces the Shakers' publishing history, including these periodicals (19), in the opening of his *Bibliography of Shaker Literature* (3–20). The Shakers bought their first press in 1823, for the Pleasant Hill, Kentucky, community. The Watervliet, Ohio, community had a press by 1832, and the North Union, Ohio, community had one by 1834.

22. For descriptions and analyses of the Era of Manifestations, see Stein (*Shaker Experience,* 165–200), Edward Deming Andrews (*People Called Shakers,* 152–76), and Sally Promey's *Spiritual Spectacles.*

23. Hollister's record of his childhood at Mount Lebanon, New York, corresponds with Briggs's account of receipt of the book, but he recalls that he was to use the book to jot hymns and the like. The diary of John Holmes at Sabbathday Lake, Maine, is probably an extant example of one of these diaries. Rather than a book of hymns and poems or a record that would allow the writer, during the last week of December, to reflect on the past year, Holmes's book is sketchy, practically blank. The few entries are so short and spotty that we gain insights to his low alphabetic literacy and must wonder how many Shaker diaries were of this quality. The degree of self-expression these little books allowed is difficult to know; Holmes's example, in juxtaposition with Hollister's and Briggs's, illustrates the variety of responses to the same institutional task.

24. That the sect's uniformity is due to the controlled reading is a statement in keeping with one he makes later; namely, that his story of his experience in one particular community (Hancock, Massachusetts) is representative for all of Shakerism. Recent studies of Shakerism have attempted to counter this myth of Shaker uniformity with explanations of Shaker self-expression. For example, Promey analyzes the expressive role of the drawings of the Era of Manifestations; Tim Reiman and Charles Muller argue for the significance of Shaker furniture; Linda Mercadante discusses the self-expression of written testimonies. Some critics, such as Diane Sasson, acknowledge both self-expression and its limitations (*Shaker Spiritual* and "Individual Experience").

We might wonder, since Lamson seems to despise the Shakers' uniformity so much, what drew him to the sect. As he explains, he saw "orthodox" Christian churches as anti-reform; as a Christian, he thought moral and social reform necessary. Specifically, abolition, pacifism, and temperance were social movements he thought necessary and saw Shakers involved in. Lamson's experience, then, dovetails with what Deignan sees as the thrust of the 1848 edition of Calvin Green's *Summary View of the Millennial Church*—their "exemplaristic features" (159).

25. Lamson also comments negatively on education in the communities. Children go to school but three months of the year until they are fifteen (girls) or sixteen (boys), only to receive instruction in writing, reading, a little arithmetic, grammar and geography, and this from teachers whose "qualifications would not be approved by a town committee." Frank Taylor, who argues that by this time in the century Shaker education was "progressive," also explains that residents of towns in which Shaker communities were located sent their children to the Shaker schools. That is, the Shaker schools had displaced public schools because of the former's higher quality. Nicholas Briggs comments on the excellence of the Shaker teachers. These apparent contradictions are one more example of individuals holding diverse views of similar situations.

26. The preface to Philemon Stewart's *Holy, Sacred and Divine Roll and Book,* published during this period, describes in some detail his reading and writing practices as well as his injunctions for the publications, distribution, and reading of them. Stewart also compiled for the ministry "The Holy Laws of Zion" (1840), a manuscript listing strict regulations of behavior that was to separate Shakers from the world. The manuscript was to be read twice yearly for six years, on the birthdays of Jesus and Ann Lee (Andrews, *People Called Shakers,* 156). See also Blinn's *Historical Record* (II, 287–91).

27. My title has been influenced by Jerome Bruner's *Actual Minds, Possible Worlds,* a reader response study that emphasizes both reasonable and emotional thought as constitutive of readers' imaginative constructing.

28. William Dean Howells writes in 1884 that the Shirley, Massachusetts, Shakers enjoyed the oral readings of Twain and Harte (*Three Villages,* 108–9).

29. The attention to Blinn's penmanship in addition to the comments about classics and fiction seem to indicate that Briggs has an aesthetic sense typical of the world's—the art or form of the manuscript is important, as is a well rounded familiarity with the literary arts. Also, the description of Blinn as a "general good teacher" counters Lamson's criticism of Shaker schools and reflects the variations among the community schools, especially across time. Lamson's experience was at least a decade earlier than Blinn's.

30. Otis Sawyer, Elder at Sabbathday Lake, Maine, from 1872 to 1884, had so many books that he had printed labels for numbering and organizing works in his library.

31. See Byrd's letter dated January 25, 1827 (Stein, *Letters*). For discussions of Youngs's coded writing and its relationship to sexuality, see Susan Matarese and Paul Salmon, "Assessing Psychopathology in Communal Societies." This essay also provides an overview of Youngs's voluminous manuscripts.

Chapter 2

Letters, Spirits, and Bodies: The Shakers' Spiritual Literacies

The letter killeth, but the spirit maketh alive.
II Corinthians 3:6

Ann Lee has been described by Shaker scholars as "illiterate" and "unlettered."[1] The labels are understandable—she left no written records, and the first Shaker publication to present an extensive picture of her life describes her as such. The first chapter of the *Testimonies Concerning the Life, Character, Revelations, and Doctrines of Our Ever Blessed Mother Ann Lee, and the Elders with Her* (1816) includes a sketch of Lee's childhood that explains that she "was very illiterate; so that she could neither read, nor write" (I, 3). Nevertheless, the *Testimonies* also include images that ask us to view Lee as "reading," for she interprets several kinds of uninscribed signs: She mystically and prophetically reads visions as well as people's minds, hearts, and bodies; and she quite reasonably and innovatively reads orally conveyed passages of Scripture. Lee "writes" or "publishes" these readings in public settings in the form of orally conveyed mini-sermons to a crowd or one-on-one lessons. Lee's reading, writing, and publishing provided her agency and autonomy in a culture and climate that relegated women to a private and emotional realm. Her literacy differs, however, from that of her female predecessors and contemporaries such as Anne Hutchinson, Ann Hibbens, and Jemimah Wilkinson in that it becomes inscribed in a volume edited by male leaders and, as I assert throughout this chapter and those that follow, foundational to the sect.[2] Dependent upon the indwelling or embodied spirit, Lee's "reading" and "writing," as delineated in the *Testimonies,* illustrates the interplay of spoken and written language and realms gendered masculine and feminine, establishing in print the parameters of what I call the Shakers' "spiritual literacies."

Shaker spiritual literacies, like all cultural literacies, have parameters and rules that the communities established and taught in various ways. Lee's emphasis on drawing from the embodied spirit to read people became coupled with the leadership's codification of bodily rituals through the Millennial Laws. These institutionalized codes, meant to develop spirituality, allowed Believers to read individual Shakers' bodies and bodily behavior, and the spirit informed these interpretive acts. Thus, the Shakers' bodies, controlled and channeled by written laws and unwritten rituals, were integrally involved in their writing and reading acts. The Shakers' attitudes toward their bodies upheld an "androgynous ideal" integral to their literacies.[3] This fluidity, not unlike the symbolic work of other Christians since the first century, appears in Shaker texts other than the *Testimonies*. Works by Benjamin Seth Youngs, Richard McNemar, John Dunlavy, and Rebecca Cox Jackson reiterate the relationship between spirits, letters, and bodies by quoting the scripture "the letter killeth, but the spirit maketh alive" (II Corinthians 3:6) and exemplifying its significance through their texts. These works illustrate the spiritual literacies, initiated by Lee, that sustained Shakerism throughout the nineteenth century.

ANN LEE'S READING

In cultures only partially "literate" or beginning to accept and embrace literacy, such as the Puritan culture of seventeenth-century New England, traces of the spoken exist in written records. "Even in literate societies," Robert St. George writes, "speech continues to be a fundamental component in the routine shaping of social reality." St. George calls attention to this "interdependency of speaking, reading, and writing" (276) as he questions the given distinction that "unlike written or material artifacts, speech is by definition ephemeral. Once uttered, the word totally disappears" (277).[4] His assertion illuminates late-eighteenth- and early-nineteenth-century Shakerism. In the *Testimonies* Shaker editors capture the power of the spoken words of Ann Lee but recognize the necessity of writing and print to do so. In contrast to the Puritan claim of the primacy of the written over the spoken (which St. George demonstrates they ironically inverted), the *Testimonies* reinforce the interplay of the spoken and the written. Rather than saying, "Once uttered, the [spoken] word disappears," I assert that once written, Ann Lee's spoken words permanently attest to the power of uninscribed signs within Shakerism.

Certainty about what Lee said and about the "facts" of her life, of course, are limited; yet Lee's speech and physical activities influenced the textual recordings of them to some degree. Studies of Revolutionary New England, the era and locale in which Lee evangelized, document events similar to those in the *Testimonies*, such as the storming of buildings housing Lee and her followers as well as other brutal assaults upon their bodies during the 1780s, in what are now western Massachusetts and the Albany, New York, area.[5] My purpose here, however, is not to validate the Shakers' veracity or accuracy but to give attention to the way the narrative records and preserves scenes of Lee's interpretive and expressive acts, reflecting images previously conveyed orally and preserved in memory. As other recent studies of the biography have demonstrated, the text's value emerges from its role as an index of the Society's status and concerns in 1816, as a record of reflective inscription by male leaders rather than as an accurate record of the female leader's life.[6]

Drawn from oral testimonies of "eye and ear" witnesses (both female and male), the edited accounts bear marks of orality and the emotional exhuberance of personal narrative while also demonstrating the "reasoned" rhetoric typical to early-nineteenth-century legal literature and *belles lettres.* Much of the *Testimonies's* power within the Society arises from this generic amphibiousness, a topic I discuss further in Chapter 4; equally valuable within it is the mutability of its heroine. Jean Humez and Marjorie Proctor-Smith, for example, have pointed to the maternal images of Lee "laboring" and feeding juxtaposed with images of Lee as a strong, independent, and somewhat masculine figure.[7] As Humez aptly concludes, "All of these possible versions of Ann Lee became part of the ambiguous heritage of later Shakerism." She suggests, "It was an advantage to Shakerism, as it responded to internal instabilities and adapted to changes in the outside culture over time, to have a sacred text that could supply so readily multiple understandings of a founder" ("'Ye Are My Epistles,'" 103). I agree that the ambiguous images undoubtedly were an asset.

More specifically I add to these assertions that images of Lee's literacy—meant to instruct other Shakers—similarly allow multiple visions. Two passages early in the volume foreground the multiple visions of literacy which inform Shaker attitudes toward reading and writing throughout the nineteenth century. In the first of these, a sketch of Lee's childhood, the editors contrast her illiteracy with her "acquired . . . habit of industry," gained as a result of working as a child rather than "being sent to school" (I, 3). The passage emphasizes Lee's bodily activity, rather than book work, as reflecting and contributing to spirituality. The second reference contrasts traditional notions of literacy and religious learning with the spiritual power Lee possesses, yet it also introduces the complex interplay between the authority of a female's personal inspiration and the need for institutional validation by "lettered" males. The passage reports Lee to have said:

"Before I came from England, there was a great lord came to see me. He had been acquainted with me from my childhood, and knew that I was poor and had no letter learning. He watched me in every movement, for I had the power of God upon me, and spoke with other tongues; and being a learned man, he understood what I said, and was thereby convicted that I had the power of God." (IX, 11)

Lee manifests spirituality through her speech, which appears to be a foreign language such as Latin or Greek, rather than ecstatic gibberish, since "a learned man" understands it. Ironically, Lee's spiritual power, triumphant in spite of her lack of knowledge of "letters," must be validated by this "learned man." This juxtaposition subtly reinforces the Shakers' dependence on traditional notions of literacy even while revamping them with their emphasis upon reading and publishing uninscribed signs. Men of "learning," as this passage and Shaker doctrinal works demonstrate, inscribe and interpret texts that reinforce Shaker faith. These two passages together suggest the interdependent elements of Lee's and subsequent Shaker literacies: Spirituality emerges from and thrives upon bodily actions as well as intellectual endeavors; the body's activities can be read as signs of spirituality; intellectualism and learning are not to be set aside but kept alongside of uninscribed messages of spirituality to advocate or validate them.

Lee's ability and willingness to read her own visions while in England set her apart as a leader and began to establish Shaker literacies. They revealed to her, for example, that the Second Coming of Christ had occurred and that the small group of Shaking Quakers of which she was a part were to go to America. They provided her the doctrine of celibacy. They also showed her the conversions, punishments, and rewards of those in the spirit world.[8] One example of such reading appears as Lee speaks to Nathan Farrington of a vision he had of "the Lord Jesus Christ, and Mother Ann by his side" (XXIII, 11). She explains to Farrington that this vision will sustain Believers "when all things else [e.g., inscribed texts] fail" (XXIII, 12). She implicitly emphasizes here both the power of uninscribed texts such as visions and the content of the vision: two people who embody the Christ Spirit.

Lee's language on several other occasions demonstrates that people, like visions, deserve to be read as texts. The spirit gave this type of skill to such other eighteenth-century religious leaders in New England as Jonathan Edwards and Isaac Backus, but Lee places the ability to read people's hearts and minds above reading of Scripture.[9] She implies the importance of placing people above inscribed texts when she quotes from the New Testament (II Corinthians 3:2), "Ye are my epistles, read and known of all men" (XXXIV, 22). On another occasion Lee addresses the danger of misplacing the site of reading (and especially, of reading about the Second Coming) onto either "natural" signs or books. At Ashfield, Massachusetts, the editors record, one Believer commented after seeing an "extraordinary" display of the Northern Lights, "It is the sign of the coming of the Son of Man, in the clouds of heaven" (XXV, 19). Alluding to the Hebrews writer's reference to "so great a cloud of witnesses" of faith that should motivate Christians to cast aside sin, endure hardship, and "run with patience the race set before" them (Hebrews 12:1), Lee instructs the Believer: "Those signs which appear in the sky, are not the signs of his coming; but the second appearance of Christ is in his Church; and Christ is come to put away sin from his people; and this is the cloud [of witnesses] alluded to" (XXV, 19).

On two occasions, recorded consecutively, Lee reads people's sexual sins.[10] In one instance Lee "reads" a young woman, whom others "thought to be very honest and chaste," as "'liv[ing] in whoredom with married men, young men, black men and boys.'"[11] Although "this declaration almost staggered" one Believer's "confidence in Mother," "the girl soon after, came forward and confessed the very things which Mother had laid to her charge." The incident strengthened the Believer's faith, showing her "beyond a doubt, that Mother had the revelation of God, and was able to see what creatures had in them" (XXV, 11–12). On the second occasion Lee speaks directly to Tryphena Perkins, a professing Christian: "'You are a filthy whore.'" Enemies "began to flatter themselves, that they were able to prove Mother a false prophetess, and determined to prosecute her for defamation. They said they could prove, to a certainty, that Tryphena was not formed like other women; and therefore could not possibly be guilty of the charge of whoredom." But Lee's reading proves accurate; Perkins "was soon found to be with child, by a married man! . . . and Mother's enemies were greatly abashed and confounded" (XXV, 4). On another occasion, "Mother said, to [Believer] Mary [Tiffany], 'I see the travail of your soul written upon you in great capital letters, and I can read them as fast as I can speak'" (XXVI, 7).

Lee's miraculous insights, her ability "to see what creatures had in them," strengthened the faith of her followers and provided examples of literacies apart from inscribed texts. Influenced by the embodied spirit, Lee's remark to Tiffany about "capital letters" also indicates her partial knowledge of inscribed texts and print culture, including the Bible.[12] A scene mentioned in Chapter 1 illustrates particularly well the traditional and innovative reading of people and Scripture that comprise Lee's literacy. According to the *Testimonies,* when widow Mercy Bishop prepared to depart from a gathering of Believers at Watervliet in 1784 to return home "with a number of her small children," Lee began to speak. Apparently moved by the woman's spirituality and physical situation,

Mother in a farewell address, commended the widow for the zeal which she had manifested in bringing her family to the Church; and then directing her discourse to those who were heads of families, and people of property, . . . she spoke much to them of their duty in giving alms, and being kind and charitable to the poor, particularly to such widows and fatherless children who were among them. After speaking considerable lengthy, and very feelingly on this subject, she requested Elder James to read a passage of Scripture in the Epistle of James, first chapter, beginning at the 22d verse. (XXX, 26–27)

The account continues, explaining that "Elder James took the Bible" and read the passage, which the volume's editors reprint. The passage, on being "doers" rather than "hearers" of the Word and on visiting the "fatherless and widows," is remarkably appropriate to the situation at hand. Next, they describe the scene's aura: "The solemn gift of God which accompanied Mother's preceeding discourse, together with the impressive feeling with which Elder James read this passage, had a powerful effect on the minds of the hearers" (XXX, 32). Here the editors emphasize God's work (the "gift of God" assisting Ann Lee) and emotion (the "impressive feeling" Elder James gave to his reading) as key to affecting "the minds of the hearers." The passage reveals that Lee disrupts traditional notions of literacy and of religious discourse—the "masculine" model of reading and publishing that supposedly elevates the mind over the body and reason over emotion—and offers instead a method of teaching that draws from mind and reason but recognizes the value of personal and emotional interaction.

Rhetorical handbooks of the period advising ministers in sermon preparation and published sermons that appear to adhere to these guidelines suggest that typically the minister would begin with a scripture and "divide" it through "reasoned" exegesis so that it could be absorbed by the minds of its readers or hearers. The divided scripture would be developed into a practical application at the sermon's close. Better understanding of Scripture—the written text—was often a prominent goal of the sermon. Of course, many ministers probably let the needs of their parishoners direct them as they chose sermon topics and the scripture to be divided; and sermon style by the late eighteenth century had shifted from the "plain style" of previous generations to more emotional methods such as those used by itinerant Methodists George Whitefield and John and Charles Wesley, whom Lee might have heard in England.[13] However, the established pattern these "masculine" sermons follow is to appeal to reason through exegesis of the scripture prior to providing a practical application that is affiliated with salvation or with bodily activities.[14]

Lee's style represents an overt reversal of this "masculine" method of sermon development. Her extemporaneous speech emerges from the "texts" of physical bodies. Only after her bodily based lesson was delivered did she turn to Scripture for supporting evidence. In this instance we see her recall the passage from the Epistle of James after seeing the widow Mercy Bishop with her children preparing to depart. She recalls the situation's "antitype" within Scripture as a proof text, as readily as her "literate" male counterparts. Her message emphasizes bodily action among human beings rather than greater intellectual understanding of Scripture. However, she does not chaotically disrupt a man who is in the midst of a "reasoned" sermon with a moment of uncontrolled, ecstatic gibberish. Rather, already in control of the gathering, she instigates a coherent mini-sermon that emerges from the bodily needs she sees around her.

The significance of bodies to Shaker spirituality and literacies also emerges in several passages where Lee speaks of the embodied forms of the spirit world. On one of these occasions, she proclaims: "If you commit sin with beasts, your spirits will be transformed into the shape of beasts in hell. I now see some in hell, whose souls are in the shape of dogs, horses and swine. They appear in the shape of such beasts as they committed sin with" (XXXIV, 2).[15] This passage about the spirit world, of course, combines Lee's attitudes toward sexual sins (the body's habits and practices) with a vision of a materialized eternal life. Several others have written at length about Shaker sexuality, an important issue for the sect, whose doctrine of celibacy has remained intact for two centuries.[16] A significance of this passage, to this book, is that it suggests the Shaker theology of the resurrection, which is directly connected to Shaker bodies, letters, and spirituality. Leaders such as John Dunlavy, Benjamin Seth Youngs, and Calvin Green consistently reaffirmed in their writings the significance of the body to spirituality through its "crucifixion" and "resurrection." They explained that contrary to beliefs of many other sects, the Society believed in only one resurrection. This spiritual resurrection occurred not at the moment of physical death or at a future day of judgment when Jesus would return from the Heavens, but when any individual "died" to the old, fleshly self and began the "regenerate" life. It began with "crucifixion" of the flesh, which included celibacy.[17] Thus ongoing judgment and resurrection—the "second coming" of the Christ—occurred at moments varying from individual to individual. For the Shakers physical death marked only one small step in the middle of the progressive resurrection life of the spirit—what one writer referred to as a mere "translation" in which the spiritual being sloughs off the fleshy casing. Because the Shakers' resurrection bodies were not yet to be obtained, winged beings but the regenerate spirit housed within physical bodies, physical bodies were not easily cast aside. The physical body was both the house of the spirit and the vehicle in which the spirit progressed toward its perfection. As Kathleen Deignan explains, "The 'body' is problematic for Shakers, since it is at once the ground of both sin and salvation" (79). Stephen Marini aptly describes the exemplary union of body and spirit in Ann Lee, a restoration of "the wedding of earthly and spiritual natures" that had been manifest in Adam and Eve before the fall: "By rooting out sin as a human being 'conceived in sin, and lost in the fullness of man's fall,' she established spiritual dominion over an imperfect body. Jesus had restored spiritual perfection, Mother Ann physical perfection to human nature, thereby completing the reunion of humanity with God" (*Radical Sects,* 152). For the Shakers following Lee's example, the body's experiences were critical to spirituality.

Lee's animated physical body, according to the *Testimonies,* inflamed spite in some but commanded respect from others. For example, one chapter opens with this bodily and spiritual "presence":

In reproving and condemning sin and all manner of evil, in feelings, words, and actions, Mother's power was beyond description. Though she would often bear with lost, dark souls, who were blinded and corrupted with sin, till her life seemed almost spent through sufferings; yet at times, when she felt a gift of God to reprove their wickedness, the power of her spirit seemed like flames of fire, and the words of her mouth more dreadful than peals of thunder; so that the most stubborn and stouthearted would shake and tremble in her presence, like a leaf shaken with a mighty wind. (XXXII, 1)

The passage focuses on Lee's actions "reproving and condemning sin," her "bear[ing] with lost, dark souls," "the power of her spirit . . . and the words of her mouth"—summed up as "her presence." Other passages in the *Testimonies* and in apostate accounts also depict this "presence" and Lee's performances.[18] For example, when Shaker editors describe Lee's physical appearance, offering a portrait to Believers who never knew her in the flesh, they move quickly from the concrete physical aspects of Lee's body to more changing, abstract aspects of her physicality such as her deportment. This movement recurs in the paragraphs that follow in the chapter, leaving out the purely physical but meandering among her words, her mental abilities, and her works.[19]

Mother Ann Lee was a woman, in nature, of a strong constitution, rather exceeding the ordinary size of women; very strait and well proportioned in form, or rather thick; of a light complexion, and blue eyes; her hair of a light chestnut brown. In appearance, she was very majestic, and her countenance was such as inspired confidence and respect; and, by many of the world, who saw her without prejudice, she was called beautiful. To her faithful children (*spoken of spiritually*), she appeared to possess a degree of dignified beauty and heavenly love transcending that of mortals. (XXXIX, 1)

Lee's "constitution," "form," "complexion," "eyes," and "hair," appearing only near the volume's end, indicate this static physical icon is less important to Believers than the animation conveyed by moving pictures of her bodily actions.

In his *Account of the People Called Shakers,* Thomas Brown similarly describes Lee's presence, though with negative connotations because, in his opinion, she transgresses gender boundaries: "Ann Lee was a woman rather short and corpulent. Her countenance was fair and pleasant, but often assumed a commanding, severe look" (330). Yet even he cannot resist turning from Lee's stature to her performance: "She sang sweetly, with a pleasant voice, but would frequently use the most harsh, satirical language, with a masculine, sovereign address. Her natural genius was resplendent, with a quick and ready turn of wit, but entirely destitute of school education" (330). Lee's bodily appearance and actions exude her spiritual presence, whether she enters a room singing, leads a group in dancing, speaks to individuals, or addresses a crowd. She displays in these instances what Humez refers to as an ability to "improvise" "as occasion demanded in order to remove or circumvent any roadblocks her gender placed in her path" ("'Ye Are My Epistles,'" 86). The improvisation is an element of her literacy, for Lee "reads" these social situations and responds in an effective manner.

Humez summarizes Lee's effectiveness as an improvisational and charismatic leader in terms some might consider "feminine": "Lee probably relied primarily upon the *emotional* impact of her presence, the dramatic appeal of her message about celibacy, and an *ecstatic* mode of worship to convince her followers *experientially* of her authority and the rightness of her leadership" ("'Ye Are My Epistles,'" 86, emphasis mine). But Lee's performative readings of and responses to given social situations—sometimes "emotional," "ecstatic," and "experiential" —demonstrate her knowing when to let reason predominate and when to allow emotional excess. Examples of Lee's bodily performances—her "reading," writing, and "publishing"—draw from and reflect both "masculine" and "feminine" modes.

The type of authority and presence Lee commands appears in several other passages as Lee reads Scripture in a way that silences, befuddles, and often angers people who hear her, not because of the supernatural, emotional, or irrational elements of the readings but, rather, because of the cleverness—the reasoning skills—she exhibits. To borrow the words Jane Kamensky has used to describe Anne Hutchinson, Lee "was beating them [men] at their own game," a "game of verbal thrust-and-parry [that] was arguably more damning than her female/prophetic mode" (193). For example, during "an assembly" in 1781, the *Testimonies* records, Mother "came forth with a very powerful gift of God, and reproved the people for their hardness of heart, and unbelief in the Second Appearance of Christ." Her "reproof" was directed specifically to the men of the audience:

"Especially, (said she) ye men and brethren! I upbraid you for your unbelief and hardness of heart."
    She spake of the unbelieving Jews, in his first appearance. "Even his own disciples, (added she) after he arose from the dead, though he had often told them that he should rise

the third day, believed it not. They would not believe that he had risen, because he appeared first to a woman! So great was their unbelief that the words of Mary seemed to them like idle tales!" (XXIII, 2–3)

Here Lee closes the message with an innovative but "reasoned" interpretation of the scripture: "His appearing first to a woman, showed that his Second appearing would be in a woman!" Through "syllogistical" reasoning, not unlike what Kamensky demonstrates Anne Hutchinson and Ann Hibbens used in the seventeenth century (192), Lee argues convincingly that the scripture's fulfillment is within herself. Lee's speech is "masculine," as Thomas Brown describes it, not only in its tone and words, but also in its cleverness and reasoning.

In the precedent-setting example of Lee's innovative interpretation of Scripture, she gives an extended explanation of who she is. Joseph Meacham and Calvin Harlow—eventual leaders—have questioned her about Pauline teachings on women being silent in the churches; in response she explains her spiritual position in Jesus' absence:

"The order of man, in the natural creation, is a figure of the order of God in the spiritual creation. As the order of nature requires a man and a woman to produce offspring; so, where they both stand in their proper order, the man is first, and the woman the second in the government of the family. He is the father and she the Mother; and all the children, both male and female, must be subject to their parents; and the woman, being second, must be second to her husband, who is the first; but when the man is gone, the right of government belongs to the woman: So is the family of Christ." (IV, 3)

The passage shows Lee reinforcing the traditional values for women in relation to men within the family and the church, but it also drastically revamps them with what Humez calls "an ingenious argument" ("'Ye Are My Epistles,'" 86), which influences Meacham's thinking: It "opened a vast field of contemplation to Joseph, and filled his mind with great light and understanding concerning the spiritual work of God" (IV, 3).

Meacham was willing to accept Lee's argument for her leadership role in the absence of the male Christ; he was willing to recognize and accept the spiritual presence she embodied. The passage continues with a gloss that describes his understanding of the female Lee in relation to the male Jesus: "He saw Jesus Christ to be the Father of the spiritual creation, who was now absent; and he [Meacham] saw Ann Lee to be the Mother of all who were now begotten in the regeneration; and she being present in the body, the power and authority of Christ on earth, was committed to her; and to her appertained the right of leading, directing and governing all her spiritual children" (IV, 5).

Lee's literacy—her ability to read and write that depends upon a spiritual presence drawing from both reason and emotion—surprises some readers into silence and spurs others to violence. The woman's silencing of men occurs neither by specific requests for silence, submission, or obedience nor by vocal command but by her unusual content and style. Although sometimes Lee's and the Elders' voices bestow miraculous spiritual power, most men's responses to Lee appear as matters of choice rather than matters of miracle.[20]

Not all who came peacefully were converted like Meacham and Harlow. Not all the crowds or mobs of people who came to see Mother Ann came with skeptical or violent intents.[21] The *Testimonies* aptly introduces not only Lee's reading but how others "read" Lee, a topic I discuss in more detail in Chapter 4. In sum, and borrowing from contemporary theories of reading, Lee's followers appear as readers willing to submit to the text—to her bodily and spiritual presence; Lee's persecutors, unwilling to submit, literally do violence to the text. These violent readings occur because the men have preconceived ideas about two "semes"—the "eschaton" and "woman."[22] Lee's presence spills over the categories within which the persecutors attempt to contain her. They have thought about the Second Coming of Christ but never imagined the eschaton to be in female form. As "woman" she was expected to be mother of a biological family and contained within domestic space. The "resisting readers"—those unwilling to submit to the "text" of Lee, namely, what she teaches and what she represents—resist but do not read "against the grain." They read not with hopes of making societal change (helping to build the "kingdom of heaven") but with desires to solidify existing social categories.[23] In contrast, Lee reads against the grain of masculine religious discourse and offers an example they choose not to follow. Lee's followers, content with the reasonable and ecstatic spiritual fullness she conveys, willingly submit to this novel "text." These instances of Lee being read by her followers, in combination with examples of her reading and publishing, establish the literacies predominant within Shaker communities throughout the nineteenth century. Lee draws from both reason and emotion to convince her audience. She conserves basic elements of Christianity (charity and respect for the truths of the New Testament) while revamping orthodox practices associated with reading, writing, and publishing. This blend of tradition and innovation, drawing from both reason and emotion, celebrates the body's role in spiritual reading and writing, and it promises dynamism and fluidity within Shakerism in the years to come.

SHAKER BODIES, LETTERS, AND SPIRITS

These views of Lee's literacies and spirituality parallel two avenues others have traveled as they have revised what appear to be firmly opposed, hierarchized gendered categories. First, others have pointed to the realm of the body as integral to spirituality; second, they have noted that some writers define the spirit or the spiritual realm as an androgynous one. In sum, these scholars ask us to consider how women subvert the hierarchized dichotomies and to rethink the dualities as unified rather than in opposition to each other. Caroline Walker Bynum writes of "medieval asceticism," for example, that it "should not be understood as rooted in dualism, in a radical sense of spirit opposed to or entrapped by body" (*Holy Feast,* 294). Male and female ascetics attempted "to plumb and to realize all the possibilities of the flesh. It was a profound expression of the doctrine of the Incarnation. . . . They were not revelling against or torturing their flesh out of guilt over its capabilities so much as using the possibilities of its full sensual and affective range to soar ever closer to God" (*Holy Feast,* 294–95). In addition to asking readers to see asceticism and discipline as a celebration of the body, Bynum highlights differences in men's and women's symbolic work. Medieval male mystics, she argues, recognized and transgressed traditional gender boundaries, whereas women became more deeply embedded in their own "feminine" space.[24] Like medieval ascetic women, Ann Lee celebrates the body and the "feminine" realm, but she also transgresses traditional gender boundaries. Clarke Garrett similarly notes the bodily spiritual work of early Shaker male and female leaders in a gendered manner. Of Lee's "ecstatic experiences," he writes, "The prevailing mood seems to have been one of celebration, of rejoicing in the presence of the divine." In contrast, "under Whitaker's leadership, the gifts of the Spirit were generally those of mortification, forcing believers to confront and overcome their own sins, especially those of sexuality" (212). Yet even what he sees as "mortification" I will argue is an acceptance of the body's power.

This ambivalent and gendered imagery, especially present in the *Testimonies,* allows Shakers to continually redefine the spiritual realm and its relationship to the body in ways similar not only to medieval writers but also to gnostic writers of the first three centuries. In *Adam, Eve, and the Serpent* Elaine Pagels explains that gnostics revised the orthodox dichotomy between mind (*nous*) and sensation (*aisthesis*) or the "nobler, masculine and rational element" associated with Adam and the "lower, feminine element, source of all passion," associated with Eve and the body (64–65). Instead, they emphasized a pairing of "*soul* and *spirit*—that is, between the *psyche* (ordinary consciousness, understood to include both mind and sensation) and the spirit [*pneuma*], the potential for a higher, spiritual consciousness" (66). Some gnostic writers associated the soul—"the emotional and mental impulses" (68)—with the female and the spirit with the male, but "many other gnostic texts reverse[d] the symbolism" (66). In all these gnostic works, however, the writers emphasized an individual's wholeness depended upon a blend of the two.

Although writing of historical periods and locales distant from American Shakerism, Pagels's and Bynum's comments offer useful points of inquiry to this study. They underscore celebrations of the body among religious and spiritual people generally considered to subdue and deny it. Many have similarly viewed the Shakers. Pagels and Bynum also demonstrate that gendered terms have been relevant to many people's spirituality, not merely by creating gendered codes of behavior, such as bearing and nurturing children, but more importantly to help them argue for a union of the dichotomies in whole and holy individuals. These two concepts underpin an understanding of Shakerism and, consequently, of Shaker literacies.

Shaker theological writings, like the gnostic writings Pagels analyzes, encourage the use of gendered terms but unify them through "the annointing spirit." This invaluable choice of an abstract term, an example of their "dissociation," as Kathryn M. Olson explains it, allows them to maintain some beliefs and change others as they write their theological tracts and autobiographies.[25] Gendered dichotomies first appear in print in 1808 as "the structural principle" in Youngs's *Testimony of Christ's Second Appearing* (Deignan, 96). Chief among "the polarities of all reality," Deignan nicely summarizes, is "the fundamental pair of male and female . . . which Youngs sets as his archetypal foundation" (96–97). Yet "we must not mistake [the Shakers] to be . . . theological dualist[s]" (Deignan 120), for "the polarities which undergird the created world are themselves utterances of the constitutive terms of God's power and wisdom. . . . The term which will translate the eternal, transcendent, and bivalent Word of power and wisdom into the historical, economic, still bivalent revelation of Father and Mother . . . is . . . the annointing Spirit who will bridge the gap" (120–21).[26] Oliver C. Hampton rearticulates Shaker androgyny in his 1880 article "Relation of Intellect and Emotion," which appeared on the front page of the Shaker *Manifesto*. Hampton illustrates how Shaker thinking diverges from that of the world by underscoring the belief in the union of these dichotomies—the necessity of both terms within a single person. He equates "wisdom and love," as he says "mankind" does, with "positive and negative, active and passive," "intellect and emotion," and "reason and religion." He explains that aspects of the "male" categories (given first in each pair) are "necessary to develop, define, explain, [and] to illustrate" the administrative details of church life, those "necessary to the existence of a self-perpetuating community," such as theology and "regulations." The "female" terms are "necessary to the development of the religious sentiment together with all the Pentecostal gifts, inspirations, ministrations from the spiritual world, prophecies, tongues, healing of disease, together with all sympathy for human suffering, going out of one's self to do good to others." The categories and functions Hampton describes reinforce the stereotypes of male and female spheres typical of the nineteenth century. Yet he concludes, "Unless these principles of wisdom and love are equally and normally developed in the individual, his or her efforts to attain spiritual perfection must necessarily be abortive."[27]

Thus Shaker pieces written near both ends of the nineteenth century emphasize these unified dichotomies within the sect. Hampton's neglect of the body, however, implicitly reflects a material-spiritual dichotomy that other Shaker scholars have noted, primarily to discuss the sect's denial of their bodies through celibacy. Among these, Sally Kitch has focused on published works from the Victorian era to argue that celibacy empowers Shaker women because it subverts the culture-nature hierarchy, which Sherry B. Ortner has described as the structural symbol system functioning in many societies. Based on the assumption that "heterosexual intercourse as a symbolic system depended upon gender theories in which males and females represented opposed and even warring subcultures that could be mediated by, but not truly blended in, sexual union" (23), she claims that "celibacy . . . alters woman's relationship to reproduction, thereby associating her with production and leadership rather than with consumption and submission" (8).[28] Kitch may appear to argue that through celibacy women become like men, thus gaining the higher notch of the dualistic hierarchy, but her argument implicitly follows Pagels's pattern by emphasizing the Shakers' redefinition of the spirit. She explains that Shakers saw both elements of the nature-culture opposition "to be human creations that stood in opposition to true or divine nature. They classified reproductive humanity in the realm of human culture that is necessarily opposed to divine nature" (50). According to her argument, the Shakers see a "warring dichotomy," but between "divine nature" and "human culture" or between "spirit" and "flesh" (50). The spirit is neither male nor female; both men and women operate freely within the spiritual realm. As Hampton writes, both terms lie within the spiritual realm. Kitch's argument elevates the spiritual in Shakerism, but with its focus on celibacy, it inevitably illustrates that the spiritual realm is symbiotic with the material realm, which includes Shaker bodies. Lee's example in the *Testimonies* demonstrates that discipline and chastity should be seen as a celebration of the body in the sense Bynum describes. However, rather than adhering to Kitch's pattern of emphasizing celibacy as a cause of the unification of masculine and feminine, I follow Deignan's example of emphasizing the embodied spirit—Youngs's "annointing spirit"—as the unifying element. As an abstract term, "spirit" allows for rhetorical dissociation in Shaker writing. As Olson has written of other Shaker dissociations, this rhetorical move allows Shakers fluidity and change.

Another distinction between my emphasis and Kitch's is that I am concerned with the interdependence of the spiritual and the material rather than arguments of linear causality. Lee's literacies in the *Testimonies* illustrate and set forth the interdependence of acts of interpretation and expression with the spirit and bodily activities. Records of the Shakers' bodily activities during their daily lives also illustrate this symbiotic relationship, and other Shaker works reinforce this interdependence, though often with a unique spin. For example, Deignan notes that the image of the body—both corporate and individual—functions as the primary controlling symbol of the Shakers' first published document, Joseph Meacham's *Concise Statement of the Principles of the Only True Church* (1790). The image of the Church as unified body—perhaps drawing from the Pauline image (I Corinthians 12)—provided individual members a sense of family and, with it, spiritual strength and support. The Shakers recognized the fluidity of the Society and the distinct personalities within it from their early years throughout the nineteenth century, but uniformity of beliefs (even beliefs in diversity and the progressive nature of revelation) contributed to images of an ideal Shaker body.

Although individual Shaker bodies manifest diverse spiritual gifts such as dancing, shaking, speaking in tongues, drawing, and writing, after Lee's death the sect as a whole manifested a unified spirituality through productivity and regulation. By the mid-nineteenth century products such as furniture, baskets, boxes, and inscribed texts were their fruits of the spirit, replacing biological children and converts; regulation of bodily behaviors as diverse as sexuality and reading and writing contributed to the productivity. With the codification of theology in print after 1790, the connections between bodily regulation and spirituality became more explicit. Some leaders, such as Lucy Wright, resisted this inscribed codification; however, the "Order and Rules of the Church" at New Lebanon circulated in a letter just after her death in 1821. Regulations known as the Millennial Laws of 1821 soon followed.[29] The behaviors regulated by these "laws" changed over the years, but at times they included prevention of Brothers and Sisters passing each other on the stairs, kneeling before and after eating, and kneeling with the right knee first, as well as restriction from playing with cats and dogs, placing right thumbs and fingers above the left when hands are clasped, not placing feet "on the rounds of . . . chairs" when sitting, and the like. Each of the laws has a purpose. Lifting feet when ascending and descending stairs, for example, prevented "wear[ing] out the carpets unnecessarily." Laws regulating diet and hygiene reflected new "scientific" beliefs of the nineteenth century.[30]

The overall purpose of these laws over the years, according to the introductions to several versions, was maintaining unity of spirit and love among Brothers and Sisters and for God. Theologians and other "outsiders" interpret the Laws, their functions, and their origins differently. The 1845 version, according to Theodore Johnson, contained "detailed proscriptions for every aspect of the Believer's daily round" and "bear the mark of the era of spirit manifestation" (40), whose ecstatic "charism" produced some institutional control. The Laws caused apostates such as David Lamson to complain that the sect was one of "total uniformity" with no freedom for personal expression (18). And Edward Deming Andrews's reprint of the 1845 version in 1953 has contributed to the popular images many outsiders have visualized during the past half century. Stein accurately suggests that the Laws strengthened the Shaker body at large by further differentiating individual bodies within it from the world; they "defined the boundaries between Shakerism and the world, establishing clear lines of demarcation between the sect and the larger American culture, both in a literal and in a symbolic fashion" (*Shaker Experience*, 67).

The Millennial Laws show that bodily experiences in Shaker communities came to be more uniform—more ritualized—after 1821. Believers maintained unique personalities and underwent unique bodily experiences, but widespread communal practices regulated by the daily rituals created a distinct body known as the United Society of Believers and began to blur the boundaries between individual and communal bodies. The Millennial Laws represent a means of maintaining the spiritual life of individual Believers by encouraging bodily habits that reinforce individuals' relationships to the body at large. Knowing these bodily codes—manifestations as well as agents of spirituality—Shakers were able to "read" other Believers' behaviors in any Shaker community.

Stein correctly assesses the Shakers' move from Lee's orally conveyed teachings to the codification of theology and morality through written works such as the Millennial Laws. He explains that the Laws "evolved out of the practical needs of the growing society"; they regulated an otherwise unwieldy number of Believers (*Shaker Experience,* 67). Equally important to this study, however, is Stein's application of Max Weber's notion of the "fundamental tension between 'charism' and 'institutions.'" Stein writes of the Shakers that their theology temporally and logically "follows religious [bodily] experience" of Lee and the founders: "By contrast with religious experience or the direct encounter with the divine, theology represents an intellectual *rationalization* of the possession of sacred values" (*Shaker Experience,* 66–67). He concludes his remarks about the "temporal and logical sequence," however, with a significant qualification: "Experience and reflection, nonetheless, are not mutually exclusive and often stand in creative relation to one another" (*Shaker Experience,* 67).

An important contention of this book is that these bodily codes reinforced by the Shakers' Millennial Laws—considered repressive and pejorative by many—actually enriched their literacies and their spirituality. First, the "creative relation" between experience and reflection continued to exist even after the Laws were established. Second, the Laws suggest the importance of what Paul Connerton calls "habit memory": "the capacity to reproduce a certain performance" such as typing, riding a bicycle, or playing the piano without thinking. Such "bodily automatisms" associated with societal rituals, Connerton argues, provide an important matrix from and in which individuals and societies often decide how to act. For the Shakers, bodily habits—exercises such as the dances that led to their popular name, behavior coded in the Millennial Laws, and reading and writing practices—inform social memory and spiritual fulfillment.

Bodily habits reinforce what Connerton classifies as two other types of social memory: "cognitive" and "personal." People use personal or experiential memory to remember and convey events, generally presented in narrative style. Within Shakerism the numerous testimonies and biographical and autobiographical writings, such as those of Ann Lee, Rebecca Cox Jackson, and Alonzo Hollister, relied predominately on this aspect of memory. Cognitive memory draws from learned "facts," such as the alphabet, the multiplication table, or names of national capitals. Shakers used cognitive memory in scriptural interpretation and its conveyance in doctrinal works such as Dunlavy's *Manifesto.* They also used cognitive memory to convey orally and in writing details such as Ann Lee's birthday and items of the Millennial Laws.

As Connerton also explains, particular genres foreground particular types of memory; mathematics tables and the classification schemata of the natural sciences, for example, emphasize cognitive memory, whereas autobiography draws from personal memory. Yet as the case studies of this book illustrate, all three types of memory inform writing and reading acts to a certain degree. For example, the elegies written at Canterbury, New Hamsphire, discussed in Chapter 6, draw from cognitive and personal memory as well as from habit memory. To write an elegy to Emeline Kimball, with whom she worked in the Infirmary for several years, Marcia Hastings drew from personal memories of the deceased. The *Journal,* which preserves these transcribed poems, includes details such as dates of birth and death, which draw from cognitive memory. Yet the performances of the elegies (both the writing acts in private and the public readings during funeral services) draw from habit memory. Shaker literacies validate cognitive and personal memory as well as the habit memories that inform such ritualized reading and writing acts.

I use "ritualized" as Peter Shaw has used it to describe linguistic behavior, to signify "any incantatory, partly unconscious use of language" (9). All reading and writing acts that draw from a symbol system ingrained in the memories of most readers should be thought of as rituals—events, actions or behaviors that are "not fully rational and controlled" (9). Although Shaw uses the words "not fully rational" and "partly unconscious," which leaves room for the roles reason and consciousness play in ritual, the emphasis on unconscious behavior and the irrational in definitions of ritual has led many to see rituals as thoughtless, empty, and stifling processes, used by leaders of a community to control followers' minds and bodies. Apostate Nicholas Briggs, for example, wrote that the Shakers' ritualized dancing had an hypnotic effect (474). I view rituals among the Shakers as acts of "fulness," fostering the faiths of those practicing them, for several reasons: First, observers or outsiders have a difficult time assessing or knowing that a particular ritual is "empty." Second, the visions ritual participants have of particular symbols vary from person to person and from moment to moment. Rebecca Jackson and Alonzo Hollister, for example, discussed in Chapter 5, read and write the symbol of Ann Lee differently from each other and from moment to moment within their narratives. A person reading cognitively or rationally at one moment may read the same text noncognitively or emotionally at another. Finally, both cognitive and noncognitive readings can be empowering acts for the participants.

Ritualized reading and writing may occur not only with genres such as autobiographies, biographies, histories, and elegies comprised of images of heros and heroines but also with individual scriptures. I use "may occur" rather than "occurs" to emphasize this type of literary act first, as one that is only sometimes employed and second, as one that is learned (unconsciously) through repetition. By writing or reading a genre or a Bible verse such as "the letter killeth, but the spirit maketh alive" (II Corinthians 3:6) again and again and again, the writer or reader who may initially think critically about the language and symbol system being used may eventually begin ritualized textual work.

Throughout their history the Shakers have recognized the value of and accepted these multiple kinds of reading acts, enabled by their views of the spirit. From their earliest days they have espoused a belief in an active and living spirit whose embodied presence has informed writing and reading acts. Its existence and significance constitute what Mary Douglas refers to as "implicit knowledge" —truths "too true to warrant discussion," manifested in the society's symbols, rituals, and myths. In periods of turmoil, such as the years of communal formation through printed theology (1790–1827) and in the ecstatic revival of the mid-nineteenth century (1828–1850), leaders such as John Dunlavy provided written explanations of the spirit and its manifestations (*Manifesto,* 38–62).[31] These written explanations "obliquely [re]affirmed" this "implicit knowledge" while they revealed the writers' struggles with contrary "truths" asserted by others within and outside of Shaker communities.[32] For example, Richard McNemar and Dunlavy attempt to define the spirit and its manifestations in *The Kentucky Revival* (1807) and *The Manifesto* (1818), respectively, as Jonathan Edwards and others had during the Great Awakening. In spite of attempts such as these to codify in writing the spirit and its work, diverse understandings of the spirit, spirituality, spiritual manifestations, and their relationship to reading and writing emerge in Shaker texts, a result of Lee's example.

The Shakers' frequent citation of the verse "the letter killeth, but the spirit maketh alive" manifests this diversified usage. The verse invites readers to understand "the spirit" rather simply in relationship to "the letter." The dichotomy may be read, for example, as a simple representation of oppositions between the mosaical law of the Old Testament and Christianity of the New Testament. Yet the verse's context and the Shakers' diverse appropriations of it complicate any oversimplification by multiplying the significations of "the spirit" and "the letter" and underscoring the integral relationships among letters, bodies, and spirituality.

Shaker writers often used the verse as a proof text; rather than explicating the verse, they cited it to prove other points. Thus analysis of their appropriations begin to unfold the verse's multiple layers of meaning. Benjamin Seth Youngs, the primary editor of *The Testimony of Christ's Second Appearing* (1808), employs the scripture as a rationale for the most weighty evidence of the Second Appearing and the establishment of the true millennial church. He acknowledges three sources people may draw from to arrive at knowledge of God and "the true Church of Christ"—ecclesiastical history, Scripture, and the testimonies of "living witnesses." Among these, "the testimony of living witnesses is considered of the highest authority and superior to any written record whatever." He continues: "As far as the builder is superior to the thing which he builds, so far the living subjects of the work of God, stand forever superior to any thing that they can possibly comprise in letters. The living testimony of God is not of the *letter*, but of the *spirit*: for *the letter killeth*, but *the spirit giveth life*" (12). This passage could be read simply as Youngs's employment of the humility *topos,* since it follows a disclaimer about the *Testimony*'s quality and status: "We are far from expecting or even wishing any of our writings to supercede the necessity of giving testimony, or in any wise prevent a further increase of light and understanding in the things of God" (12). Yet the disclaimer and the passage that follows present in unison Youngs's emphasis on the primacy of personal testimonies and bodily manifestations (over written texts) in fostering spirituality.

More than half a century later later Rebecca Cox Jackson uses the scripture in her autobiographical writings to explain her ability to understand three difficult books that appear to her within a dream: "I should have the spiritual meaning of the letter revealed in my soul by the manifestation of God. This revelation, then being in Heaven, was the true book which must come to give us the true meaning of the letter—as 'the letter killeth, but the spirit maketh alive'" (Humez, *Gifts of Power,* 290). Jackson uses the verse to validate not only the spirit's assistance in the reading of inscribed texts but also the revelation of God through "mystical" and personal experiences such as dreams. Thus the passages by Jackson and Youngs reflect the diverse work and embodiment of the spirit. In this case the "more literary" male emphasizes the spirit's embodiment in people while the less literary female emphasizes the spirit's assistance in the interpretation of the letters within books. The writers invoke understandings of the spirit they need to assist them in the historical and material moments in which they live. This openness to the spirit's work contributes to writers' abilities to draw upon the spirit as needed, informing and complementing the literacies that have empowered them as they live within the Society.

The verse's context, which Lee supposedly knew, encouraged such diverse readings. Prior to the summary statement, "the letter killeth, but the spirit maketh alive," the Pauline writer explains to his audience, Christians at Corinth, "Ye are our epistle written in our hearts, known and read of all men: Forasmuch as ye are manifestly declared to be the epistle of Christ ministered by us, written not with ink, but with the Spirit of the living God; not in tables of stone but in tables of the hearts" (II Corinthians 3:2–3). The writer complicates the letter-spirit dichotomy of verse 6 by referring not only to "letter" as *gramma* (anything written or inscribed) but also to "letter" as *epistle* (a body of writing). And human beings, human hearts, and the spirit replace stone, paper, and ink as media—tools and agents of the writing act. Thus when the *Testimonies* (1816) editors record Lee saying to her followers, "Ye are my epistles," they underscore her use of the verse to emphasize (as Youngs does in the *Testimony*) spirituality embodied in humans and reading that includes interpreting human hearts and bodies. Yet her citation also indicates, as Jackson's use of the passage does, her reliance on the inscribed letters of Scripture.

The passages from Jackson and Youngs attest to the major implication of Lee's teaching—"the letter" by itself is death. Whether a human body or an inscribed document,"the letter" receives life from the spirit. In a kind of circularity, however, Shaker spirituality depends upon both inscribed texts and bodily experiences. In addition, the examples of Jackson and Youngs reveal that readers and writers of the word "spirit" read and write their own understandings of "spirit" into texts as needed, some associating it more nearly with the rational work of the mind, and some connecting it to emotional or less rational feelings of hearts and human bodies.

In sum, the Shakers classify as a work of the spirit what Stein refers to as the "creative relationship" between theology and experience and what Linda Mercadante refers to as "religious imagination." Mercadante, who like Stein considers the relationship between "experience" and "doctrine" in Shakerism, sees the "religious imagination" as the link "between experience and theological idea": "Experience can be translated into new images and concepts only when the religious imagination is allowed to operate freely" (51).[33] Mercadante privileges the "testimony" as the key genre for empowering individuals and sustaining religious groups because it allows the religious imagination to work freely; it allows innovation in personal expression and, subsequently, in doctrine. She writes:

A testimony is a hermeneutical act, a "collision" of perspectives, where an individual's life story and encounter with the divine is interpreted within the framework of a given belief structure. Here the personal and the communal meet; experience and doctrine are fused together. In addition, the movement is dynamic, as individual believers, through these acts of interpretation, sometimes also affect or change the understanding of the communal faith story. Writers are active in this process, shaping the narrative in the same way as the belief structure does. (128)

However, the examples of Youngs's and Jackson's readings and writings of the word "spirit" and the other examples included in this study—analyses of doctrinal treatises, histories, biographies, and elegies—demonstrate that other genres function in this way as well. Readers and writers of these can be as active and dynamic as those of testimonies.

Through a belief in a spirit that operates through bodily experiences as well as mental reflection, the Shakers allow room for innovation in personal expression and, subsequently, in doctrine and bodily codes. Sometimes the spirit is more closely associated with the senses and the emotions than with the mind. In these instances Shakers submit to "the pleasure of the text"—to emotional, experiential readings where readers' life experiences cause them to read themselves into texts, to displace quite easily the images of people within them for images of themselves. This type of literary work occurs with narratives such as the *Testimonies* (1816) and personal narratives of other Shakers. Forms of typological reading, not unlike readings of the Bible or of *Pilgrim's Progress*, these interpretive acts depend upon symbol systems working within and shaping the culture. The systems are sometimes rationally invoked and sometimes unconsciously interpreted through habit.

These ritualized reading and writing acts, noncognitive as they were at times, gave individuals within particular communities a framework to rely upon when a need, such as whether to leave Shakerism or not, arose. Yet the ritualized reading also grounded innovative and creative ways of reading and writing. That is, although Believers learned the codes of Shaker literacies within institutionalized communities, the codes themselves allowed for innovation because of the notion of an embodied spirit, exemplified initially in Ann Lee. Lee's interpretation of people's bodies and minds, of mystical visions she saw, and of mystical voices she heard established the reading of uninscribed texts as a significant part of spiritually informed reading. The uninscribed texts of visions and voices, written in the mind, the heart, and the memory, encouraged private acts of reading; they allowed some independence and autonomy, some "charism" within the "institution." The belief that the spirit operated apart from inscribed texts allowed Shakers to receive new revelations and to instigate new religious practices for the community as a whole. Thus, for example, the Shakers changed their worship practices during the Era of Manifestations and continually revised the Millennial Laws throughout the nineteenth century. Yet spiritual literacies also allowed innovative readings of inscribed texts. The spirit assisted Shaker leaders such as Richard McNemar and John Dunlavy in reading the Bible in a new way. They drew from their training as "reasonable" interpretors of Scripture, their cognitive memories and habits of reading religious tracts and scriptural passages, and their personal memories of people to write inscribed texts that serve as doctrinal handbooks to the Shakers' spiritual literacies.

NOTES

1. Sally Kitch refers to Lee as "the illiterate daughter of working class parents" (8). Jean Humez begins a piece on Ann Lee imagery, "Illiterate herself, Ann Lee is reported to have called her followers 'my epistles, read and known by all men'" (*Mother's First-Born,* 1) and describes her on another occasion as "an illiterate working-class Englishwoman" and an "unlettered female prophet" ("'Ye Are My Epistles,'" 83). Stephen Stein writes that "Ann Lee's illiteracy [was] a limitation that fueled her rejection of all writing" (*Shaker Experience,* 9).

2. Hutchinson and Hibbens were accused, like Lee, of heresy and witchcraft. Jane Kamensky has analyzed their speech as it is recorded in court documents in "Governing the Tongue: Speech and Society in Early New England." For more on Hutchinson's speech, see also Patricia Caldwell's "The Antinomian Language Controversy." Jemimah Wilkinson, the "Publick universal friend" who roamed revolutionary New England dressed in "masculine" garb, left a manuscript account of her "transfiguration" and one anonymously published work, along with other written records. See Susan Juster's "To Slay the Beast: Visionary Women in the Early Republic," which also includes a brief comparison of Wilkinson to Ann Lee.

3. Suzanne Thurman, "The Order of Nature, the Order of Grace," employs this term to discuss gender roles in Shakerism (10).

4. On the "oral residue" among early New England literates, see David Hall's *Worlds of Wonder.* Other discussions of the relationships between orality and literacy include Robert Darnton's *Great Cat Massacre,* M. M. Bakhtin's *Rabelais and His World,* and Margaret Spufford's *Small Books and Pleasant Histories.*

5. In addition, the *Testimonies* includes references to Lee, accused of witchcraft and of being a man in woman's clothing, having her clothes ripped from her by members of the mobs. As Carol F. Karlsen has documented in *The Devil in the Shape of a Woman,* such accusations and treatment of women who transgressed societal norms were prominent in the mid- and late seventeenth century. She also suggests that these actions and attitudes among common people did not die away as soon as the church and state offically relinquished such beliefs and practices. Although Lee lived much later than the period of New England witchcraft trials Karlsen discusses, it is quite probable that she endured such physical and emotional brutality. For the best recent analysis of Lee's activities in New England, see Thurman. On mob violence in the period, see Peter Shaw, *American Patriots and the Rituals of Revolution.*

6. Stein has written, for example, that "the resulting story—no less valuable for the process of collection and editing—has historical relevance more for the time of its collection and composition than for the earlier ages that it purports to describe" (*Shaker Experience,* 9). Humez's rigorous "'Ye Are My Epistles'" exemplifies this approach. Humez explains, for example, the leaders' dual reasons for composing the piece: "to defend itself from external enemies and internal political problems" (*Mother's First-Born,* 5). She also writes that the text's "contradictions" in Lee imagery "derive in part from real tensions within Shakerism at this time over the meaning of her ministry and over the authority of female religious leaders in general" (*Mother's First-Born,* 5).

7. Proctor-Smith writes, "In naming Ann Lee as Mother, the Believers not only acknowledged her role in giving birth to and nurturing the Society, but they also recognized in her the revelation of the Mother-aspect of God." She "is portrayed as an individual of authority and power, with a decisive role to play in the work of redemption" (*Women,* 146–48). Linda Mercadante summarizes, "the range of attributes for both Mother Ann and Jesus were broad. And Mother Ann, more than Jesus, was portrayed as not only stern and

judgmental, but also as nurturant, motherly, and empowering" (138). Humez explains that although Lee appears at times as "a poor, weak woman," at others she "emerges as a towering, awe-inspiring, and even frightening figure: a strict, even harsh, mother, whose reproofs are remembered clearly for thirty years; or a terrifying seer and prophet, who reported flying with visionary wings through the heavens and the prisons of hell" (*Mother's First-Born,* 6).

8. She says on one occasion: "'I see multitudes of the dead, that were slain in battle, arise and come into the first resurrection;—I see Christ put crowns on their heads, of bright, glorious, and changeable colors!'" (XXIII, 9).

9. See William G. McLoughlin's *Isaac Backus and the American Pietistic Tradition* (1–22) on the "new light" tradition of "reading" these personal experiences. Edwards discusses his ability to read the manifestations of the spirit in "A Faithful Narrative" and "A Divine and Supernatural Light."

10. Central metaphorically as well as literally, these two passages continue one of the textual strategies I discuss in Chapter 4—they recreate Lee as a purist, sexually speaking. In addition to her few explicit teachings against sexual union even between husbands and wives, other passages contribute subtly to this depiction of Lee's bodily chastity.

11. This comment categorizes men in a way that echoes the compartmentalizing within Shaker villages when communities were "brought into order" after Lee's death; Believers were assigned to "families" according to a spiritual hierarchy and age. It also reflects the racial stereotyping recorded in many Shaker documents, a topic of Chapter 5. On another occasion within the *Testimonies,* Lee is recorded to have had a vision of a man "as black as a negro," described as such because of his sinful condition (XVII, 2).

12. Lee's scriptural knowledge, as specifically as it is depicted here, may have been sharpened by the editors of the *Testimonies.* Thomas Swain explains that in the 1816 version Lee is recorded to give paraphrases of biblical passages but in the 1888 edition she says "the complete Biblical verse[s] verbatim" (57). Yet it is quite probable Lee knew Scripture well from absorbing it aurally over the years.

13. Marini writes, "The relationship of the sects [of revolutionary New England, such as the Shakers] to Whitefield was particularly intimate and substantive" (153–54). Lee was a "convert" or "adherent" to him at one time (*Testimonies* [1816], IX, 3–4). Marini explains the predominance in their theologies of orality and experientialism, focusing on a "schema" of "the lineaments of the history of redemption," rather than "sophisticated philosophic disuptations of Evangelical Calvinism and Arminianism" (153–54).

14. On New England sermon style, see Teresa Toulouse's *Art of Prophesying.* In "Resurrecting Life" I provide two examples of "rational" Puritan sermons structured to meet audience members' needs of consolation. Hugh Blair's *Lectures on Rhetoric and Belles-Lettres* reflect the shifting style of sermons of the late eighteenth century, influenced by successful itinerants such as Whitefield.

15. On Lee's laboring with those in the spirit world (XXVII); on the judgment of both righteous and wicked (XLII, 1; V, 5).

16. Most recently, Glendyne R. Wergland ("Lust") and Susan McCully have revisited this topic, considered previously by Louis Kern (*An Ordered Love*) and Lawrence Foster (*Religion and Sexuality*).

17. See Dunlavy's *Manifesto* on the resurrection (Part III); on the union of the spiritual with the material (38–39). Marini summarizes this Shaker theology, drawing especially from the works of Meacham, Youngs, and Green (*Radical Sects,* 148–55). Youngs and Green write, for example, "'When he renounces the will of the flesh, and is subject to the will of the Spirit; then he is raised from a death of sin to a life of righteousness; and this is his resurrection'" (Marini, *Radical Sects,* 153). Kern also discusses the relationship between

sexuality and theology (76–90).

18. Humez notes "the impressive nature of Ann Lee's own appearance," "the power of her example and her words," and her use of "personal experience storytelling as an important teaching tool" ("'Ye Are My Epistles,'" 91, 102, 98).

19. James Fitch also uses the categories of "words" and "works" to create a verbal portrait of Puritan woman Anne Mason (Madden, "Resurrecting Life," 242). This appears to be a commonplace of verbal portraiture of spiritual women. See Laurel Thatcher Ulrich ("Vertuous Women Found," 22).

20. As he delineates the spirit's work in *The Manifesto,* Dunlavy describes the Shaker belief that "man" is a "free, moral agent" with a "rational spirit" that is "the representative of God" and that leads him to act based on judgment of empirical evidence (38–40). On one occasion in the *Testimonies,* however, the responses to Lee appear miraculous. When a group of "unruly men" appeared on horseback during a meeting, Lee's request that they "draw back" eventually affects the horses and the men: "The men refusing to obey, she raised her hand, and with great power and authority, cried aloud, 'Draw back, I say, or I'll smite the horse and his rider.' On uttering these words, all the power of resistance seemed instantly to be taken from the men, and their horses immediately ran backwards, from the house" (XIX, 29–30).

21. "Captain of militia" Phineas Farnsworth, though not moved to convert as Meacham was, also responds with noticeable silence to Lee's innovative and convincing reading of Scripture. In "the latter part of January, 1782," Farnsworth appeared at the Square House in Harvard "with a large company of men, to drive them [the Believers] off, unless they would promise to be gone by such a time." Lee draws her response from Scripture: "Ye that say, To day or to morrow we will go into such a city, and continue there a year, and buy and sell, and get gain: Whereas ye know not what shall be on the morrow. . . . For that ye ought to say, If the Lord will, we shall live, and do this, or that" (James 4:13–15). According to the *Testimonies,* Lee replied to Farnsworth, "'I expect to go tomorrow, if it is God's will.' . . . After some conversation, he took his leave of Mother, promising not to molest her, seeing she was going away tomorrow. 'Yea,' (said Mother,) 'I expect to go tomorrow, if it is God's will; but I will return again the next day if it is God's will, for all you.' The Captain, feeling himself bound, said no more" (XIII, 5–6).

22. This behavior echoes the violence against women in Puritan culture, which Ann Kibbey demonstrates was an extension of Protestant iconoclasm in *The Interpretation of Material Shapes in Puritanism: A Study of Rhetoric, Prejudice, and Violence.*

23. In *The Resisting Reader* Judith Fetterly contends women who read "against the grain" by resisting images of masculine heroism contribute to social change.

24. She writes:

Men, who were dominant, used symbols to renounce their dominance. Reversals and oppositions were at the heart of how symbols worked for men. . . . To women, however, male/female contrasts were apparently of little interest; . . . Women saw themselves not as flesh opposed to spirit, female opposed to male, nurture opposed to authority; they saw themselves as human beings—fully spirit and fully flesh. And they saw all humanity as created in God's image, as capable of *imitatio Christi,* through body as well as soul. (*Holy Feast,* 296)

25. Olson defines "dissociation" as "an ingenious rhetorical move through which multiple elements of a single concept are differentiated and arranged hierarchically. . . . One aspect is endorsed while its devalued partner is given new coherence within the particular system of thought" (45). She contends that "when evidence meeting one's knowledge criteria

discredits a highly valued knowledge claim, one may use dissociation to revise one's knowledge criteria, or rules of evidence, rather than reject the knowledge claim. The advantage of such a practice is that it protects the knowledge claim by moving to a higher level of abstraction than the level of evidence" (46). In this case, the knowledge claim is that of the embodied and ever-present spirit that influences reading and writing acts (she refers to the belief in progressive divine revelation, which of course is a manifestation of the active and living spirit); the incompatible evidence is the concrete description of what texts were written and read during Shaker history. As Olson describes, the beauty of this dissociation is that it "not only renders irrelevant the immediate complication, but also immunizes the thought system from similar future incompatibilities" (46).

26. Deignan's thrust is probably a reaction to such critics as Louis Kern, who labels the Shakers dualists (76).

27. Hampton writes: "In looking around us and into the general structure of the universe, the most palpable and obvious departments we can discover therein are the dual ones of male and female. The origin of these may be traced to the no less palpable principles of wisdom and love, a duality observable in all the dispensations of Divine Providence and for aught we know to the contrary, a duality constituting the Infinite mind itself" (1). Because this language echoes Margaret Fuller's "Woman in the Nineteenth Century," Hampton possibly drew from her work; or perhaps Fuller drew from Shaker theology.

28. Kitch acknowledges and draws from the works of Amanda Porterfield, Nancy Cott, Barbara Welter, Carroll Smith-Rosenberg, and Ann Douglas, which argue in sum that in nineteenth-century America, "religion . . . helped to modify both actual and symbolic female domestic confinement in general" (Kitch, 42). Mainstream Protestantism "valorized allegedly female traits such as intuition and spiritual and emotional sensitivity, which were routinely devalued in other public domains" (42). Kitch argues that "in less traditional sects . . . women fared even better"(42). The celibate Shakers, for example,

examined the symbolic premises of female confinement to the natural familial domain, and they rejected them as incompatible with the spiritual order. . . . The rejection of subordination and confinement did not necessarily mean the rejection of all traditional female activities, or of female gender identity, however. Rather, the incorporation of spiritual, transcendent symbolism into female gender identity by these groups sometimes promoted a kind of female superiority, particularly in spiritual affairs, that privileged female qualities. (43)

Both Kitch and Bynum build upon Ortner's article "Is Female to Male as Nature Is to Culture?" which has received much critical attention. Kitch writes, for example, that Carol MacCormack "objects to Ortner's use of structuralism because it ignores data that disprove its models"; "women can be seen as mediating between nature and culture rather than as languishing in the natural realm. Women also play active roles in marriage and agree to their own 'exchange.' Structural analysis also fails to account for female power in a number of societies" (Kitch, 44, n.7). Kitch agrees with Ortner that "such failures do not necessarily invalidate the endurance of a symbolic system" (44, n. 7). Bynum recognizes that Ortner's work has been criticized for its "universalist" bent; however, she explains, she does not want to imply that there is "abject truth" to these dichotomies nor that "medieval women espoused such a dichotomy," but "that this is the pattern symbols fell into in male writing and religious practice between 1200 and 1500." She also notes that Ortner has tried to revise her earlier theory in *Sexual Meanings* (*Holy Feast*, 414, n. 14 & 15).

29. See Theodore Johnson's historical introduction to the 1967 reprint of the 1821 version.

30. Thurman discusses the Harvard and Shirley Shakers' use of "cutting edge" medicine and homeopathy (160–66).

31. For an overview of debates about the spirit's work during the Era of Manifestations, see Sasson, "Individual Experience."

32. According to Douglas, when people challenge these truths with apparently "explicit knowledge"—that is, when cultural conflicts arise between the "real" and the ideal—the "implicit knowledge" is as least "obliquely [re]affirmed" as the society attempts resolution and compromise (3–4).

33. She writes, "Doctrine and experience were *intentionally* yoked" (122, emphasis mine) and "the Shakers valued experience over doctrine" (5); "experience, rather than scripture, Christian history, or any definitive theological corpus, was always the primary source and norm" (51).

Chapter 3

Doctrinal Guides to Spiritual Literacies: McNemar's *Kentucky Revival* and Dunlavy's *Manifesto*

Figures and shadowy representations are not the substance;
yet they are not false or fraudulent.
—John Dunlavy, *The Manifesto,* 1818

Richard McNemar and John Dunlavy converted to Shakerism during the Kentucky Revival, when missionary Believers from "the east" appeared with the story of Christ's Second Appearing. The charismatic Revival had begun in 1799 among congregations of Presbyterians at Paint Lick and Cane Ridge, Kentucky, and Turtle Creek, Ohio. Seven leaders of the "New Light" Presbyterians or "Schismatics," including McNemar and Barton W. Stone, offically broke away from their more conservative counterparts in 1803. Stephen Stein describes leaders of the movement as "factious liberals [who] gave voice to a theological Arminianism based on the principle of biblical authority . . . [and] combined a commitment to democracy with a fervent anti-institutionalism and a radical congregationalism. They believed the indwelling spirit of Christ was the bond of religious unity" (*Shaker Experience,* 58).

The radical "bodily manifestations" of the indwelling spirit during the Revival years included "praying, shouting, jerking, barking, or rolling" (McNemar, 69)—actions not too much unlike the early manifestations among Believers in Christ's Second Appearing in New England. Thus when John Meacham, Benjamin Seth Youngs, and Issachar Bates appeared in the West in 1805 to explain that the millennium of spiritual presence and perfection had begun, ushered in by Ann Lee, many such as Dunlavy and McNemar soon attached themselves to this new sect and helped establish communities of Believers.[1]

These Shaker communities in what are now Kentucky and Ohio have been recognized for contributing to the sect the intellectual grounding that drew some converts throughout the nineteenth century and that made it more respectable to the world.[2] Among the western Shaker writers of theology, McNemar and Dunlavy inscribed two texts which articulate and illustrate Shaker literacies in similar though complementary ways. Dunlavy's *Manifesto* (1818) and McNemar's *Kentucky Revival* (1807) serve as doctrinal handbooks to spiritual literacies in that they illustrate the "creative relation" of reflection and experience to theology and doctrine; they reflect the intertwining of "cognitive," "personal," and "habit" memories. The men's conversions, like their literacies, are dependent upon beliefs in the progressive nature of truth and revelation, in reasoning as a key factor in conversion, and in the indwelling spirit, exemplified initially in Ann Lee. However, as each writes his text—with a claim that it is directed to potential converts—he chooses to emphasize these beliefs to varying degrees.

Remarkably, references to Lee are almost absent from these and several other works male Shaker leaders composed during the sect's formative years, although the 1816 *Testimonies* and works by apostates published before 1827 focus on her. The first published doctrinal work, Joseph Meacham's *Concise Statement of the Principles of the Only True Church* (1790), for example, omits any mention of Lee by name. Meacham devotes twenty-four pages to a typological reading of Daniel and Revelation to set forth the four "dispensations of God's Grace to Fallen Man." When he argues that the final dispensation began in 1747, he includes only an oblique reference to Lee, as he explains Christ's Second Appearing was "'revealed by one to others'" (Deignan, 87).[3]

Dunlavy similarly includes only one reference to the controversial woman in his lengthy *Manifesto*. Lee's absence from these early works has been attributed, and accurately so, to the writers' concerns with rationalizing their faiths.[4] As Deignan has written, Dunlavy's one reference to Lee by name basically "answer[s] the accusation that the Shakers have put Ann in the place of Jesus as the Christ" (126). The one early writer who breaks this pattern is Youngs, whose *Testimony of Christ's Second Appearing* includes the first biographical sketch, a precursor to the 1816 *Testimonies*. Dunlavy's omission of Lee "is particularly significant since Dunlavy was, after all, a convert of Youngs, and it was Youngs who had raised Ann Lee to an exalted christological status" (Deignan, 126). Thus "Dunlavy takes up the delicate task of reexpressing Shaker christology in terms more acceptable to the orthodox ears of his Calvinist critics who accused the Shakers of supplanting Jesus with Ann" (Deignan, 138). These differing presentations of Lee and the relationship between Youngs and Dunlavy underscore two important elements of Dunlavy's faith (and that of other Shakers): First, his conversion was based in part on a personal relationship rather than "pure" reason; second, Shaker theology of the embodied spirit allowed an openness to varied interpretations of Lee's exemplary status.

Although Lee appears to be absent from these works, she is, in fact, the absent presence informing and supporting them. Without Lee's claim to embody fulfillment of prophecy, and without the power of her physical and spiritual presence before men such as Meacham and Dunlavy, they would not have read her into Scripture as they did, nor would they have written their works. Thus in the process of omitting Lee to explain rationally the Shaker faith in the sect's formative years, these authors articulated, illustrated, and helped to codify the literacies she established. They reinforced the paradoxical dependency of spiritual literacies upon both inscribed and uninscribed texts as they wrote theology and history to unify the Shaker church, a church founded upon the presence of the indwelling spirit.

As Deignan points out, Dunlavy and Meacham emphasized the spirit's presence within all members of the millennial church rather than the presence of the Christ Spirit solely in Ann Lee (84). This emphasis infiltrates Shaker literacies, as these men inscribe them, in two ways. First, Lee's spiritual life causes them to revise ecclesiastical history, describing themselves as living in the millennial kingdom of heaven on earth. To accomplish this revision, these writers depended as acutely on knowledge and reading of Scripture as leaders of other Christian sects. They were, like their archenemies, systematic theologians who depended upon Scripture; the differences between them emerged from differences in the foundations of their systems. For the Shakers the foundation was the belief in the presence of the Christ Spirit in Lee. Second and consequently, these writers explained, the spirit's presence in Believers closed the gaps between "shadowy type" and "reality." Spirit-filled Believers lived in a world of "presence," where signs were not marks of "absence" but infused with meaning. The meaningful signs they read were not only inscribed texts but, as Lee had established, uninscribed signs such as bodies and oral testimonies of other Believers.

The works of Dunlavy and McNemar illustrate their need to graft their newly received testimony of Lee and the millennial church onto what they already knew about Christian eschatology. In many ways they were "already written" by the discourses of Protestant sects that had worked through Scripture to explain reasonably their particular understandings of the "last days," the spirit's manifestations, and the correct hermeneutic. Unable to leave this type of reading and reasoning behind, they brought it to the convincing oral testimonies of Shaker missionaries from New England, binding the two together in their theology and history.

A dense and lengthy theological treatise organized by topic, Dunlavy's 520-page work came to be known as a key reference work rather than a text to be meditated upon, for it exhibits patterns of tedious Calvinistic exegesis, albeit with a Shaker spin. Dunlavy overtly provides an "institutionalized" and "rational" reading of Scripture, heavily sprinkled with Greek and Hebrew renderings of the verses he cites as proof texts to argue for his understanding of topics such as "On the Being of God," "Of the Truth of Revelation," and "Of the Resurrection." As Deignan explains, "Dunlavy is preoccupied with presenting Shakerism in the categories of strict evangelical faith, refashioning these to illumine his Shaker gospel. . . . [He] is influenced by the stock themes and controversies of evangelical Calvinism more than anything else" (126).[5] McNemar exhibits in his work intellectual qualities similar to those of his brother-in-law Dunlavy—he frequently quotes Scripture and occasionally uses Greek or Hebrew. But in contrast to Dunlavy he adopts a rather easily absorbed chronological and narrative style for his 119-page history, the Shakers' first bound volume. McNemar's work reflects the importance of his experiences during the years of revival in northern Kentucky and southern Ohio; his reading of people and events serves as the basis for his narrative and his argument for the role of the spirit in reading its bodily manifestations.[6]

Each work, however, depends upon other types of interpretive acts as well. Although Dunlavy does not mention it, his writing also draws from his experience in the Kentucky Revival, and McNemar draws from his understanding of the Shaker doctrine he has learned, though he mentions it only periodically and supposedly tangentially within his narrative. For example, McNemar's narrative begins as an intellectual history, describing the schism between "orthodox" Presbyterians and the New Lights as a result of the charismatic revival. To describe the schism, however, he delves into theology, which is obviously colored by his Shaker bias. McNemar and Dunlavy claim to write their works for the world, and they do so in the heated "atmosphere of controversy" surrounding the Kentucky Revival (Deignan, 126).[7]

The world, however, is not unitary. As M. M. Bahktin has written, "Language—like the living concrete environment in which the consciousness of the verbal artist lives—is never unitary. . . . Actual social life and historical becoming create within an abstractly unitary national language a multitude of concrete worlds" (*Dialogic Imagination,* 288). These "worlds," which Bahktin also refers to as "stratifications," are sometimes intentionally "expropriated" by writers such as McNemar and Dunlavy. McNemar's and Dunlavy's works' prefatory remarks and title pages, the styles they exhibit, and references to imagined readers by name point to the multiple stratifications of discourse these writers employ and in which they are engaged. In addition to writing to "outsiders," consisting of both seekers and enemies, they address other Believers who needed or wanted "reasoned" theology and history, and they write for themselves. Analysis of what appears to be their "abstract linguistic discourse," when "cut off from the fundamentally social modes in which discourse lives, inevitably comes across as flat and abstract" (Bahktin, *Dialogic,* 259). Rather, when we consider the "multitude of concrete worlds" in which these men live and write, the fulness of their Shaker literacies emerges.

Defending the faith they had accepted and convincing themselves in the process of writing to others, McNemar and Dunlavy rationalized and reinforced the spiritual conversions they had recently undergone. Geoffrey Harpham describes conversion as "a constant, ceaseless process," as "the unchanging condition of our existence" (48). Yet he distinguishes two parts of the process: an imitation and a remaking. Imitation is an initial commitment to an ideal brought about by a mentor, a teacher, or reading of a text. Remaking, the second, less superficial part of conversion that reinforces the first, occurs through inscription of a spiritual autobiography, through "translating the self out of selfhood and into discourse" (48). By nature of its association with the self in discourse, remaking, or the secondary conversion, occurs not only through writing spiritual autobiography but also with the writing of any religious genre, such as McNemar's and Dunlavy's polemical works. In sum, a writer's audience is to a certain degree "always a fiction"; a writer's "self" is the primary invoked reader (Ong, "The Writer's

Audience"). Thus Dunlavy and McNemar write in the styles and genres each needs to convince and reconvert himself.[8]

The proclaimed audience for each, however, is the seeker of religious truth. In the opening paragraph of his preface, for example, Dunlavy asks, "How shall the inquirer know with whom to cast his lot?" (i). He implies his book will help the inquirer find the "true" Church. McNemar's title page includes the phrases "With a Brief Account of the Entrance and Progress of What the World call Shakerism ... Presented to the True Zion-traveller, as a Memorial of the Wilderness Journey." As a "*memorial,*" the history implies the "Wilderness Journey" is over—the Millennial Kingdom of Zion has been reached.[9] Yet the presentation of the memorial to "the True Zion-traveller" implies there are those still traveling—either within Zion (those who have already converted) or on their way to the Millennial Kingdom (those seeking the "true" Church). These imagined readers, the dense writing styles and "masculine" genres of McNemar and Dunlavy imply, were men of Christian traditions not too much different from themselves.[10]

The men similar to themselves included the writers' enemies as well as seekers. McNemar's *History,* for example, includes a section directed pointedly to Barton W. Stone. According to McNemar, Stone had seceded from the Springfield (Ohio) Presbytery as a result of a desire "to examine the scriptures separate and judge of them according to their internal evidence"; "to take them according to their own proper sense, and prove that they no where countenanced those evils that abounded in the churches, but the contrary" (11). This notion of a (singular) "proper sense"—a divinely "well-wrought urn"—had been a part of Protestant hermeneutics for centuries.[11] It had contributed for decades to the sectarian spirit upon which the nation was founded and that continued to ferment in the nineteenth century, influencing not only Stone but also Shaker theologians.

Stone distinguished between his own followers as those of "the true gospel" and the Shakers as those of "wild enthusiasm." The Shaker apostate Thomas Brown quotes Stone as having written:

You have heard no doubt before this time of the lamentable departure of two of our preachers, and few of their hearers, from the true gospel into wild enthusiasm, or Shakerism. They have made shipwreck of faith, and turned aside to an old woman's fables, who broached them in New England about twenty-five years ago. These wolves in sheep's clothing have smelt us from afar, and have come to tear, rend, and devour. (352)

Stone seems almost embarrassed that something as "enthusiastic" as "an old woman's fables" could have drawn away two of his colleagues and "brothers" from "the true gospel"—the faith based upon and drawn from *the* "proper sense" of the Scripture. McNemar and Dunlavy, who claimed that understanding of the truth of Scripture was "progressive," also argued for "right" readings.

Dunlavy, like McNemar, rails against Stone, addressing the entire final part (IV) of *The Manifesto* to him in the form of a letter. Section I of Part IV begins, "Barton:—I have inscribed this letter to you as being the most proper person to whom I could direct it, to answer the proposed ends" (411). In other areas of the text, he refers to other "enemies" that shape his argument: He refers to works by Timothy Dwight, grandson of Jonathan Edwards, and by William C. Davis, a premillennialist in Carolina. Dwight has been described as "a mediator between Old Calvinism and New Divinity" and "inclined toward Scottish epistemology" (*Dictionary of American Religious Biography*). He possessed a strong belief in the revelation of Scripture and led a campus revival at Yale in 1802 (coinciding historically, and not insignificantly, with the revival in western Kentucky of which Stone was a part).[12] And Davis, a premillennialist, depended upon a close reading of Scripture for his belief that the second coming of Christ would occur in 1847.

Knowledge of these references within the Shaker treatises and the men's attitudes toward biblical interpretation enriches our understanding of the Shaker theologians' sense of audience and purpose. McNemar and Dunlavy, concerned with maintaining the appearance of reason and intellect they had evinced in their earlier faiths, continue to do so through their argumentative styles, which draw heavily from Scripture and from ecclesiastical histories (written by theologians of the world). In an attempt to counter Stone and others like him who considered Shakers full of "wild enthusiasm"—followers of an uneducated, allegedly illiterate female, these men used their theology and history as a means of illustrating their higher order reasoning skills and their literacies through scriptural exegesis and citation.

Dunlavy uses Scripture more explicitly and frequently than McNemar. In this regard Dunlavy's text complements McNemar's, which emphasizes spiritually infused people as the primary ones to be read. McNemar quotes from the Bible and delineates Shaker doctrine, but his explicit and implicit emphasis is on knowledge drawn from divine revelation apart from Scripture. Dunlavy's excessive use of Scripture in every case explains Shaker differences, probably in an attempt to illustrate the Shakers' similarity to other sects in their rationalism and their belief in the Bible. Dunlavy's text first appeared eleven years after McNemar's, just after the 1816 *Testimonies* and prior to the establishment of the Millennial Laws, thus reinforcing the sometimes logical order between experience and theology. Dunlavy appears to have been attempting to counterbalance these more narrative and emotional texts centered on Lee's life and, like the other men, responding to accusations from outsiders with a rational theology. I refer to it first here because it articulates more explicitly than McNemar's the hermeneutics of the Shakers' spiritual literacies.

Among the "themes and controversies" Dunlavy rationalizes in *The Manifesto* are the work and presence of the Holy Spirit, discussed, for example, in his lengthy third section on the Resurrection. Dunlavy's explanation of the nature of Jesus' resurrection fulfills several purposes other than the more explicit ones. Primarily Dunlavy explains the spiritual rather than physical nature of Jesus' resurrection body through scriptural exegesis. Secondarily he elaborates on the necessity of figurative language (i.e., typology) and a speaker's or writer's accommodation of language to his or her audience. In addition to these more explicit tasks, he implicitly argues for the value of Scripture, an implied concern of his invoked audience, because many outsiders such as Daniel Rathbun had accused the Shakers of not using the Bible or, at least, not using it properly. Finally, the passage validates the human body as a sign or symbol that when infused with the spirit deserves to be properly read.

In this section of his work, Dunlavy provides an exegesis of biblical passages where the apostles fail to recognize Jesus when he first appears to them in bodily form after the crucifixion. Dunlavy differentiates among the disciples' reading of Jesus' resurrected body described in the Gospels, later apostolic writings about resurrection bodies after Jesus' ascension, and his own reading of both these sets of scriptures. Reworking a classical Christian argument about the nature of Jesus' body during this period, Dunlavy focuses not only on the nature of the body but also on the necessity of this bodily representation of a spiritual being. That is, he distinguishes between representation and reality or, in contemporary linguistic terms, between signifier and signified. The Deity's use of a representative body in the case of Jesus, Dunlavy explains, demonstrated not a divine will to deceive the early disciples but a mark of wisdom, an understanding of the gap between signifier and signified for most readers.

They received [from the Deity] such evidences of the truth as their weaknesses required, and their infancy in spiritual things admitted; for they were yet unacquainted with the distinction between the natural and spiritual creation—between the old man and the new. And there could be no deception in his [Jesus'] appearing to them in the old creation, or body, or an assumed body in the appearance of the old, until they were convinced of his resurrection, his being alive and his really appearing to them, and until they obtained more correct knowledge of his true character in the new creation. (332)

Following this line of thought—these disciples had not yet received the spirit and thus did not have the ability to read spiritually—Dunlavy proceeds to the second part of the classical argument, the discrepancy between Jesus' references to a physical life after death in the gospels (as in the story of the rich man and Lazarus) and the apostles' references in the Epistles to resurrection bodies (I Corinthians 15). Dunlavy argues that Jesus used a different kind of language to talk about life after death than later writers did because his audiences—mostly Jews—had no concept of resurrection; in contrast, the primary audience the apostolic writers addressed—Greek converts to Christianity—did. Thus he justifies Jesus' and the gospel writers' uses of figurative language and simultaneously expresses his own understanding of typological readings: "Figures and shadowy representations are not the substance; yet they are not false or fraudulent, when they subserve the purpose of conveying evidence to the understanding and of establishing truth. The disciples were yet in nature, the Holy Spirit being not yet given, and needed natural and perceptible representations, to confirm them in the faith of that substance which is spiritual" (333). The illustrations and language used to discuss the Resurrection effectively, therefore, varied. But because they had not yet fully received the spirit, all the first-century followers (and, by implication, all those who lived prior to Ann Lee) understood nothing other than figurative language. Their conditions as part of "natural creation" necessitated their being addressed "in such language as they could understand." Dunlavy summarizes, "They were obliged to dwell greatly in the letter, and leave the true spiritual substance to be learned by future experience" (337).

Believers in Christ's Second Appearing, Dunlavy's contemporary brothers and sisters, however, dwell in the spirit and read accordingly. Dunlavy refers to this spiritually infused reading while explaining why the Shakers did not participate in the Christian ritual he refers to here as "the Lord's Supper." The crux of Dunlavy's argument reflects Shaker literacies that come to light in comparison to their neighbors in New England—those who followed the Calvinist tradition as well as those who did not. Dunlavy summarizes, "Eating the Lord's Supper . . . proves the absence of Christ." He reminds readers that Scripture (I Corinthians 11:26) asserts to those participating in the ritual, "Ye do show forth the Lord's death till he come." Since the Shakers believe in Christ's presence in their Millennial Kingdom, they do not practice the ritual. To further delineate the difference between themselves and members of sects that do, he writes, "Neither can it avail any thing for them [other sects] to plead that he is with them in Spirit; for Christ is the Spirit, and where he dwells in Spirit, there he dwells in reality" (246).

The debate he enters, over the Lord's Supper and the presence or absence of Christ within it, harkens back to debates of the Reformation and of Puritan New England that continued among theologians throughout the eighteenth century and into the nineteenth. The debates, essentially about the gap between finite humanity and the infinitude of the Deity, centered upon the question: Did the elements of the Lord's Supper embody the corporeal Christ (and his spirit), or were they merely signs pointing to his presence in a transcendent realm, which covenanted believers in the faith could perceive and experience? As early as the 1520s Martin Luther had argued that they contained the "real bodily presence of Christ," whereas Ulrich Zwingli argued that they contained his spiritual rather than corporeal presence (Holifield, 8). Zwingli argued that humans could not possibly ingest and embody an infinite God; whereas Luther argued that because God had become incarnate as Christ, humans could follow this example and did so in part through partaking of the bread and wine. Calvin followed Zwingli's argument, insisting that Christ's presence was too great to be contained in these finite items, "signs" of God's covenant with humans. To see them as more than signs was to limit the freedom and infinitude of God and the Holy Spirit (Holifield, 18). However, because he did not want to demystify the sacrament (as he believed Zwingli had done), Calvin redefined the Holy Spirit and its manifestations and emended Zwingli's argument by saying Christ did not need to be ingested to be spiritually present at the Supper.

New England Puritan leaders for the most part followed the pattern Calvin established. Concerned with not following "popish" traditions but also not wanting to lose the relevance of the sacramental designs of God's covenant, they sought to articulate the spiritual presence of the infinite God within the earthly realm of his finite creatures. Others in New England, as what has come to be known as the Antinomian Controversy reveals, did not see this unbridgable gap between creator and created. In 1637 the Boston midwife Anne Hutchinson "claimed to receive immediate revelations from God, without the aid of the audible or visible Word"

(Holifield, 142). In general, her followers claimed that "only the immediate witness of the Spirit could enduce the presence of justifying faith, and that salvation resulted solely from the Spirit's direct activity, entirely apart from the instrumentalities of the material creation, whether ordinances of the visible Church or creaturely faculties of men" (Holifield, 141). Although John Cotton of Boston's First Church initially sided with the Hutchinsonians, he eventually saw their claims as dangerously heretical because they implied that "the believer somehow transcended creaturely finitude" (Holifield, 141).[13]

The orthodox within American Protestantism, through the time of the Shakers, followed Cotton's tradition. The elements or "emblems" of the Lord's Supper pointed to a transcendent reality rather than being corporeal or spiritual reality themselves. Attempting to maintain the mystery of the sacrament, some ministers tried to emphasize the Holy Spirit's presence during the Supper, though they articulated that neither spirit, body, nor blood was ingested when bread and wine were. Dunlavy directs his comment, "Neither can it avail any thing for them to plead that he is with them in Spirit," to those who adhere to the belief that Christ's spirit is present, though his body and blood are not. He differentiates Shaker christology and pneumatology from such beliefs by concluding, "Where he dwells in Spirit, there he dwells in reality." As Dunlavy's *Manifesto* records their theology, the Shakers' "reality" existed within the pneumenal realm. In thus unifying spirit and reality, Dunlavy appears to overlook and deny the corporeal. However, this world of spirituality, since the time of Christ's Second Appearing, could be merged with the world of the flesh. I use the word "could" to emphasize that the worlds of spirit and flesh were not always one, or at least were not always *seen* as one. Those people who were able to merge flesh and spirit, or to be filled with the Holy Spirit, which allowed them to do so, constituted the "true" Church of Christ. These Believers in Christ's Second Appearing lived the Shaker "resurrection" life of the spirit marked by celibacy and, sometimes, charismatic gifts. Their visions of these signs and others, because of the presence of the embodied spirit, differed from those without.

The Shaker position was similar to that of "radical" groups such as the Quakers, who met with derision, physical abuse, and exile in New England because of their belief in an indwelling spirit. Although the relationship between the early Shakers and the Quakers of mid-eighteenth-century England and America is difficult to establish because of the lack of records kept by Shakers during Ann Lee's life, the similarities between the theology of the two merit a brief excursion into Quaker linguistics.[14] The Quakers had eradicated the Reformed sacraments of Baptism and the Lord's Supper, and their understanding of the "inner light" afforded by God's spirit living within believers also affected their attitude toward and use of language. For example, because speech was a carnal element necessary to "natural man," they held up silence as both a means of achieving and a sign reflecting spiritual perfection. Silence allowed them to hear God's voice speak within. For orthodox Christian groups the Scripture was *the* Word of God, but for the Quakers, "the Scriptures were rather the tangible reports of the Word of God that was *in* those who spoke and recorded them" (Bauman, 25–26, emphasis mine).

The written word was one step removed from the immediacy of the divine in the spoken word.

Richard Bauman sees Quaker thought and practice as "the logical extreme" of "the Protestant tendency," as described by Walter Ong, to strip away symbols and rituals by "a progressive interiorization of the word" (29). However, "By making the voice of God within man the core religious experience of their movement, the Quakers elevated speaking and silence to an especially high degree of symbolic centrality and importance" (31). That is, they replaced traditional icons and rituals with new ones, which centered on language in oral form. One of these was the act of being silent, another the form of speech that was uttered. In addition, "Speaking became a metaphor for all human action . . . which was thereby encompassed by the same moral rules that governed verbal activity, that is the stripping away of superfluity and carnal indulgence and the maintenance of a 'silence' of the flesh in all things" (Bauman, 30–31). In a sense the Quakers were attempting, like Christ, to *be* the Word. Thus even their bodily actions, including speech, became symbolic; they asked outsiders to read their bodily practices and abstinences as texts.

McNemar's *Kentucky Revival* underscores Shaker bodies as texts more than Dunlavy's *Manifesto* does, perhaps because like the 1816 *Testimonies* his selected genre is more overtly grounded in personal experience than Dunlavy's. Like Dunlavy's theological work, McNemar's history also provides a hermeneutic; in a rhetorical move that perhaps predicts Dunlavy's, McNemar refers to this world as one of "reality." He writes, "*The believer* travels out of the use of shadows and signs, ceremonies and forms of worship, to which he might have been strongly bigoted while in bondage under the law. . . . [A] blessed reality, an enduring antitype, is wrought in *the believer*" (83, emphasis mine). As difficult as it may be for literary critics to imagine a world free from shadows and signs, McNemar's emphasis on the Believer—rather than on the type, sign, or text—reiterates and further explains how Shakers access the realm of reality to which he and Dunlavy refer.[15] The spirit within an individual validated personalized readings—of Scripture, other written texts, people, visions, or any other sign.[16]

The spirit giving life to "the letter"—in this case, the objects perceived—is highlighted in another section of the history, in which McNemar describes and explains his understanding of the "supernatural," spiritual gifts of the Revival: "We must first believe the report concerning the invisible, before we can see the object face to face, and actually possess it. And the firm belief of a thing will produce great effects, both on the mind and the body" (37). The temporal and causal relationship between belief in and possession of the spirit parallels Dunlavy's teaching on the spirit. Belief (for Dunlavy, a reasoned belief) precedes receipt of the spirit (52; 59). Ironically, possession of the spirit assists people in reading others who testify to the Second Appearing of Christ. Those in Kentucky who did not believe, according to McNemar, failed to do so because they failed to submit both to the spirit and to the texts at hand—the spiritual and bodily manifestations in other people.

McNemar provides throughout his history several specific examples of people with appropriate and inappropriate literacies. He nostalgically glorifies the early

Believers in New England for their ideal literacy: "It was not immediately to the Scriptures they applied for light, but to that transporting spirit, which opened clearly to the mind, those mysterious things, recorded in Scripture" (65). He refers to the Shawnee, among whom Shaker missionaries have worked, as exemplary because they claim people can know their "great spirit" without going to school or learning to read. He writes that this method "is the best kind of knowledge" (113). He closes this section by comparing the exemplary Shawnee to Stone and his cohorts, who refuse to see the "great spirit" revealed and working apart from Scripture. He writes elsewhere of the spirit's work, "The believer has to make a final settlement with an old systematic idea, that the spirit of God speaketh invariably in the scriptures" (81); in contrast, "the greatest evidence, the true believer receives, . . . is the divine light" (82). Distinguishing himself on another occasion from systematic theologians who have made an icon of the Bible, he writes, "I dare not worship a book, and my soul recoils at the idea of worshipping that Spirit which originally suggested these words" (106).

These passages underscore McNemar's personal involvement in the text he writes as well as the stance he takes. In perhaps the strongest statement of his attitude toward Shaker literacies, he explains his own conversion to the sect: "I have had the documents open before me, without covering or disguise, i.e. the people who had set out to be righteous, and follow Christ, in deed and in truth" (106). His statement that the people are the documents and his claim that the documents are "without covering or disguise" issue the message that Shakers read not only written texts such as Scripture with immediacy but also people—living, embodied texts—who surround them.

This primacy of "the Word within" rather than Scripture, along with their doctrines of celibacy and confession, their church hierarchy, and in later years their communal lifestyle, led enemies of the Shakers to compare them to Deists and Roman Catholics.[17] The works of Dunlavy and McNemar certainly depend upon attitudes toward reading, science, and reason similar to those of Deists; yet they also depend upon attitudes toward biblical interpretation similar to those of systematic theologians such as Stone, Dwight, and Davis. Shaker leaders, well schooled in Scripture and previously leaders in other Christian sects, set themselves apart by their understanding of the first cause, by the foundation of their system—the events surrounding Ann Lee's life. Because of their reading of her embodied spirit, they read Scripture and especially prophecy about the Second Coming of the Christ differently.

McNemar's and Dunlavy's works demonstrate that in these formative years of Shaker theology the readings of two types of texts—the inscribed texts of Scripture and the embodied texts of people—dialectically contributed to personal knowledge and to the sect's inscribed theology. Memories of personal experiences, cognitively recalled "facts," and "habits" of reading Scripture intertwine to inform Dunlavy's and McNemar's reading and writing acts. Their literacies and literary acts illustrate and articulate that for the Shakers both people and inscribed texts were living when filled with the Holy Spirit, and the fullness came quite often from the eyes of the spirit-filled reader. There were no "gaps" between the signifiers or symbols of these texts and the "reality" they represented, for signifier and signified were fused in one indivisible sign. As a fusion of body and spirit, of the divine and the corporeal, Ann Lee was the primary example of what others could be as well. Images of Lee, remembered and memorialized (both explicitly and implicitly) in Shaker literature, reinforced the faith of early converts after her death and of the Believers of succeeding generations who knew her only through "reading" these memorial images.

NOTES

1. For another version of the conversions, see "Sketch of the Life and Experience of Issachar Bates."

2. Stephen J. Stein (*Shaker Experience*, 57–87); Edward Deming Andrews (*People Called Shakers*, 70–93).

3. Several works discuss Shaker theologians in the context of other American millennialists. See Robley Whitson's *Two Centuries of Spiritual Reflection* (6–14), Stephen Marini's *Radical Sects of Revolutionary New England*, Stein's *Shaker Experience* (57–87), and Henri Desroche's *American Shakers*. For a discussion of typological readings by postmillennialists other than the Shakers, see James West Davidson's *Logic of Millennial Thought*.

4. According to Kathleen Deignan, "Meacham consistently diverts attention from the controversial Mother of Christ's Second Appearing" (87). She explains:

Given his [Meacham's] personal relationship to Lee, and her tremendous spiritual influence on him and all the early Believers, his omission of her in connection with the fourth dispensation has very clear and deliberate theological significance. As the earliest written document of Shaker faith in the Second Appearing, the *Statement* radically underscores the Believers' faith that Christ had come, not in a person but in a people. The Second Appearing is neither the return of Jesus nor the advent of Ann, but the gathering of a Church for the final redemptive work of gathering all men and women into the eschatalogical community of the resurrection. (84)

Meacham's emphasis, then, is not on Lee per se. To him Lee's embodied spirituality is not unique but is exemplary of the indwelling spirit available to all members of the true Church of Christ.

5. Deignan's is the most lengthy and in-depth analysis of Dunlavy's work. Like Deignan, Stein discusses *The Manifesto* in relationship to other theological works, but he focuses more on the social and historical setting within which it was constructed than on the volume's content. He describes the work as "less accessible to Believers and outsiders alike" than other Shaker theological works and histories, and he writes that Dunlavy "constructed his volume as a negative critique of classic Reformed dogma." The work "recasts Shaker beliefs and practices in the mode of contemporary nineteenth-century Protestant apologetics" (*Shaker Experience*, 75).

6. McNemar explains that his narrative depends upon the moving personal testimonies of Shaker missionaries Meacham, Youngs, and Bates, who described their life of perfection. He writes: "If a historian cannot be disinterested and unbiased, it is necessary that he be honest;—and therefore I acknowledge, that nothing ever presented itself to me, that so powerfully interested my feelings as the above testimony" (77).

7. Of the print wars the Shaker missionaries to the west caused, Stein writes that the conversions of Dunlavy, McNemar, and other New Light ministers "legitimized the claims of the missionaries and thus fueled the hostility of the sect's opponents, especially those belonging to the Christian part. Barton W. Stone, splitting with his former colleagues, became an ardent enemy of the sect; he denounced the Shaker apostles as the 'vortex of ruin'" (*Shaker Experience*, 60).

8. Deignan implies Dunlavy's need to convince himself when she writes of his similarity to his enemies, "It is not clear whether Dunlavy himself shared their suspicions [about Lee's claims], but he succeeds in developing a Shaker christology alternative to Youngs's . . . by avoiding all mention of Ann Lee's name" (138).

9. The act of establishing a memorial for travelers has a biblical precedent (Joshua 4:6–9).

10. As Nina Baym's recent study indicates, nineteenth-century women read and wrote histories, genres often considered masculine. It is equally possible women may have picked up these volumes; however, Ann Douglas's study of gender and nineteenth-century print culture (*Feminization*) indicates the primary writers and readers of this genre were males.

11. See Perry Miller's *New England Mind*.

12. Dwight wrote in his *Travels in New-England and New-York* (III, 149–69): "[Shaker] doctrines are so gross that they can never spread far; while the industry, manual skill, fair dealing and orderly behavior of the Brotherhood, render them useful members of society" (qtd. in Richmond, II, 39).

13. See also David Hall's *Antinomian Controversy*.

14. Early Shaker records and numerous histories by outsiders describe the young Ann Lee as participating in a group of Shaking Quakers led by John and Jane Wardley in England. Recently, Clarke Garrett has challenged the Wardley's connection to the Quakers, but he does point to similarities of doctrine (*Spirit Possession*, 142). Stein also challenges the previously assumed relationship by pointing to the Quakers' quietness and inwardness during this period. He believes the French Camisards had more influence on the Shakers than the Quakers did (*Shaker Experience*, 3–4).

15. At least one Shaker writer recognizes ever-present gaps. The preface to Benjamin Seth Youngs's *Testimony* acknowledges the inadequacy of writing and rhetoric for both the learned and the unlearned (xii–xiii). Yet he, too, depends on the Holy Spirit to fill the gaps and focuses on Lee's example of embodied spirituality.

16. Literary theorists may recognize this emphasis on the Believer as similar to the personalized readings validated by reader response theory, and they may recognize the difficulties of breaking away from claims to a "right" or "privileged" reading in realms where institutional authority exists. As readers might imagine, Shaker literacies provoked conflict within the Society on several occasions. I discuss the conflict between personalized and institutionalized readings in more detail in Chapter 5, on Rebecca Jackson's literacy. On conflicts in the Harvard community during the Era of Manifestations, see Diane Sasson's "Individual Experience."

17. See, for example, Thomas Brown's *Account of the People Called Shakers* (226–30) and David Lamson's *Two Years' Experience among the People Called Shakers* (27–30).

Chapter 4

(Ad)dressing Naked Bodies with Pious Suffering: Writing and Readings of the 1816 *Testimonies*

In 1816 the Shakers published the *Testimonies Concerning the Life, Character, Revelations, and Doctrines of Our Ever Blessed Mother Ann Lee, and the Elders with Her*. The *Testimonies's* purpose, as indicated in the "preface," was "to *preserve* 'A Faithful Record' of those precepts and examples [of Ann Lee] for the *instruction* of the next generation of Shakers" (Swain, 10). As Jean Humez has explained, Shaker editors Rufus Bishop and Seth Y. Wells compiled the text in response to pressures and persecutions from "outsiders," who continued behavior that had begun in mid-eighteenth-century England and revolutionary New England; yet they also recognized the importance of teaching the growing number of younger Shakers about Lee, as the preface states ("'Ye Are My Epistles,'" 88–89). In fact, the text's primary use was within the sect rather than as a proselytizing tool. John MacLean's bibliography of Shaker works asserts that "this book was used solely by the elders, and was sometimes called the 'Secret Book of the Elders'" (32), noting that only twenty copies were published.[1] The limited number of copies and MacLean's reference to the Elders' hold on them indicate not only the text's internal circulation but also the probability of material within the *Testimonies* being read aloud to Believers. The power of these orally conveyed images of Lee, I argue here, emerges in part from their receptors' knowledge of fictional and nonfictional narratives of female piety and from the evocation of sentiments through sensational and graphic images of bodily suffering. In so doing, they reinforce the acceptance of both reasoned ways of knowing and emotional ways of knowing and the interaction of nonverbal and literate modes of communication within Shakerism.

This analysis of the writing and readings of the *Testimonies,* then, discusses *what* the volume presents through its structure and images, *why* it employs such strategies, and the *implications* of these presentations for later Shakers. The striking images of Lee's suffering and piety were intended in part to counter the accusations of naked dancing and other acts of "sexual immorality" and bodily promiscuity apostates and other outsiders levelled against the Shakers generally and Ann Lee in particular.[2] I suggest that editors Bishop and Wells intentionally omitted any references to the accusations they hoped to counter because of their awareness of the ability of even verbal depictions of naked bodies to disrupt the narrative; instead they selected and arranged images of female piety and suffering common to popular narratives of the period. I place these images of Lee in three categories: First, as other Shaker scholars have noted, Lee appears as a nurturing and supportive wife and mother.[3] Second, in perhaps the most emotive passages in the text, Lee suffers both physically and emotionally for herself and for others' sakes; readers visualize or read her body as it undergoes such trials. Finally, Shaker editors present Lee, even though an unattached or "loose" woman, as aboveboard in her sexual behavior. In addition to adhering to images of female piety in order to counter the accusations of Lee's sexual sin and unfeminine behavior, the text's images and structure break away from traditions in ways that free Shaker men and women from constraints imposed by gender; they propose an androgynous spirituality instituted by celibacy, as Sally Kitch has argued, and a new concept of "marriage" that looks beyond gendered boundaries and biological propagation, ideals popular in the nineteenth century. The *Testimonies's* inscription and its implied readers demonstrate that Shaker literacies include reading bodies and their spiritual manifestations and responding emotionally to such signs.

REVISING SENTIMENTAL STRUCTURES

An argument about the narrative's structure and its appeal to the sentiments necessitates a description of the text as a whole, a 405-page, forty-three-chapter volume. Providing a structural overview, Thomas Swain dissects the first part of the work's longer title, *Testimonies Concerning the Life, Character, Revelations, and Doctrines of Our Ever Blessed Mother Ann Lee, and the Elders with Her,* to underscore four topics—"Life," "Character," "Revelations," and "Doctrines"—as organizing principles.[4] He describes the first twenty-two chapters as a narrative biography "present[ing] the life [and character] of Mother Ann, . . . beginning with her birth and life in England and ending with her life and death in America, and including such events as her arrests, incidents with the mobs at Harvard and Shirley [Massachusetts], and her travels from one community to another" (10–11). In contrast to these chapters, "which are related in a historical sequence, chronologi-cally," Chapters XXIII–XXVI inscribe "the revelations that Mother Ann manifested at various times" without attention to chronological sequence. This second section of mystical prophecy is followed by ten chapters (through Chapter XXXVII) that present "the doctrines Mother Ann stressed in her ministry." Then, according to the order suggested by the title, "the concluding chapters, XXXVIII–XLIII, were further sketches of the life and character of Mother Ann, Father William Lee, and Father James Whittaker" (10–12).

Although he does not analyze explicitly the narrative structure, Swain implicitly presents the work as reasonably planned by the editors and introduced to readers by the title, which accurately forecasts the chapters that follow. The initial biographical sketches, which include depictions of Lee's persecutions, would immediately appeal to readers' sentiments. The sensational first section of the narrative, if it won readers' respect for Lee, would prepare them for the section of mystical prophecy, or her miraculous "revelations," and for the presentation of her difficult doctrinal teachings, such as crucifixion of the flesh through celibacy. This argument for the significance of the text's "reasonable" order presumes that Shaker readers need to be convinced through reason and that they would read the entire text in order. One could argue that the readers—previously covenanted Shakers—need not be convinced of Lee's authority; they already believe. However, because conversion is a continual process, this reasonable order would have served as a faith-strengthening and instructive text to those who had not had the opportunity to be "eye and ear" witnesses to Lee's testimony and were perhaps learning of the numerous accusations being levelled against her and the sect during the first part of the nineteenth century. Members of the "rising generation," familiar with the Shakers' legal struggles within the world, would need countertexts to strengthen their faiths as much as outsiders would need them to alter their attitudes toward the sect.

One also could argue *against* a structural reading by asserting the unlikelihood that Shakers would read the text in its entirety, from cover to cover. Although some Shakers may have considered the complex structural overview, most Shakers, especially those who received the text aurally, would not. In fact, the sections are not so neatly divided as Swain would have us believe. Appeals to readers' sensibilities run throughout, as do doctrinal teachings and accounts of Lee's mystical abilities. Location of these images is significant for those who want to analyze the text's structure, but most readers or listeners influenced by the text would not consciously consider their locales.

So what purpose does a structural analysis serve? It suggests the social and historical circumstances shaping the text and Shaker leaders' attitudes toward countering them through literature. For example, almost as an aside to his readers, Swain describes the last two chapters of the *Testimonies* as the "suffering and punishment which apostates endured after they had left the Truth and no longer were Shakers" (12). Following his pattern of narrative description, Swain gives no comments about how or why these last chapters break away from the topics the title suggests. These chapters of judgment mark a dramatic shift from the text's earlier topics, where Ann Lee and her followers receive earthly punishments. Yet they clearly give the Shakers the upper hand and the last words; they present the Shaker church as the one being rewarded and to be rewarded in the future. These two chapters serve as Lee's verbal *coup de grâce:* In addition to marking the oral residue within the text and Shakerism by echoing the New England folk tradition of administering curses, they counter the detrimental effect of apostate accounts upon Believers' spirituality.[5]

Humez, who also provides a structural overview, fully acknowledges pressures from both inside and outside the sect that shaped the *Testimonies's* structure, dividing the text according to the narrative voices and types of Ann Lee imagery they convey. She describes three styles that contribute to the work's "patchwork or multilayered nature": personal experience stories told by Lee's first American converts about their contacts with the awe-inspiring woman; a history or travel narrative of Lee's two years of evangelistic missions in New England, where she is described as a "female victim," often from an omniscient point of view; and Lee's first-person narrative of her life in England, recalled by Believers who heard her tell these stories. These three types of narrative and the ambigious images of Ann Lee which they convey were "an advantage" to Shakerism, Humez argues, "as it responded to internal instabilities and adapted to changes in the outside culture over time" ("'Ye Are My Epistles,'" 103). Two important points emerge from Humez's analysis: In addition to underscoring the Shaker editors' response to accusations from the world as they shaped this powerful and influential narrative for those within the sect, she asserts, these ambiguous images allow readers to draw from them as they needed at particular moments in their spiritual lives.

I employ both these elements of Humez's analysis—one centered on writers and the other on readers. The volume, consciously compiled by the editors, counters several forces working against Shaker faith by representing the traditions of Shaker theology and literacies. The text exhibits the writers' reasoning skills as well as their belief in the value of emotions and sentiment. The *Testimonies's* structure and narrative patterns suggest that Believers who offered their recollections orally and editors Bishop and Wells, who shaped the text, relied upon several rhetorical models many Americans knew: doctrinal treatise, history, biography, captivity narrative, spiritual autobiography, and sentimental novel. For example, the *Testimonies* follows the patterns of the conventionally "masculine" genres of doctrinal treatise, history, and biography when it employs the omniscient, authoritative voice and includes dates, names of people, and locations of events. In these instances the editors appeal to reason to convince both outsiders and insiders of the veracity of the Lee story. More important to the majority of Believers than the text's "reasonable" elements is the *Testimonies's* appeal to readers' emotions, accomplished in much the same way as late-eighteenth- and nineteenth-century sentimental works. I use "sentimental" to refer to fictional and nonfictional accounts that appeal to readers' "sentiments" or emotions, often through vivid images of human suffering. The conventions of plot and character typical to these works, supposedly more popular with female readers, complement the text's "reasoned" characteristics. By examining these popular conventions and ways in which the *Testimonies* offers alternatives to them, we begin to understand the power of the tales for other Shakers.

Several literary critics have offered explanations, relevant to this analysis, of why sentimental works are as appealing, successful, and powerful as overtly "reasoned" nonfiction and *belles lettres* whose meanings are ambiguous. Like the novels of the period, as Cathy Davidson describes them, the *Testimonies* includes dialogue that softens and humanizes the authoritative voice and allows readers to "sit in on the conversation." Its heroine, not a world-renowned male such as Jesus or General Washington, offers to young Believers, especially females, a model of success that is not beyond their grasps. Similar to Davidson's argument of the appeal of female role models in the texts of the early Republic, Jane Tompkins explains that the appeal of popular nineteenth-century narratives generally labeled "sentimental" (such as Susan Warner's *Wide, Wide World* and Harriet Beecher Stowe's *Uncle Tom's Cabin*), arises from their "embrace of the conventional": stereotypical characters and plots that emphasize pietistic traits such as self-abnegation and suffering along the "way" to an eventual reward—a palatial home and reunion with family and friends in heaven or the earthly reward of marriage to a Christian spouse. As she explains, "A novel's impact on the culture at large depends not on its escape from the formulaic and derivative, but on its tapping into a storehouse of commonly held assumptions, reproducing what is already there in a typical and familiar form" (xvi). Nina Baym refers to this typical storyline—where quite often a heroine is justly rewarded with physical and/or spiritual union with an ideal mate in earthly or heavenly marriage—as the "overplot" of woman's fiction, and Joseph Allen Boone labels it the plot of "romantic wedlock."

In addition to accessible plots and voices, sentimental narratives create what Karen Sanchez-Eppler refers to as "bodily bonds" between readers of and characters in the genre. The narratives brings together emotion and physical sensation

as the eyes of readers take in the printed word and blur it with tears. Reading sentimental fiction is thus a bodily act. . . . This physicality of the reading experience radically contracts the distance between narrated events and the moment of their reading, as the feelings in the story are made tangibly present in the flesh of the reader. . . . In sentimental fiction bodily signs are adamently and repeatedly presented as the preferred and most potent mechanisms both for communicating meaning and for marking the fact of its transmission. (100)

Ann Jessie Van Sant, who draws from eighteenth-century science to trace the emergence of the genre in the period, also underscores bodies' involvements, as both objects observed in the text and subjects provoked to response by perception when reading. The presentation of Ann Lee's body in the *Testimonies* similarly engages Believers' bodily involvements in reading or imagining it, thus pointing to the body's role in Shaker literacies.

In addition to the emotive images, accessible plots, and conversational voices, however, Davidson has suggested much of the power of these texts emerges from the ways in which they were read. Her argument that the sentimental novel carried political power by providing women new perceptions of their traditional roles depends upon two supporting tenets. First, she argues that the multivocality of the novel allowed readers to imagine themselves in roles other than as passive receptors of authoritative, didactic, and omniscient voices. Second, she asserts that private reading allowed women to exercise independence in thinking (43). In sum, because novel reading encouraged personal interpretation, the increase in novel reading in the early Republic posed a threat to the "elite minority [such as ministers and political leaders] to retain a self-proclaimed role as the primary interpreters of American culture." As described earlier, the *Testimonies* is multivocalic; yet the private reading spaces Davidson writes about appear not to have been available to such an extent for Shakers, whose reading and writing time was controlled and limited by the "elite minority" within the sect. Nonetheless, the striking images within the volume provoked Shakers' emotions; and by the mere nature of emotive symbols and their interpretation, the reading of the *Testimonies* allowed some individualized interpretation. Davidson's and other critics' approaches thoughtfully provoke this reading of the *Testimonies's* formulaic aspects, the placement of a strong female at its center, the ways in which the Shaker story of Lee counters cultural traditions, and an analysis of its impact upon Believers.

When Shaker Believers and editors began sharing and compiling stories of Ann Lee's life, they may have struggled with how to tell her story. They most likely, however, turned quite easily and subconsciously to the models of narratives about women that many Americans knew. The plot and character of one such popular and influential narrative, John Bunyan's *Pilgrim's Progress,* provides a framework that allows us to see the ways in which Ann Lee's journey in the *Testimonies* adheres to and veers from the linear trajectory typical to it. Bunyan's allegorical work is appropriate for several reasons: First, in Part II Bunyan tells the story of a female's quest; male editors and Believers retelling the story of Lee reiterate such gender crossing, demonstrating what they believe spiritual people should be. Second, it elicits a note on the relationships among allegories, spiritual narratives, and "sentimental" works. As Davidson, Baym, and others have shown, many nineteenth-century readers who opposed fiction and novels in concept accepted in practice narratives whose purpose was spiritual or moral improvement; in fact, the genre boundaries contemporary literary critics use were unknown to many of these readers. The allegorical or fictional story of Bunyan's Christiana, which includes dialogue and images of suffering, mixes narrative techniques as does the *Testimonies*; a primary purpose of both, however, is spiritual improvement.[6] Finally, because of its great popularity alone *Pilgrim's Progress* merits comparison to the *Testimonies*. As David E. Smith has shown, many nineteenth-century writers concerned with changes in the American religious climate used Bunyan's pattern to tell their own versions of the Christian pilgrimage; the work was widely read and widely known in America from the time of its publication in 1678 (Part II in 1684) through a peak in popularity then. Louisa May Alcott's "little women" perform a version, and Harriet Beecher Stowe lists it in 1852 among the volumes common on the bookshelf of the typical New England household (*Uncle Tom's Cabin,* 173). Such popular tales contain vital force as communities pass them along, even in oral form. Shakers would have been familiar with the plot and character it conveyed to the American public.[7] Certainly Ann Lee's behavior while traveling bears a marked resemblance to that of Bunyan's Christiana.

Bunyan's Christian, the well-known pilgrim who journeys toward God, arrives in the Celestial City at the close of Part I. At the opening of Part II Christian's wife, Christiana, provoked by a dream vision, sets off on her spiritual journey. She, like

Lee, travels not alone but with a female companion, her children, and male protectors. Referred to more than once as a "poor" and "weak" woman, Christiana escapes victimization by rape early in her travel (179–80). Lee, also described as a poor, weak woman, is victim of physical assaults shameful to "true" women—on one occasion she has her clothes ripped off (XXI, 6–18), perhaps because some believe her to be a witch or a man in woman's clothing. In addition to her dreams and visions, Christiana "reads" other nonverbal signs along the way and learns from them (181); Lee does likewise (XXVI, 8). Christiana speaks proverbs to her traveling companions, including her children, whom she catechizes. Lee continu-ally teaches her followers, whom she views as her spiritual children. These actions mark both women as evangelists, concerned about the souls of friends and family. As they journey, both women sing hymns and dance to make their ways lighter (because their suffering is immense) and to celebrate God's guidance. These actions of Christiana were commonplaces of eighteenth- and nineteenth-century narratives meant to foster spiritual growth. It is not coincidental, then, that throughout the *Testimonies* Lee appears constructed in relationship to images of Christiana that reinforce "woman's sphere." Lee concerns herself with "feminine," domestic duties—with feeding her people, with their having a place to live, and with teaching or "catechizing" her children. Also, her practice of celibacy within marriage (before her husband, Abraham, leaves her) foreshadows and reinforces the concept of the passionless Victorian "angel in the house," which was prominent by the 1830s (Nissenbaum; Cott, "Passionlessness"). Bishop, Wells, and Shakers passing along tales of Lee thought of her in relationship to their culture's ideals, ideals that were transmitted orally as well as in written narratives read silently.

In spite of the numerous similarities between the two women on their journeys, the *Testimonies* present images of Lee that differ from those of Christiana and show her transgressing traditional boundaries of the "female sphere." Bunyan's Christiana, for example, follows her husband's path to the Celestial City, but Lee initially leads her husband. She aims for a spiritual destination different from Abraham's. Likewise, whereas Christiana learns by the guidance of the male "Interpretor" to read signs around her as she travels (183–88), Lee's reading is a gift born of the spirit. Lee often teaches her male traveling "companions," depicted as equals or as her children rather than as her protectors, how to read Scripture. For example, she revises Pauline teachings on women being silent in the churches in a way that convinces Joseph Meacham of her authority (IV, 3). The "children" Lee guides and teaches are symbolic rather than biological, and her catechizing of them is less formal than (i.e., not as "reasoned" and "doctrinal" as) that of Christiana. Bunyan inserts dialogue to illustrate the children's formal catechism (204–7); Bishop and Wells record Lee's pithy proverbs, memorable because of their brevity and appropriateness to the moment. Christiana celebrates her children's marriages to pious spouses, but Lee celebrates celibacy—either within marriage or as an alternative to it. In fact, a major part of Christiana's goal in reaching the Celestial City is reunion with her husband, Christian, who has previously arrived there. Lee's "travel," however, aims at a higher kind of marriage—spiritual union between Believers and the Deity. And Lee's "travail" results in spiritual rather than biological childbearing. At the close of the *Testimonies* Lee neither finds herself happily married to the proper man nor rejoining her husband in the palatial halls of heaven. Instead, on her deathbed she envisions reunion with her brother, William, and proclaims her marriage to another female, "Mother" Lucy Wright, who has, at the time of the *Testimonies's* publication, succeeded Lee as another powerful female leader. Thus the Shaker narrative both parallels and breaks from the sentimental trajectory as its structure and imagery present alternatives to widely embraced notions of sexuality and marriage. This revision, as I will discuss in this chapter's conclusion, places the narrative in the category Boone labels "counter traditional" and suggests implications for Shaker "readers"; for now, however, I will address ways in which the *Testimonies* counters the immediate concerns emerging from apostate accusations in the years of the early Republic.

SHAKER SPECTACLES: (AD)DRESSING NAKED BODIES

In the final chapter of the *Testimonies*, following even the deathbed scene of Ann Lee, the editors record: "At Watervliet, in the presence of Cornelius Thayer, William Scales and others, Mother said, 'I saw William Scales in vision, writing that which was not according to the simplicity of the gospel; and the evil spirits hovered around him, and administered evil to him. They looked like crows.' And Mother reproved William sharply" (XXVI, 8). William Scales's name in this passage may be easily read over or judged as insignificant; however, Scales's name also appears in apostate Thomas Brown's *Account of the People Called Shakers* (1812). The references to Scales in the texts published only four years apart, two among many attempts by Shakers and apostates to give their respective works authenticity and validity by referring to people by name, are neither incidental nor accidental. To counter accounts such as Brown's the Shaker editors include prophecies such as this one, perhaps remembered only after Scales's apostasy actually came to pass, parallel to Peter's denial of Jesus as the Christ in this regard.

In addition to the judgment's careful placement near the end of *Testimonies,* as described previously, its brevity is also significant. Brown's reference to Scales provides much more information than the Shaker work does, describing the man as one who "had been liberally educated and had read much; had belonged to the society several years, and for awhile had been zealous in the cause" (327). The thrust of Brown's comments about Scales, however, centers upon his bodily activity as a Shaker. Brown explains that Scales on one occasion "stripped himself naked and testified his faith": "'Naked came I into the world, and naked must I go out; and naked must my soul stand before God, as naked as my body now stands before you. It is my faith that sin has been the cause of shame, and my soul must become divested of shame, and as completely stripped of sin as my body is now stripped, or I can never stand before you in the world of spirits'" (327–28). Brown's reference to Scales's actions as illustrative of his righteousness may appear outlandish to contemporary readers. However, as Richard Bauman has documented, such acts of "going naked" were quite common among seventeenth-century Quakers. Quite possibly, then, Brown accurately describes Scales's testimony.

Why, then, does the *Testimonies* omit any references to such practices among late-eighteenth-century Shakers? And why do Brown and other apostates such as Daniel Rathbun and Amos Taylor not only refer to the Shakers' "going naked" within their works but make the act into a spectacle?[8]

Exploring the "going naked" phenomenon from both metaphorical and sociological perspectives illuminates the impact of the accusations in Brown's apostate account and the imagery and structure of the *Testimonies* as a response to his work. Bauman describes the Quaker act of "going naked as a sign" as integral to Quaker hermeneutics, which sought to "'break down the boundary between literalness and metaphor, between conceptions and things'" (86).[9] As he explains, "The physical acting out of the metaphors . . . the intersemiotic translation from the verbal to the physical codes enabled the act of communication to seize the attention of onlookers especially effectively, by making visible the semantic anomaly" by which metaphors work. Metaphors work because of the inherent anomaly between the "literal truth values" of the two terms involved; they depend upon the readers' noting the discrepancy, which is only arresting in its verbal form if the readers have sensitive receptive and imaginative skills (86). That is, for example, William Scales's *saying* he stands naked before God—the verbal act—is not as arresting as the bodily act—his *standing naked* before other humans as a metaphor of his spiritual nakedness before God.

This sort of "performative metaphor," however, is most "intelligible and effective" within its ritual framework. "Acting out certain metaphors in other settings may make them more strongly noticeable, but relatively less intelligible as metaphors" (Bauman, 87). A problem for the Quakers, Bauman summarizes, was that actions they intended others to read as metaphors conveying spiritual messages "shocked and alienated most others and prompted accusations of shamelessness and immorality against the Quaker movement" (93). The reason outsiders to the sect misread the metaphors was that the sign of "going naked" was "saturated with literal truth value. The act of displaying one's naked body in public . . . was so striking and shocking in its own right that it tended to engage the onlookers' attention so wholly at that level that they were prevented from looking beyond the arresting literal fact for a metaphorical meaning" (92). If the discrepancy between the "literal truth values" of the two terms of a metaphor is not noted, as was the case with going naked, the sign does not work as its creators intend.

The Quaker incidents Bauman describes illuminate the case of Scales using his naked body to testify about his Shaker spirituality. The Shakers' hermeneutic, as the works of John Dunlavy and Richard McNemar explain and illustrate, parallels the Quakers' in its attempt to "break down the boundary" between signifier and signified, between shadow and reality. They use their bodies as signs embodying and pointing to a spiritual reality. Yet the breakdown of the boundaries can lead to problems; as Scales's use of his physical nakedness as a metaphor for his spiritual condition illustrates, it was so "saturated with literal truth value" that it was misinterpreted (or uninterpreted) by outsiders such as Brown, who viewed it as inappropriate, un-Christian behavior.

Brown reinforces the inappropriateness of the Shaker practice of "going naked" by including at least two other references to it in his *Account*. These sketches connect the act to promiscuity, lewdness, and sexual sins of the flesh rather than to metaphorical, ritual action, although he describes them as recurring elements (i.e., rituals) of Shaker religious life. Brown carefully distinguishes between "going naked" and the "lewdness" of sexual intercourse, but he associates the former with what he sees as other socially unacceptable bodily behaviors the Shakers practice, such as the excessive use of "spiritous liquors."

Those reports that have been the most circulated are, that they not only stripped and danced naked in their night meetings, but sometimes put out the candles and went into promiscuous intercourse; and that the Elders had connexion [*sic*] when they pleased, with such women as they chose; and that they concealed the fruits of it by the horrid crime of *murder*! It was also reported, that many of the Shakers, by order of the Elders, were castrated. (336)

The "connexion," the "murder," and the "castration," he goes on to say, cannot be confirmed; however, he claims he can "confidently" attest to the stripping and dancing naked.

Two important aspects of Brown's descriptions emerge in the other references to these rituals: His sources of knowledge emerge as other than his own experiences in the Church, and he implicitly delineates the differences between the visions of outsiders who want to gaze upon the spectacles and insiders who participate. Of the dancing naked as a purification rite, for example, he writes using the past tense, indicating that the ritual no longer existed when he joined the Shakers; he gathered the story from others: "In order to mortify the carnal mind, their dances *were* excessive; and the various methods they practiced to mortify and try that which they called the root of all evil [sexual intercourse], *were* truly astonishing" (322, emphasis mine). As he continues the passage, he clearly imagines his readers as part of the curious outsiders, arousing interest by calling attention to the gap he leaves: "Several things which took place, for the sake of modesty, are here omitted" (322). Although pleading modesty, he continues, promising both pleasure and truth with the narrative:

But I may observe thus far, that *they stopped every avenue of their houses, so the world's people, as they called them, could not see them, and had one or two of the brethren out to watch*; they then stripped themselves and danced naked, when the gift of order came from Mother Ann so to do; . . . Several were whipped, and some were ordered to whip themselves, as a mortification to the flesh. A young woman by the name of Elizabeth Cook, was stripped and whipped naked, by Noah Wheaton, for having desires towards a young man.—Abiel Cook, her father, hearing of it, prosecuted Noah Wheaton for whipping his daughter naked. (322–23, emphasis mine)

The phrasing embedded in the center of this passage indicates the Shakers' recognition of the power of the metaphorical acts. If these rituals actually occurred, they reflect (as Clarke Garrett, Lawrence Foster, and others have noted) the leaders' attempts to control sexual desire, deployed through other physical actions, the dances.[10] The passage indicates the relationships between desire, power, and attempts to control sexuality, as Michel Foucault has described them in *The History of Sexuality*. Here the desires for power, in conflict with each other, infiltrate those both inside and without the religious community. The "stopp[ing] every avenue of their houses" indicates the Shakers knew outsiders, who *desired* to see, would not understand these metaphorical acts. The passage interesty begs the question of *why* outsiders desired to see. The simple answer, of course, would be to prove the Shakers are transgressing societal laws about sexuality; as Foucault's work suggests, though, the spectacles would satisfy outsiders' own repressed desires for pleasure and power gained from gazing upon others different from themselves, especially those transgressing societal laws.

Brown appears to have drawn this description from apostate Daniel Rathbun, whose printed account circulated among apostates and other curious outsiders; for in another passage, Brown indicates that he records what Rathbun told him. This passage, which more overtly demonstrates sexual desire, also presents conflicts between Shaker males and the female Ann Lee. Perhaps in this passage Brown succumbs to direct quotation of Rathbun because he wants to deflect responsibility for having observed such erratic and sexual behavior; yet, unlike the other passage, he wants it to have the validity of an eyewitness account and thus attaches Rathbun's voice to it:

"One day," said he [Rathbun], "in the afternoon, William Lee, having drank very freely, fell asleep; when he awoke, he ordered the brethren (in number about twenty) to be assembled, I being one with them. William Lee then informed us, that he had a gift to rejoice—and ordered us to strip ourselves naked; and as we stood ready to dance, Mother Ann Lee came to the door of the room with one of the sisters. William Lee requested her to stay out, as he had a gift to rejoice with the brethren. Still she persisted. He said to her again, *Mother, do go out—I have got a gift to rejoice with the brethren; and why can't you let us rejoice? you know if any of the sisters are with us, we shall have war.* " (290)

The emphasized sentence concludes with a shift from Rathbun's descriptive and summarizing voice to an explanation of Lee's violent phrase "we shall have war": "That is, [we shall] have to fight against the rising of nature" (290). The definition seems to be Rathbun's rather than Lee's or Brown's, but regardless of the explicator, the meaning is clear. According to the explication, the presence of male and female Believers in the same room, according to William, will unnecessarily and unwantingly arouse the males. In contrast to the potential "war," the scene presents male bonding that promises a peaceful rejoicing. But the peaceful rejoicing gives way to violence, as the female Lee asserts herself:

But as she would not retire, he pushed her out, and shut the door against her. Then she went round the corner of the house, and attempted to get in at a window. Lee prevented her. She came to the door again, with a stick of wood, and stove it open. Lee met her at the door. She struck him with her fists in the face. He said, the smiting of the righteous is like precious ointment. She then gave him several blows in quick succession. At each of which he made the same reply. At last, the blood beginning to run, he lost all patience, and exclaimed, before God you abuse me; and presented his fists and struck her, and knocked her almost down. I immediately stepped in between them, and cried out, for God's sake, Father William, don't strike Mother! I had rather you would strike me. The brethren, who had stood waiting [*sic*] the event, then gathered round and prevented further blows. There was hard threatening on both sides. Thus ended the gift of rejoicing. (290)

The scene presents Ann Lee transgressing "laws" of gender by wielding the bloody weapon not only because she wants to enter the space designated "male" but also because as testimonies of her life record, she does not seem to struggle with the temptation of "rising flesh." The female Ann appears to believe that men and women should be able to participate jointly in "the gift of rejoicing."[11]

Brown acknowledges the act of "going naked" as a "gift" that had "entirely run out" at the time of his interaction with the Shakers. If Brown's record is accurate, the Shaker practice of "going naked" was relatively short lived, perhaps because like the Quaker practice that preceded it by a century, it caused persecution. Shaker records, including the *Testimonies*, do not refer to the practice at all, probably because writers and editors recognized the failure of outsiders to read the metaphorical performances appropriately, and rightly so, since the metaphorical boundaries blur for those on the outside, even for contemporary readers who seem to understand the close relationships between bodies, spirituality, and sexuality. Nakedness, verbally inscribed within a text, much as the uninscribed, physical behavior of "going naked," prevents nineteenth-century readers from using reason to understand the whole of what is being said. Brown's generally "reasonable" historical narrative demonstrates the phenomenon; when interrupted by these incidents, the narrative becomes extremely emotive and irrational. Many engaged with his argument, however, would read over these narrative inconsistencies or ruptures because they already know the narrative: The Shakers transgress social norms. The easy acceptance of the "irrational" reading of the naked body, as Joy S. Kasson has argued, involves placing it within a known narrative. Writing of Hiram Powers's frequently viewed nineteenth-century statue of a naked Greek slave, aptly titled *Greek Slave*, Kasson explains that the artist "attempted to present an attractive female subject encased in a narrative that would simultaneously invite and repel erotic associations" (176); however, "Powers insisted on the importance of the narrative framework, which provided what he called the circumstances that could justify depiction of a nude subject" (178).[12] Writers of sentimental fiction also depended upon this type of placement to justify their seduction plots. In Susanna Rowson's *Charlotte Temple* (1794) and Hannah Webster Foster's *Coquette* (1797), both popular in the nineteenth century, the female characters' seductions and sexual intimacies are not totally explicit, yet their authors depend upon readers' filling in the gaps with their knowledge of how narratives of such "promiscuous" acts end—with the death or social demise of the female victim.

Quite often the authors present characters reading these female bodies according to the sexual narratives they know, which runs counter to readers' knowledge of these females' bodies. In these instances, it is not what the body has actually done but the way the body is presented in narrative that presents "truth" to the readers. Similarly, Brown's *Account* and the Shaker *Testimonies,* regardless of Ann Lee's actual behavior (which is forever a "purloined letter"), presents "truth" for their respective readers, who have already written the narratives.[13] For example, when the virtuous ministerial suitor of the coquette in Foster's tale, Ernest Boyer, unexpectedly catches Eliza Wharton in the garden in "clandestine intercourse" with the rake Peter Sanford, Boyer reads the scene as a sign of Eliza's "coquetting artifice" and accuses her "of having an intrigue with Major Sanford" (133–35). In spite of Eliza's tears and her pleas that he hear her explanation of her innocence, Boyer reads the scene in the only way possible for him: A virtuous woman who had proclaimed her relationship to one man would not be found in such a position with another. A similar reading occurs in *Charlotte Temple* when the rake, Belcour, attempts to win Charlotte from Montraville, the father of her illegitimate and unborn child. Montraville appears at Charlotte's cottage one afternoon, "and without calling the servant he walked up stairs, thinking to find her [Charlotte] in her bed room. He opened the door, and the first object that met his eyes was Charlotte asleep on the bed, and Belcour by her side" (84). Montraville reads the scene in the only way he knows how—as a sign of Charlotte's infidelity. In *Charlotte Temple,* however, unlike the scene in *The Coquette,* readers discover what Montraville is unable to learn—that Belcour "conceived the diabolical scheme of ruining the unhappy Charlotte in his opinion for ever" by "laying himself by her side," without her knowledge, so that Montraville would find them thus. Both Foster and Rowson present their female characters as victims of impious men, but these scenes also demonstrate that once women allow themselves to be placed in compromising positions, their bodies will be read in ways beyond their control. As Kasson has suggested, the societally known narrative directs the readers to accept the sexual image with a given frame and perspective. The nakedness and sexuality are present, yet accepted because controlled in a given way.

Shaker editors seem to be aware of the problems of appearances of nakedness and sexuality and wish to be reasonable about how they will appeal to readers' emotions. They omit references to nakedness, replacing images of disruptive naked bodies with images of pious and virtuous bodies of the Believers and of the woman they emulate, Ann Lee. Sexuality and sensuality appear within the *Testimonies,* but only in scenes where Lee reads and judges others' behavior. She appears as the wise, pure, and successfully married mother—a Mrs. Temple or a Mrs. Wharton—rather than the wayward daughters Eliza or Charlotte.

One passage that shows readers Lee's sexual purity and her ability to read others' sexual intentions occurs when a man tries "to put his head to her bosom": "While Mother was at Shirley, there came a man to see her, who made a great profession of christian love, and wished to have his love acknowledged by Mother, and, in a fondling manner, attempted to put his head to her bosom. Instantly the power of God came upon her, and she arose and led him into another room to Elder James, 'Here (said she) is a man full of religious devils'" (XXXVII, 10). Lee's actions as a sexually pure and wise woman here complement actions as dutiful wife and mother at other textual sites. As in the world's narratives of female piety, however, Lee's appearance as the suffering victim perhaps arouses more emotions than any other images.

Images of Lee in the text's first chapter establish the precedents of suffering and female piety for the remaining narrative. In describing Lee's childhood, the editors put forth accepted gender roles as they record: "Her father, though poor, was respectable in character, moral in principle, honest and punctual in his dealings, and industrious in business. Her mother was counted a strictly religious, and very pious woman" (I, 2). Also according to gender roles, in ruling his household, Lee's father rules over and against women's sexual "looseness"—seen in his daughter's mere reference to "cohabitation." The first chapter explains that when as a child Lee "admonished" her parents about their "fleshly cohabitation," her father "threatened and actually attempted to whip her; upon which she threw herself into her mother's arms and clung round her to escape his strokes" (I, 5). According to the editors' authoritative, narrative voice, this event was "an early and significant manifestation of the testimony she was destined to bear, and the sufferings she was destined to pass through in consequence of her testimony." However, the scene also mirrors the period's understanding of gender roles. On this occasion Lee's mother's arms provide a haven from brutality.

Depictions of Lee as a wife and mother—albeit asexual in those roles—complement this picture of sexual purity. Passages such as the one below, which depict Lee taking children into her arms, reveal her understanding of the nurturing maternal body. On one occasion her motherly behavior saves her, emblematic of the power of these pictures of Lee's presence upon those who read and hear the accounts. "Persecutors" have appeared on the scene, "demand[ing] *to see the old woman*." The passage that follows illustrates the error of the italicized phrase as it describes not an abusive old woman but Lee as a nurturing mother:

Mother was, at this time, standing in the midst of the assembly, with a young child of Nathan Farrington's in her arms; but feeling a gift to go into another room, which she could not do, without passing through the mob in the hall; she, therefore, with the child in her arms, took hold of young Mehetabel Farrington, and bid her go forward, and stop for nobody; and thus they passed through the mob, into a more retired room. (XX, 24)

Her bodily contact with the Farrington children—one in her arms and another at her feet—demonstrates her motherly concern for their safety while it protects her from harm. Although not Lee's biological children, they serve as human shields, saving their spiritual mother. On another occasion she takes Nathan Farrington's youngest daughter, Esther, "into her arms," kisses her, blesses her, and remarks, "This child is a Believer; she is my child" (XXXI, 17). Immediately following this passage, the *Testimonies* depicts "Mother Ann" instructing children how to pray, which included kneeling, asking for grace, asking to be good, and thanking God for "victuals" (XXXI, 18).

Shakers were to be thankful to God for victuals but not completely reliant upon Providence. In response to accusations about the sect's covenant in favor of shared property, against the grain of American yeoman farmers' beliefs in individualized productivity, the editors explain that Lee "felt . . . that it was the duty of Believers to provide for their temporal support, and not always be idle dependents on the bountiful and miraculous hand of Providence" (XI, 30). Thus the references to Lee's concern with "lay[ing] up stores of provisions" so that her "family" of Believers and her guests will have nourishment not only demonstrate her desire to nurture, her hospitality, and her wisdom but also her industry—all characteristics idealized by women in the colonies and the early Republic.

These concerns mark Lee as an ideal wife as well as an ideal mother, or "angel in the house." Other passages describing Lee as a wife adhere to eighteenth- and nineteenth-century notions of female piety. On one occasion, she sends a female follower and her children home to the husband and father who "fell away and became very bitter" (XVI, 12). She explained her actions: "She is his wife, and I will not keep her here so" (XVI, 13). Demonstrating another case of spousal affection, the *Testimonies* records that after Lee and her followers arrived in New York from England, her husband, Abraham, "was visited with severe sickness: to nurse and take care of him in this sickness, required her whole time and labor. This duty Mother performed with the utmost care and attention." Both Abraham and Ann had been employed, but "their earnings now ceased, and they were reduced to extreme poverty" (II, 2). Lee filled woman's proper role by leaving her employment to care for her first priority, her husband and his bodily needs.

In addition to presenting Lee as a righteous, moral, and pure Christian woman, a wife dedicated to her husband's physical and spiritual needs (rather than his sexual desires), and a mother dedicated to providing for her children, the *Testimonies* includes numerous images of Lee's fulfilling gender roles typical of the age by suffering because of her faith. The text begins with Mother Ann's "suffering" as a child in the first chapter, and the images abound throughout, ending with her death, probably brought about by physical persecution. These images could accrue emotive power for readers as they progress through the narrative, or they could influence readers individually, as they read or hear a single account. But these examples of Lee's suffering, and that of other Believers as well, undoubtedly affect readers because of their physicality.

Lee's suffering appears in two forms, which convey much of the text's overall force: In the first type Lee "suffers," "labours," or "travails" for lost souls—some deceased, some living; in the second type, outsiders physically persecute her. Both types of incidents affect the emotions and cause readers to sympathize with her. The latter type of suffering mimics that of females in popular American captivity narratives. The commonplaces of physical suffering such "captive" women as Mary Rowlandson undergo include, for example, starvation, walking great distances, sleep deprivation, and sleeping on the hard, cold ground. Lee endures these hardships as well as being beaten.[14] Both types of suffering appear within the first chapter. As they reappear throughout, they continually remind readers of Lee's bodily reality and the role of the body in spirituality. Even for those readers who do not read cover to cover, the frequency and, in some cases, length of these kinds of passages suggest that readers cannot come away from the text without sensing Lee's bodily suffering.

In the passages where Lee "suffers" for lost souls, the narrative actually presents little of her body. The somewhat vague descriptions of her "labour" refer to her pacing the floor, lying in bed, or uttering moans or cries (perhaps not unlike acceptable depictions of women in childbirth). The narrative describes her, for example, as "walking the floor and labouring under the power of God," prior to prophesying to her followers in New England (XXIV, 12). She labored "with the dead" during all hours of the night, singing so loudly that she woke those around her (XXVII, 25). This laboring for others was perhaps more exhausting to readers than it appears—out of context and with its lack of vivid depictions of her body—for the term "laboring" begins to accrue meaning earlier in the text. It appears in several well-known and oft-cited passages where Lee "labors" for herself. Of the day she referred to as her spiritual "birthday," Lee vividly recounts her body's movements:

I cried to God three days and nights, without intermission, that he would give me true desires.
    I was, sometimes, under such sufferings and tribulation, that I could not rest in my bed anights; but had to get up and walk the floor. I feared to go to sleep, lest I should wake up and find myself in hell. When I felt my eyes closing with sleep, I used to pull them open with my fingers, and say within myself, I had better open my eyes here, than to open them in hell. (VI, 2–3)

Another passage encourages readers to visualize the bodily activity associated with Lee's laboring during the nights in New England. She recalls: "I often rose from my bed, in the night, and walked the floor in my stocking feet, for fear of waking up the people" (VII, 4). Another vividly presents the effects of this "laboring" upon her body: "I travailed in such tribulation, wringing my hands and crying to God, that the blood gushed out from under my nails, and with tears flowing down my cheeks, until the skin cleaved off" (VII, 19).

    In the first of these depictions, the precedent-setting account of Lee giving birth to herself, the "laboring" necessary "to prepare her for a far greater work," results in physical changes in her body:

In watchings, fastings, tears and incessant cries to God, she labored, day & night, for deliverance from the very nature of sin. And under the most severe tribulation of mind, and the most violent temptations and buffetings of the enemy, she was often in such extreme agony of soul as caused the blood to perspire through the pores of her skin. . . . Sometimes, for whole nights together, her cries, screeches and groans were such as to fill every soul around her with fear and trembling, and could be compared to nothing but the horrors and agonies of the damned in hell, whose awful states were laid upon her, and whose various agonies she was, by turns, made to feel.
    By such deep mortification and sufferings, her flesh wasted away till she became like a mere skeleton. . . . [H]er earthly tabernacle was so reduced that she was as weak as an infant; and was fed and supported by others, being utterly incapable of helping herself; though naturally of a sound and strong constitution, and invincible fortitude of mind. (I, 9, 11–12)

Although the editors write that "her cries, screeches and groans . . . could be compared to nothing but the horrors and agonies of souls under sufferings for the violation of the laws of God," the metaphoric language of the passage evokes images of childbirth. Lee, the "laborer," is also "as weak as an infant"; she has given birth to herself.

Two other narrative sites refer to this incident. One account repeats her becoming "like a skeleton" (VII, 15); the other refers again to the "bloody sweat [that] pressed through the pores" (VII, 18). Both accounts also use infant imagery. In the first, Lee says "a kind of down came upon my skin, until my soul broke forth to God . . . and my flesh came upon me, like the flesh of an infant" (VII, 15). In the second, the account reads, "I became as helpless as an infant. And when I was brought through, and born into the spiritual Kingdom, I was like an infant just born into the world" (VII, 18). This incident of Lee cleansing herself from sin through labor—recorded three times in the narrative—serves as a preparatory act to the laboring for the sake of others, which follows. Readers or hearers of the repeated brief references to Lee's "laboring," especially any who had experienced the pains of childbirth, would react sympathetically to her suffering.

If readers or hearers of the earlier suffering passages were not able to imagine Lee's "laboring" for others—its metaphorical message and its physical manifestations—they could probably imagine the widespread physical persecution of all Believers, including Lee's primary example. Depictions of Lee's suffering due to physical persecutions by skeptics and unbelievers, similar to the passion week scenes of the biblical Gospels in effect, had the power to evoke sympathy and arouse other emotions. After opening images of Lee's father threatening to beat her for "admonishing" him for "cohabitation," the text of the *Testimonies* indicates that her brother actually did. Angered by her "singing by the power of God" and refusing to answer his questions, she explains, "he then beat me over my face and nose, with his staff, till one end of it was very much splintered. . . . He continued beating till he was so far spent, that he had to stop and call for drink. . . . He then turned the other end of his staff, and began to beat me again" (VIII, 15–16).

Numerous brief incidents that occur in England, as vivid as this initial beating, appear next in the narrative: Lee is kept fourteen days in a stone prison where, she claims, "I could not straiten myself" and "had nothing to eat nor drink, except what I sucked through a pipe-stem, that was put through the key-hole of the door once in twenty-four hours" by one of her supporters (XIII, 3). Ordered "to advance" along a road, she "was soon knocked down with clubs; and after [she] got up, and began to walk, [she] was kicked every few steps, nearly two miles." She "then felt as if [she] should faint with thirst, and was almost ready to give up the ghost, by reason of the cruel abuses" (VIII, 18). On another occasion, she explains, "a mob . . . dragged me out of the house by my feet, till they tore the skin off my face" (VIII, 34). On yet another occasion, a mob put her in a cart and drove it through the streets, where "people . . . threw mud, horse-dung, and all manner of filthy stuff, which they could get, into my face" (VIII, 37).

This vivid physical suffering involves Lee's followers as well as herself. In England Elder William Hocknell, for example, is "thrown into a *bulge-place*"—"a deep vault of human excrements," a note explains. After he got out and changed his clothes, the mob "beat and abused" him, rolling him "in a mud slough" and leaving him "wounded," with his "head in a gore of blood" (VIII, 22–23). In New England, the suffering differs only in its extensiveness—the passages lengthen and the number of victims increases. The editors devote the majority of almost six chapters to this persecution, the most violent of which occurs in Petersham and Harvard, Massachusetts, and New Lebanon, New York.[15] In one example from these chapters, "a violent-spirited stout man" thrusts one Believer through a door with such force that "instantly the blood gushed forth, and ran down [the Believer's] face and bosom." On another occasion Valentine Rathbun, an Elder in the Baptist Church, came to persecute Believers, including his son. As the *Testimonies* describes, "The old man mounted some steps, and taking an advantageous position, with a large hickory staff, he levelled several strokes at his son's head, with such violence, that his scull was laid bare nearly three inches in length" (XIX, 7).

These kinds of descriptions incrementally build a case for the Believers and for Ann Lee. Always a desired object, Lee sometimes escapes the persecution, when the mobs fail either to identify her or to locate her. A scene at New Lebanon typifies the others in the sentiments it arouses through bodily violence:

They [the mob] seized the brethren, one after another, and dragged them out with the most savage violence. Richard Spier was three times thrown out a back door, which was very high from the ground. Some were drawn out by the hair of their heads; some were taken by four or five men, one at each arm and leg, and pitched, headforemost, with great violence, into a mud puddle near the door; some had their clothes badly torn.

. . . Mother was, at this time, in a back bedroom, separated from the rest of the people by a ceiled partition. The ruffians strove to enter the room where she was; but were kept back by the brethren who guarded the door: After a considerable struggle, they succeeded in tearing down the ceiling of the room, seized Mother by her feet, and dragged her, in a shameful manner, through the parlour and kitchen, to the door. (XXI, 6–7)

A carriage chase ensues, with Lee in the getaway vehicle her followers had prepared. The mob cuts the horses' reins, beats a Believer who attempts to lead the horses anyway, and tries to upset the carriage at a small bridge, where one among them falls down the "precipice." The mobster soon regains his place riding alongside the carriage and "violently seize[s] hold" of Elder James in an attempt "to precipitate him headforemost upon a rock" (13). Another Believer intervenes, and Elder James escapes with only broken ribs.

The destination of the chase is the home of Judge Grant, who was to hear Lee's indictment. Upon their arrival, "Mother was dragged into Grant's in such a rough manner, that her cap and apron were torn off" (18). A note explains that "John Noyes—the constable, had greatly abused Mother, and struck her, several times, with his staff, before Grant's face; particularly one severe stroke across her breast, the mark of which she carried for sometime afterward." After some verbal wrangling between Lee and Grant, Grant orders her "put . . . under keepers":

The constable, and two other ruffians . . . took her, and in a very abusive manner, dragged her out of the house, and along the street, about fifteen or twenty rods, to the new house.

Mother felt extreme anguish, from the cruel abuses of these men, who vented their enmity by beating, griping, and pinching her as they dragged her along. She cried out, and said, "Must I give up my life in your hands?" But regardless of her cries, they dragged her along into the house, and up stairs, as though she had been a dead beast, and then thrust her into a room, where she sat down and cried like a child. (XXI, 21–22)

The physical abuse and violence of these occasions leaves Lee with signs her followers, and recipients of the *Testimonies,* read. In an authorized exposure of her body, reminiscent of Mary Rowlandson's references to her wounded side or Elizabeth Ashbridge's references to her abuses by her husband, Lee

showed them the bruises she had received from the cruel persecutors. Her stomach and arms were beat and bruised black and blue; and she, and the sisters with her, affirmed that she was black and blue all over her body; and indeed, it was not to be wondered at, considering how much she had been beaten and dragged about: She wept, and said, "So it has been with me almost continually, ever since I left Neskeyuana; day and night—day and night, I have been like a dying creature." (XXII, 3)[16]

These incidents of physical suffering by Lee and her followers affect the emotions and cause readers to sympathize with them. Lee's suffering not only parallels the trials pious Christian women were expected to bear, as demonstrated in popular narratives of the first part of the century; it also forecasts the suffering and behavior of such female characters as Harriet Jacobs's Linda Brendt and Frances Harper's Janette Alston, who appeared in sentimental narratives later in the century. Lee, like Harper's and Jacobs's women, respectively, subverts gender roles through teaching celibacy and spiritual agency apart from mainstream religious institutions.[17] Thus Believers could view Lee as a Christian heroine who both maintained and subverted traditional roles.

WRITING AND READING THE FINAL IMAGES OF LEE: A SUMMARY

Depictions of Lee's final illness and death—her ultimate physical suffering—provide glimpses of Lee not only living but also dying within the social constraints of her time, revealing her nontraditional attitudes toward church leadership, marriage, and gender relationships. Like the ideal virtuous woman of eighteenth- and nineteenth-century literature who is prepared for death, Lee meets it with neither fear nor struggle.[18] On her deathbed she expresses a desire to go "home," and she visualizes people and objects ready to greet her in the spirit world she will enter. The *Testimonies* records:

Soon after Father William expired, Mother said, "Br. William is gone, and it will soon be said of me, that I am gone too." She was, afterwards, often heard to say, "Well, I am coming soon." She would then say to those who were present, "Brother William is calling me." Sometimes she would say, "Yea, Brother William, I shall come soon."

. . . she breathed her last, without a struggle or a groan. Before her departure, she repeatedly said to those around her, that she was going home. A little before she expired, she said, "I see Brother William coming in a golden chariot, to take me home." (XXXIX, 30–31)

The passage also demonstrates a reunion of biological relations, typical of nineteenth-century scenes of the afterlife. Yet here the references to William Lee indicate a unity and harmony counter to the sibling rivalry Brown's *Account* presents.

Prior to this deathbed scene, in her final illnesses Lee claims her marriage to another female: "Immediately Mother Lucy, who took care of her, in her last sufferings, came and took hold of her hand, and asked her to go in [to her room]. Mother answered, 'I will; I will be obedient to you Lucy; for I am married to you, and I will go with you.' And they went in together" (XXXVII, 24). According to Shaker interpretations, Lee here passes the torch of leadership to another female. Additionally, her statement "I am married to you" may be read as Lee's assumption of the "feminine" passive role she took on earlier in the narrative as she described herself as the "bride" of Jesus, while she bestows the "masculine" role of husband and leader upon another female.[19] The "marriage" may be read as symbolic of the unique union between women in Shakerism, which Rosemary Gooden describes as "gospel union" and "gospel affection." These relationships differed from those in the world in two ways: First, the women were committed to celibacy rather than waiting for husbands to free them from their bonds to other women. Second, Shaker women were cautioned against developing one-to-one friendships; rather, they were encouraged to be in union with all Sisters. Thus the Shaker Sisters' spiritual marriages were asexual, unproductive from the perspective of biological offspring, and polygamous. Through her life as depicted in the *Testimonies,* Lee drastically revises the "marriage" plot typical to narratives of the period.

Boone classifies nineteenth-century works that counter the tradition of the plot of romantic wedlock into two categories: those by male authors such as Herman Melville and Mark Twain that present heroes who reject marriage and select instead a quest into unknown territory (20), and those by female authors such as Sarah Orne Jewett and Charlotte Perkins Gilman, who present heroines who select single life within a community of women. The narrative styles of the latter works, he writes, "are governed by the logic of incremental repetition, in which seemingly disconnected or random events circle around unchanging truths and settings, rather than by the causality of linear plotting intrinsic to the love-plot" (21). This "narrative organization . . . mirrors but simultaneously refutes the protagonist's societal circumscription: Its transformation of her circular entrapment into nonlinear rather than causally ordered patterns of narrative quietly undermines the tradition of logocentrism that has governed Western thought and shaped its standard fictions" (281). The *Testimonies* fits neither of Boone's gendered counter traditional formats completely. Lee, like the male characters whom Boone describes, faces physical and psychological challenges during her (spiritual) quest; yet through its nonlinear narrative and Lee's "marriage" to Wright, the text also presents being single and bonded to other women as a viable option for freedom and empowerment. Thus the text offers female readers multiple models for countering traditional images of womanhood.

Lee's profession of marriage to Wright, in addition to revising the concept of romantic wedlock as Boone describes it, uses the present tense verb "am." Even in the midst of her physical death, Lee refuses to relinquish her connections to living Believers. Shaker editors and Believers providing the testimonies sought to capture Lee's presence and immanence through these multiple sketches of her voice, her conversations with followers, and vivid depictions of her own and others' treatments of her body. Because Lee continues to live spiritually through the inscribed sketches in the *Testimonies,* other Shakers such as Rebecca Cox Jackson, discussed in the next chapter, are able to live spiritually as well. These Believers received images of Lee's deathbed marriage and others that served as keys for them as they read and wrote their own spiritual journeys within and against the traditions of their culture.

NOTES

1. Humez provides a history of the text's composition, describing leaders' interviewing of "'old Believers'" and arrangement of the material "into chapters organized around certain themes" ("'Ye Are My Epistles,'" 88). The editing is generally attributed to Bishop and Wells. MacLean appears to extrapolate from a note Alonzo Hollister wrote in one copy and in a letter to William Ward Wight: "Only 20 copies of this edition printed under Mother Lucy's ministration" (Richmond, I, 15–16).

2. For the most concise overview of these accusations in apostate accounts, see Clarke Garrett (195–213). See also Stein (*Shaker Experience,* 15–18), Andrews (*People Called Shakers,* 40–47), and Foster (*Religion and Sexuality,* 30–35).

3. The best historically grounded discussion of this maternal imagery appears in the works of Proctor-Smith (*Women in Shaker Community*) and Humez ("'Ye Are My Epistles'"). See also Proctor-Smith's "'Who Do You Say That I Am?': Mother Ann as Christ."

4. Several critics analyze the *Testimonies* with attention to other concerns. Proctor-Smith considers the images in relationship to those of woman's "sphere" and the "cult of true womanhood" (*Women in Shaker Community,* 204–5). Sasson writes about the volume as a precursor to later Shaker autobiographies or testimonies (*Spiritual Narrative,* Chapter 1). Deignan analyzes maternal imagery in relationship to the Shakers' systematic theology (50–58).

5. As the editors summarize, "It has most generally happened, that reprobates and persecutors have either been fugitives and vagabonds upon the earth, or have died some untimely and extraordinary death. They have not died the common death of man, nor been visited with the visitation of other men" (XLII, 5). Scales is one of these vagabonds (XLII, 16–25). As Hall points out using the well-known account of Francis Spira, these tales of judgment were oral commonplaces in New England culture (*Worlds of Wonder,* 132–35).

6. Of the blurred boundaries between fiction and nonfiction from the years of the early Republic through the antebellum period, Jane Tompkins has written,"Antebellum critics and readers did not distinguish sharply between fiction and what we would now call religious propaganda. [Susan] Warner, for instance, never referred to her books as 'novels,' but called them stories, because, in her eyes, they functioned in the same way as Biblical parables, or the pamphlets published by the American Tract Society; that is, they were written for edification's sake and not for the sake of art, as we understand it" (149). In fact, as David

Reynolds has pointed out, ministers began to adapt sentimental narrative style, shifting "pulpit oratory . . . from an expository and abstract mode of explicating religious doctrine, to a mode in which sensational narratives carried the burden of theological precept" (qtd. in Tompkins, 153). See also Davidson (40, 53–54).

7. My approach differs from Sasson's; she writes in her analysis of Shaker autobiographies that few Believers would have read Bunyan's work (*Shaker Spiritual,* 18). As noted in Chapter 1, Shaker records indicate that leaders awarded young Believers Milton's *Paradise Lost* (also among Stowe's list of popular titles) and *Life of Washington;* whether they read these works or not, many Shakers knew of them. Hall documents the power of orally conveyed narratives and images with the case of the Spira tale in early New England (132–33). I underscore the interplay of orality and literacy in conveying commonplaces of Bunyan's narrative.

8. Garrett (195–213) provides the most thorough discussion of these early apostate accounts, although he does not discuss the issue of Shaker spectacles as I do here.

9. Bauman draws much of his information on Quaker hermeneutics from other studies, most notably Jackson I. Cope's "Seventeenth Century Quaker Style," from which he takes this quote (726).

10. Foster (*Religion and Sexuality*) and Garrett discuss this early period of Shaker dance; drawing from Foucault's theories, Susan McCully analyzes relationships between women inherent in the nineteenth-century rituals.

11. The scene also presents a conflict between biological relations, Brother William and Sister Ann, resolved in the *Testimonies's* scenes of Ann's death. Shaker leaders, concerned with images of the church's revised concept of family unity going beyond biological ties, present harmony and love between the two rather than any type of power struggle.

12. Kasson also writes, "Powers presented a woman in a chaste and tranquil pose, but the narrative suggested by the sculpture implied violence and sensuality" (175); the subject of the harem was "a forbidden realm in which viewers confronted their own erotic desires" (175).

13. See Jacques Lacan's "Seminar on 'The Purloined Letter.'"

14. In *White Captives* June Namias provides an in-depth analysis of images of captivity in America through the nineteenth century. Laurel Ulrich discusses the power of the images within colonial America (*Good Wives,* 202–35).

15. Garrett historicizes these persecutions and suggests reasons for their intensity (195–213).

16. Rowlandson's frequent references to the wound in her side (344, 346, 347) provide a stark contrast to the attention the "sexually loose" female natives call to their bodies through physical adornment (356). The Quaker Ashbridge presents herself as an emotionally and physically abused wife. The physicality of her abuse appears, for example, in a scene where her husband forces her to dance "till Tears affected [her] Eyes, at Sight whereof the Musician[, reading her abused body,] Stopt and said, 'I'll play no more'" (600).

17. Neither Alston nor Brendt marries; although each character attempts to live by moral codes acceptable to mid-nineteenth century female readers, each also emphasizes alternatives to the image of the married "angel in the house."

18. For discussions of this commonplace, see Douglas, "Heaven Our Home," and Tompkins (128).

19. Lee's claims of marriage to Jesus are not new; they have biblical precedent and echo the claims of medieval mystic Margery Kempe and Puritan poet and minister Edward Taylor (*Preparatory Meditations,* 115).

Chapter 5

Reading, Writing, Race, and Mother Imagery: The Literacies of Rebecca Cox Jackson and Alonzo Giles Hollister

Rebecca Cox Jackson (1795–1871) and Alonzo Giles Hollister (1830–1911) lived in different Shaker communities and probably never met "in the flesh." Yet the authors and their spiritual narratives, considered together, offer insights into the impact of physical experiences upon Shaker literacies. Their literacies—different from each other in origin and in the number of inscribed texts read and written—draw from their gendered, racial, and historically situated experiences. Nonetheless, both Jackson and Hollister celebrated and drew life from Ann Lee's examples. In fact, these writers and their narratives also illuminate ways in which the sect's spiritual literacies, instituted by Lee and reinforced through the *Testimonies,* provide individual Believers spiritual sustenance and freedom even while they work within the constraints of Shakerism and the genre called spiritual narrative.[1] Further, because Jackson's writing predates Hollister's by half a century, they demonstrate shifts in the types of literacies predominant within the sect. Jackson's personal testimony exemplifies the genre used at mid-century by leaders for internal strengthening and evangelism. Hollister's writing, more heavily saturated than Jackson's with the world's literary discourses, reflects the Shakers' employment of the world's devices to preserve spiritual literacies near the end of the nineteenth century. He continues the "masculine" tradition leaders such as Richard McNemar and John Dunlavy established in the early decades of the century, but he creates a Shaker archive for researchers rather than an active, working library for possible converts.

This analysis of Jackson's and Hollister's literacies responds in part to Linda Mercadante's recent examination of female god imagery in Shakerism. She had hoped to discover that having a female aspect to the Deity greatly empowered female Believers. However, having considered numerous personal written testimonies, she concluded that "Shaker believers' actual use of female imagery for God in their personal expressions of faith was uneven and sporadic. Many believers' religious experience does not seem to have been deeply affected by these images" (16). In addition, she learned that among those Believers affected by the imagery, "men were equally as likely as women to use female Christ imagery in describing their religious experience" (150–51). Inviting further study of the topic, she asked: "Why were some believers more likely to be positively affected by female imagery than others? It would be interesting—possibly more from a psychological than a theological point of view—to find correlations between members' gender, background, time in the community, and their choice of imagery" (143). I submit that both Jackson and Hollister *were* positively affected by female imagery; however, given their "gender, background, [and] time in community," the ways in which they were empowered by memories of Lee differed. Jackson, who came to Shakerism as an adult, inscribes herself following Lee's patterns. As Jean Humez has written, "Jackson's career as a female religious leader presents some striking parallels with that of Ann Lee, as Jackson herself was aware" (*Gifts of Power,* 39). Several implicit allusions to Lee within her life story demonstrate that Jackson saw herself or "read" and "wrote" her life according to the *topoi* of Lee's biography. In general, her ecstatic visionary experiences and explications of them, her challenges to male-dominated religious institutions, her decisions to practice and preach celibacy (which eventually led to separation from her husband), and her persecution by unbelievers mark areas where the black woman inscribes her life within the parameters of the Lee story. Jackson differs from Lee in her desire for increased alphabetic literacy, a desire influenced not only by the historical period in which she lives but also kindled by her race. She aspires to power in part by adhering to the patterns of the dominant culture; yet as she follows Lee's example, she continually joins the realm of reason and inscribed texts with the realm of orality and bodily presence through an emphasis on an active and embodied spirit.

Jackson's adherence to Lee's pattern attracts Hollister. He lived almost his entire life as a Believer and played a key role in publishing and preserving many of the Society's texts in the late nineteenth and early twentieth centuries. As Diane Sasson and Humez have noted, Hollister edited and preserved Jackson's narrative, a text and a task he described as "a treasure."[2] He wrote in his "Reminiscences," "I greatly enjoyed the copying, evenings and mornings and sabbath days" (189). For Hollister, Jackson is an African-American mother figure, exhibiting the literacies established by Lee, who provides spiritual and emotional sustenance and wholeness during the years he was editing her text and writing about it. During these years of several institutional shifts within Shakerism, he reads the woman depicted in the narrative as a racial and gendered "other," and he rewrites her into his own narrative as an ideal, representing the past and forecasting a possible future for Shakerism.[3] Hollister's fascination with Jackson and mother imagery emerges, I believe, from his becoming more tightly enmeshed in the realm of inscribed texts, which coincides with the sect's numerical decline. In addition to mother imagery, two other topics within Hollister's narrative—his literacy and his relation to his "home"—manifest and confirm his increasing isolation, his anxieties over communal losses, and his attempt to maintain traditional Shaker values in the face of these changes. Hollister nostalgically recalls the mystical fervor of his youth as he ages and approaches physical death; he may have found that writing the narrative could heal his general feeling of loss (and, perhaps, conflicted views of his masculinity) and sense of powerlessness.

Although both Hollister and Jackson use images of Lee in their narratives to validate their pasts and imagine possible futures for themselves and for the sect, they differ in their uses of writing. In many ways Hollister and his narrative clearly fall into the "masculine" realm. For example, the narrative focuses more on "externals," is more "linear and chronological," and is less expressive of humility than Jackson's, which is more internally focused and "cyclical and associational."[4] In addition, Hollister writes, late in his life, a more distanced, retrospective account; Jackson records her reflection nearer to the time the events occurred, providing a fragmented journal rather than a sustained, retrospective life-story. In sum, Hollister situates himself through his writing and reading in the past, whereas Jackson situates herself in the present. Their actions, corresponding with their reading and writing, also differ. Perhaps as a result of her racial and gendered experiences, Jackson carries within herself a sense of home she can create anywhere. Her reading of Lee imagery therefore propels her to leave the community at Watervliet to establish her own community in Philadelphia. Hollister's reading of mother imagery comforts him as he stays within the communal home he has known for almost his entire life. He imagines others will be drawn to Shakerism by reading inscribed doctrinal texts or reading uninscribed mystical signs.

This reading of Hollister's and Jackson's spiritual literacies depends upon the interplay of "narrative selves"—the subjects Jackson and Hollister constructed in their spiritual narratives—and "historical selves." Reconstruction of the historical subjects (Jackson and Hollister) depends upon what we know of them as writing subjects. Numerous works other than Hollister's "Reminiscences," written by him and other Shakers, contribute to the contours of his "historical" self and my reading of his narrative; in fact, the limitation of my analysis to Hollister's narrative, rather than to all his works, may be said to provide a skewed vision of his literacy. However, the picture available through the narrative and other accounts I mention provides a useful contrast by which Jackson's literacy, and that of other "less literate" Shakers, may be more fully understood. In the case of Jackson, little other than her spiritual narrative exists. To reconstruct the spiritual lives and literacies of Jackson and Hollister as presented in the narratives, I consider first each writer's references to inscribed texts and alphabetic literacies. Second, I examine their uses of mother imagery, often associated with Lee, to determine the impact of her spiritual literacy upon them. I also consider how each writer employs discourses of race within Shakerism and nineteenth-century American culture. Finally, I propose that the examples Lee provides allow first Jackson and then Hollister to sustain themselves by reading and writing imaginatively. Through these literacies they visualize possible worlds for themselves and future Shakers. In spite of the world's visions of racially and gender-driven categories, they act in the present according to these visions.

Robert A. Orsi's and Caroline Walker Bynum's positions on the polysemic nature of religious symbols illuminate Jackson's and Hollister's uses of mother imagery, race, and spiritual narratives. According to Orsi and Bynum, symbols provide creative spaces in which the imaginations of participants in religious rituals operate. As Orsi writes in his analysis of female devotion to Saint Jude:

> Religious traditions must be understood as zones of improvisation and conflict. The idea of "tradition" itself is the site of struggle, and historically situated men and women build the traditions and counter-traditions they need or want as they live. Finding meaning in a tradition is a dialectical process: women worked with the form and structures available to them, and their imaginings were inevitably constrained by the materials they were working with. Still, through the power of their desire and need, and within the flexible perimeters of devotional practice, they were able to do much with what they inherited. (160)[5]

Participants' imaginative work with symbols of religious rituals such as writing spiritual narratives is shaped by their physical experiences, which include behavior influenced by gendered and racial realms both within and outside Shaker communities. In this case Jackson's literacy and imaginative work allows her to recognize the constructed racial and gendered boundaries and to move physically between them as she chooses. Hollister's literacy and imaginative work enable him to visualize Jackson's empowerment and to strengthen himself by seeing his own textual endeavors and the divine spirit bringing others to Shakerism.

REBECCA COX JACKSON:
READING AND WRITING HERSELF AS MOTHER

"I am only a pen in his hand"

When Rebecca Jackson describes herself as a pen in God's hand (107), she uses an image that is not surprising for a spiritual writer. In this case, however, Jackson refers not to her submissive role as God's scribe, mechanically or mystically writing in ink with her hand the divine messages God inspires, but to her ability to *be* the pen. Jackson's metaphor refers not to her writing of inscribed texts in private but to her "reading" people and "writing" in response to them as a public minister. On the occasion of this comment she asks God to give her "a discerning eye" to see through people, "understanding" that would allow her to distinguish "truth" when they spoke it, and "suitable answers" to give them orally in response to their questions and comments. The ironic twist brought about by the pen metaphor in this context—an image of writing used to vivify acts of aurality and orality—emphasizes the recurrent interplay between inscribed and uninscribed reading and writing in Shakerism, important to Jackson both as she acts prior to inscribing her story and as she records her life. The reading and writing Lee exemplified sustains Jackson as she struggles with her life as an African-American woman within the predominantly white religious sect.[6]

In short, the situations in which Jackson finds herself because of race and gender lead her to read and, subsequently, to reject and to revise the codes of the symbol systems within which she operates—first among the "free" blacks affiliated with the male-dominated African Methodist Episcopal (AME) church in the Philadelphia area and second among the Shakers at Watervliet, New York. Jackson's attraction to the Shaker codes and her ability to revise them depended upon the spiritual literacies their theology allows. But in spite of what Mercadante calls the sect's "gender inclusive god-imagery" (15), Jackson experienced conflict with Shaker leaders because of her race. However, Shaker literacies honoring inscribed and uninscribed texts and innovative readings of symbols offer her agency in otherwise repressive and limiting situations as she reads her visions to lead and create her own group of Believers in Philadelphia.

One of the few African-Americans known to live the Shaker lifestyle, Jackson is known as much for her racial difference as for her mystical powers. Unlike many other writers considered in this study, Jackson and her works have been analyzed by several others, including Nellie McKay, Joanne Braxton, William L. Andrews, and Alice Walker. They have discussed Jackson's writings in the context of personal narratives by black women and in relation to other Shaker narratives, highlighting the impact of her race as she associated with the sect. In addition, they have commented on the spiritual visions that structure Jackson's writings, the interpretations Jackson gave them, and her decisions to live according to the guidance provided by the visions and interpretations provided.[7] These decisions in the 1830s tore her away from her involvement with the AME church, caused her to practice celibacy and eventually leave her husband, and directed her to preach as an itinerant in Pennsylvania, New York, Connecticut, Rhode Island, New Jersey, and Massachusetts. In the 1840s they brought her to live with the Shakers at Watervliet, and in the 1850s they guided her to leave that community to lead her own band of Believers in Philadelphia, where she died in 1871. In comparison to comments about her visions and race, little has been written about how Shaker attitudes toward reading and writing contributed to Jackson's empowerment.[8] The exception is Katherine Clay Bassard's more recent discussion of nineteenth-century African-American women's autobiographies and literacies. Of Jackson in particular, she emphasizes, as do I, the Shakers' hermeneutics as critical to Jackson's ability to revise. Rather than focusing on Jackson's revision of Ann Lee's biography, however, Bassard points to the influence of AME spiritual autobiographer Jarena Lee (161–62, n. 16).[9] I respond to and build upon the work of Bassard and others as I discuss the interplay among Jackson's race, gender, visionary skills, and her literacy.

Evidence of Jackson's reading and writing even prior to joining the Shakers exists in several somewhat fragmented manuscripts, which she began to write only after arriving at Watervliet during the 1840s. Only two are in Jackson's hand, one of which is an "incomplete autobiography, 146-pages long, unparagraphed and unpunctuated" (Humez, *Gifts of Power,* 65).[10] Another manuscript version of

Jackson's autobiography exists in Hollister's handwriting. Moved by Jackson's story, he copied "an incomplete narrative autobiography and . . . 'several small books' in Jackson's handwriting, arranged by him according to date" (Humez, *Gifts of Power*, 65). The works had been given to Shaker leaders at Watervliet by Jackson's close friend and spiritual sister, Rebecca Perot, and eventually found their way into Hollister's hands. Humez's careful historical and textual analysis of these manuscripts resulted in her recent critical edition of Jackson's writings, the first published version. Drawing primarily from the pieces in Jackson's hand, Humez notes significant variations that occur in Hollister's and another later manuscript version. Humez's edition basically follows chronological order, according to dates in which the pieces were written (not necessarily the date of the recorded event or vision).

Even in Humez's edition, Jackson's writing often reflects a loose association of thoughts which some readers may see as fragmentary and hard to follow. Nonetheless, the self-editing comments on many of these occasions reveal Jackson's awareness of stylistic and organizational concerns. Humez suggests that these notations indicate Jackson may have planned to revise her work at a later date. The chronologically organized writings of Humez's edition together with Jackson's comments about reading and writing reveal her ever-increasing interaction with inscribed texts. This change parallels shifts in writing and reading practices within Shakerism as it also reflects shifts in Jackson's abilities, habits, and desires. From her early years Jackson exhibits a desire for increased alphabetic literacy—a belief in Harvey Graff's "literacy myth": Literacy contributes to the individual's (as well as her society's) progress and development (3). Jackson's drive may be in part a desire to be like the dominant race, as Henry Louis Gates and other scholars of slave narratives have asserted is typical of early African-American writing.[11] However, as Bassard has noted, the forms of these written works present differing views of the rewards of literacy; Jackson's stated goal is always spiritual rather than economic improvement. She recognizes that in her religious circles people in positions of power and authority are those who read and write inscribed texts. She may subconsciously want such communal power and authority, but she presents alphabetic literacy as a tool for *spiritual* growth rather than economic progress. In her narrative she continually reminds herself and other readers that only spiritually informed literacies are worthwhile.

Throughout her writing she shows that books validate her lived experience and, additionally, that her understanding of the texts—assisted by the spirit—is progressive. In January 1855, for example, Jackson refers to herself and her group of spiritualists as "only in our ABC's as it regards the true knowledge" (253). The spirit directs Jackson not only in her reading and understanding but also in her writing. On one occasion she echoes the opening of the book of Revelation, which she probably knew: "I was told at the beginning to write the things which I seen and heard, and write them *as* I seen and heard" (170). The passage also echoes the spiritually inscribed volumes by Shakers Paulina Bates and Philemon Stewart, texts prominent during the Era of Manifestations when Jackson came to Watervliet and that she records having read. Their visionary influence, as well as John's apocalyptic text, emerges in Jackson's record of literacy.

Jackson's description of her literacy during her early life and ministry in Philadelphia establishes that which she manifests later, during the years she interacts with the Shakers. She describes her ability to read and write inscribed texts as "a remarkable providence of God's love," explaining that she "had a great desire to read the Bible" after her conversion and sanctification experiences (107). Greatly "griev[d]" by her brother's promises to teach her to read and his lack of commitment to them because of his own physical constraints, and "hurt" by his unsolicited editing of letters he inscribed for her as she dictated, Jackson records that she heard these words spoken to her: "Be faithful, and the time shall come when you can write" (107). She also records the remarkable day:

One day I was sitting finishing a dress in haste and in prayer. This word was spoken in my mind, "Who learned the first man on earth?" "Why, God." "He is unchangeable, and if He learned the first man to read, He can learn you." I laid down my dress, picked up my Bible, ran upstairs, opened it, and kneeled down with it pressed to my breast, prayed earnestly to Almighty God if it was consisting to His holy will, to learn me to read His holy word. And when I found I was reading, I was frightened—then I could not read one word. I closed my eyes again in prayer and then opened my eyes, began to read. So I done, until I read the chapter. . . . When my brother came to dinner I told him, "I can read the Bible! I have read a whole chapter!" "One thee has heard the children read, till thee has got it by heart." What a wound that was to me to think he would make so light of a gift of God! (108)

Jackson's account emphasizes twice the source of these interpretive acts as other than cognitive or rational: First, when she becomes "frightened" by her reading, prayer enables her to continue; second, when her brother doubts her ability to do more than quote from memory, she underscores her reading as "a gift of God." Jackson's reliance on the spirit for help with reading appears in several other recorded occasions of her pre-Shaker years. For example, she describes a prayer meeting she led at her house where her innovative "reading" and "opening" of Scripture is due not to her own power but to the power of God working through her: "I read nearly a whole chapter in Isaiah. (I was impressed to open the Bible and read wheresoever my eye lit. So it was in Isaiah.) Then I began to open the Scriptures in a way I never heard nor never thought nor never saw before, and the power of God truly filled the room" (104–5). Although the spontaneity of the passage selection and reading mimics that of "mainstream" Christian women such as Mary Rowlandson, whose *Narrative of the Captivity and Restauration of Mrs. Mary Rowlandson* (1682) was read and republished well into the nineteenth century, or Susan Warner's heroine, Ellen Montgomery, of the popular sentimental novel *The Wide, Wide World* (1850), it differs in that the reading revises rather than reinforces widely accepted interpretations of Scripture.[12]

Jackson's spiritual reading also includes, like Lee's, the ability to read uninscribed texts of several types—people, dreams, and visions. As the epigraph to this section notes, she refers to herself as a pen in God's hand as she prays for insights into people; she soon writes and demonstrates she has received the gift.

Her ability to read visions recurs throughout the narrative. In "The Dream of the Cakes," for example, she sees a room full of white people eating three huge cakes she made from only small spoonfuls of batter. During a later occasion of public "opening" of Scripture, she suddenly interprets the earlier dream:

[W]hen I got there the house was full, and all around the door, and they were nearly all white people. And when I saw the table, book, and candle, I like to fall, my knees smote together. I cried out aloud, "Lord Jesus, if Thou has sent me here to preach, clothe me with Thy power! And if Thou has not, make me a public example before this people!" And in a moment, as it were, I was wrapped up in a mantle and clothed with power. And while I was speaking, I saw that this was the people that ate my cakes off of the griddle and out of the fire and out of the ashes in 1831. (126)

In addition to revealing Jackson's ability to read visions, the passage demonstrates that Jackson associates literacy with authority—an authority she holds in high regard and even fears. The "table, book, and candle," signs of ministerial authority (in this case, in front of a white audience), send her to prayer. Rather than eschewing the power, however, she rises to her spiritual call.

Jackson's reading of visions, Scripture, and people eventually leads her to break from AME and other "orthodox" affiliations. As she explains, "My eyes and my understanding were greatly opened and enlightened—my eyes opened to see into the way, into the very heart and thought of the people. And I saw the state of the churches and their destructions, that they would all come down. Many passages of Scripture were spiritually unfolded to my mind and I testified against the churches" (137). Jackson's testimony against the churches, like Lee's teachings, emerges partially from an inscribed text, but she relies upon a spiritually driven, innovative rereading of it. The results, like Lee's, are persecutions and conversions. Jackson notes, "And while I was speaking, the people looked as though I ought not to be suffered to live" (137). The changes or conversions occur, however, through a combination of spiritual force and reason—her textual "proof" of the message: "But when I had opened the subject and then proved it by the Old and New Testaments, then some of their countenances were changed" (137).

Thus in spite of the Shakers' openness toward uninscribed texts, their female elements of the godhead, and their ecstatic or "feminine" elements of worship, which, as I discuss below, attract, sustain and empower Jackson, she adheres to "masculine" models as well, looking to the Bible and other inscribed texts for authority and validation. In fact, Jackson's conversion to Shakerism partially depends upon one of their inscribed texts, and she frequently dreams or has visions of books and their interpretations.

Jackson reveals the authority of inscribed texts in a lengthy passage describing her receipt of a Shaker text in fall 1836. A man who had been living with the Shakers came to her after he heard her speaking and, according to her record, said, "The Spirit told me to give thee this book to read. And if thee understands, thee must keep it. And if thee don't, thee can give it to me again" (140). Jackson takes the book, but rather than reading it herself, she hands it to her companion, Martha, who prior to returning it reads a section justifying dancing as a form of worship. Because at this point in her life she "read[s] no books but the Bible," Jackson does not open the volume until seven years later, when she "was told, 'Open the book and look into it.'" The reading that follows, as Jackson describes it, is experiential and divinely directed rather than rational: "I opened on a part of my own experience. I opened at a passage that condemned the works of the flesh in the regeneration, as it was shown to me from heaven, and which no mortal had ever told me" (141). This reading validates her knowledge about celibacy, arrived at previously by personal experience and divine revelation. As Jackson explains, "If the spirit and substance of which the book treated had not been revealed" in her, she "might have read it [the book] all the days" of her life without understanding it. She summarizes, "For the letter killeth but the spirit makes alive" (144–45).[13] Nonetheless, "this book [the "letter"] was an earthly companion" for her during a period in which she "had none to converse with that had seen these wonderful things" (144). Thus she presents once again the conflation of orality and literacy in Shaker spirituality.

In addition to receiving this and other physical books that validate her experiences and provide her companionship, Jackson frequently receives books symbolically and in dreams and visions, signs of the value she bestows upon inscribed texts. For example, in 1843 a Shaker Sister "under spirit influence" gave her an immaterial "Book of Orders" [probably "the Holy Orders of the Church" (Humez, *Gifts of Power,* 170, n.31)] and a pair of spectacles" (170). In a dream of 1843, angels give her "a little book." Jackson writes, "When they were given to me, it was made known to me" that the book "was to give me knowledge" (174). When she awakens from the dream, she records, her "knowledge of spiritual things increased" (174).

The incident of Jackson's first Shaker text and her reading of these dreams exhibit that her understanding often comes after her initial reading. Knowledge, acquired by the spirit's aid, arrives later, after her mere "functional" and independent decoding of alphabetic symbols, in much the way Lev Vygotsky has described the "zone of proximal development" in children's acquisition of higher order thinking skills. In this case, however, Jackson attributes the higher stages of growth to the spirit's teaching, rather than to the guidance of more learned adults.[14] For example, of Philemon Stewart's *Holy, Sacred and Divine Roll and Book,* she writes, "I received this blessed book into my hand in August 1846, and I read it. And March 4, 1847, I began to understand it, for which I am truly thankful to the God of the Heaven, who gave me understanding, through our Blessed Lord and Mother" (209). Of reading "Holy Mother Wisdom's Book," Paulina Bates's anthology of gift messages, Jackson writes that she "received counsel in the most feeling and tender manner, from Holy, Ever-blessed Mother Wisdom" after she "laid the Holy Book away" (263). She records in 1863 that while spending the day "in prayer, and watching, and reading, and fasting from all evil, I was greatly blessed and instructed in the spiritual meaning of the written word of God, and my soul was strengthened and enlightened in the true work of God" (283).

Even while justifying inscribed texts and looking to them to validate her understanding, she thus continually ascribes authority to the uninscribed workings of the spirit. Her "Dream of the Three Books and a Holy One" underscores the significance of uninscribed and inscribed texts, the spirit's assistance, and because she reinterprets the dream four times, the progressive nature of her understanding. In January 1836, prior to breaking away from AME traditions or discovering the Shakers, Jackson sees her husband, Samuel, hand her over to a white man who leads her consecutively to three tables. A book lies open on each. The white man tells her, "'Thou shall be instructed in this book, from Genesis to Revelations'; 'Yea, thou shall be instructed from the beginning of creation to the end of time,' and 'I will instruct thee—yea, thou shall be instructed from the beginning of all things. Yea, thou shall be well instructed. I will instruct'" (146). The man, who seems to be in Shaker garb and has "a father and a brother's countenance," also appears after the dream during her "waking" hours. She writes, "And after that he taught me daily. And when I would be reading and come to a hard word, I would see him standing by my side and he would teach me the word right. And often, when I would be in meditation and looking into things which was hard to understand, I would find him by me teaching and giving me understanding" (147). Although she does not identify the teacher and the books when she first records the dream, they represent Jackson's belief in the authorities of inscribed texts and white men. In the first reference she describes the three books as identical, representing her inability to read inscribed texts without assistance, but in the second reference Jackson describes the three books as distinct sources of knowledge. Eight years after the vision she writes: "I received some light concerning the three books which I saw in 1836. The first was the book which the Spirit taught me. The next was the book which Jesus, who is Christ the Lord, the Father of the new creation, taught me. The third is the Book which the Bride, the Lamb's wife, is now teaching me daily, and out of which the last trumpet is sounding" (204). The books represent steps in her progress of spiritual understanding: direct revelation from the spirit about celibacy, better understanding of the Scripture in relation to her AME background, and knowledge of Shaker teachings about the Deity and the millennial church, taken from published doctrinal works as well as from oral teachings. Among these, however, Jackson grants the spirit priority, for as the passage continues it dwells on the "first" book rather than the other two: "The Spirit first taught me that I must be separated from all earthly ties before I could become a pilgrim, and then I would have power over the world, the flesh, and the Devil, for these are united all in the earth and through the earth" (204). Jackson would have gained this new under- standing of the spirit's prominence over the Bible and Shaker doctrinal texts in 1844 because she had been under the influence of Shaker theology.

Jackson rereads the vision again in 1858 in a way that validates her life experiences and sustains her spiritually. Soon after she received a blessing from Paulina Bates and others to lead the "family" of Believers in Philadelphia, as she reads Bates's "Holy Mother Wisdom's Book," the spirit gives Jackson the new interpretation: "It was made clear to my mind, the cause why God in His mercy showed me in 1836 the three books that were then to be revealed—that I was the one chosen to make it known in this city" (278).

Jackson records a fourth instance of reading the vision, prompted by meditation upon uninscribed memories rather than by reading an inscribed text. In 1864, the final entry in Humez's edition, Jackson writes: "And while I was looking in my mind at the three books which I saw in a vision of God in 1836 . . . it was made known to me the meaning of the three books, and why they were opened in the middle. And also the meaning of the word that was spoken to me at the time I saw them" (289). After briefly rewriting the dream, Jackson explains that she has believed that the first book was the Bible, since she was to be instructed "Genesis to Revelations," but she has been troubled by the interpretation because she was told "it was *to be* revealed" and she knew that "we had the Bible already" (289). Her new understanding in 1864, however, is that the first book *is* the Bible. She explains the future imperative "*to be* revealed": "Being told that I should be instructed in it, from Genesis to Revelation, meant that I should have the spiritual meaning of the letter revealed in my soul by the manifestation of God. This revelation, then being in Heaven, was the true book which must come to give us the true meaning of the letter—as 'the letter killeth, but the spirit maketh alive'" (290). Thus Jackson's new understanding underscores such "new understandings" as an inevitable result of spiritual readings. Her new understanding of the other two books, Paulina Bates's *Divine Book of Holy and Eternal Wisdom* and Philemon Stewart's *Holy, Sacred and Divine Roll and Book,* also points to the spirit's work in illuminating inscribed letters. She emphasizes that she had this vision in 1836, before these volumes were "written by mortal hands" between 1840 and 1843. Although these two texts had fallen out of favor with many Shaker leaders by 1864, Jackson continued to view them as "contain[ing] the mystery of God to the children of men, in time and in eternity." These two works reflect Jackson's continued interest in the mystical manifestations that had been at the heart of the revival, the period in which Jackson came to the Shakers at Watervliet.

In light of Jackson's ever-increasing interaction with inscribed texts, from her miraculous receipt of "the gift of reading" in the 1830s through the time of her leadership in Philadelphia in the 1850s and 1860s, it is possible to say Jackson is becoming more involved in the "masculine" world of texts and religious leadership. However, her reading may also be seen as an act of female piety and discipline, quite common and highly encouraged in the era, both within Shakerism and in the world. Like that Ellen Montgomery exhibits in *The Wide, Wide World,* Jackson's reading demonstrates her view of texts as validating and authorizing her experience, of giving her life meaning to a certain degree. Yet Jackson's writing and reading, like the textual work Harriet Jacobs exhibits in *Incidents in the Life of a Slave Girl,* resists and revises the codes of the dominant culture.[15] Jackson's literacy allows her to move among "masculine" and "feminine" and racial realms as needs demand.

"And was I not glad when I found that I had a Mother!"

Shaker theology enhances Jackson's movement between these often dichotomized realms; yet her experiences prior to meeting the Shakers, according to her narrative, contribute to her conversion. The narrative, for example, includes an abundance of mother imagery. Shaker women in general, Shaker leader Mother Lucy Wright, Holy Mother Wisdom, and Mother Ann Lee all seem to have influenced Jackson spiritually as mother figures. References to her "natural" mother and grandmother indicate her interaction with her biological relatives and her own activities as a mother and woman prior to becoming a Shaker influenced her understanding of the sect's gender-inclusive theology. Jackson's writing depicts, as Nellie McKay has described, that she learned the culture of free African-American women of the nineteenth century. The mother figures in her early life in Philadelphia worked, earned money, and gained leadership roles in prayer circles. She learned from them the importance of spiritual community and relationship, even as she learned a kind of independence.[16]

Jackson was raised by her grandmother until "between three and four," when she returned to her newly remarried "natural" mother; however, she maintained a close relationship with this early mother figure, writing later that she "loved [her] grandmother very much" (120). Her descriptions of two dreams about her grandmother demonstrate their mutual affection. One of these accounts also provides a glimpse of Jackson's relationship with her biological mother. Although her mother had threatened to whip her for relating a dream predicting her stepfather's death, Jackson wrote, "she was one of the best of mothers, and I bless the memory of her" (240). Jackson's mother believed in the visionary gift her daughter displayed, which probably contributed to the daughter's respect.

These two mother figures and Jackson's loss of them at a fairly young age (the grandmother died when Jackson was seven, the mother when Jackson was fourteen) demonstrate her ability to relate to more than one female authority figure and suggest why she so easily moved into a "mothering" role. She had learned that one of woman's responsibilities was to serve as a mother to any children that had the need. Jackson writes that even as a child she had assumed domestic responsibilities: "I always was faithful in work from my childhood, never inclined to play like the rest of my mother's children" (85). Her domestic work most likely included caring for children.[17] This sense of responsibility as a "mother" appears again as Jackson describes her burden of work as an adult female in the 1830s and her desire to "get learning": "Having the charge of my brother and his six children to see to, and my husband, and taking in sewing for a living, I saw no way that I could now get learning without my brother would give me one hour's lesson at night after supper or before he went to bed"(107).[18]

Jackson also displays her relationship with her biological mother in a vision she received in 1849, after converting to Shakerism. In response to a prayer to her "Heavenly Parents" (Father God and Holy Mother Wisdom), expressing concern for her deceased and spiritually "lost" mother, Jackson sees her sleeping peacefully in the midst of a garden of "sweet flowers in full bloom." She also learns that her mother has become "a caretaker of children," a Shaker position. The implication is that her mother converted to Shakerism once she had passed to the spirit world, a belief quite common during this period of Shakerism. Jackson's concern and relief shows her continued care for this early mother figure. Post-Freudian readers may interpret Jackson's separation from her mother as a young child, her mother's three marriages, and her mother's early death as contributing to some hostility or at least ambivalence toward the woman that she was supposed to love. Similarly, Jackson's description of her mother's threat to whip her may be read as a sign of Jackson's latent fear of or anger directed toward her mother. The daughter's dream of her mother's conversion to Shakerism and peaceful eternal sleep might be understood similarly as a psychological resolution of guilt she experienced over ambivalent feelings toward her mother or over her own departure from her family to become an independent itinerant and Shaker.[19]

Set against these numerous references to mothering in her life prior to Shakerism, Jackson's lack of comments about father figures is obvious—she appears to have been raised in their absence. She refers once to her mother's second husband, a sailor who was probably often away. Jackson's only comments about him come in the description of the dream foretelling his death (which actually occured soon after the dream) and his punishment in Hell. Her mother remarried, but we learn nothing of the new, third "father." While this dream and the absence of other paternal references in descriptions of her pre-Shaker life may be read as manifestations of Jackson's desire to remain connected to her mother or to other women, Jackson does not seem to have a fear of or hatred for father figures. She eventually married, and she desired a relationship with a Father God. She also refers positively in her writing to the man in her "Dream of the Three Books" having a "father's and brother's countenance" (147). What becomes clear through these passages is that her relationships with men were secondary to those with women. Even while desiring autonomy and separation, motivations that were manifest in relationships with men and father figures, Jackson maintained a sense of connection to mother figures and to other women.

From the women she knew early in life, she also learned that mystical, spiritual power was not to be overlooked, and even as a child she began to develop her ability to interpret and live according to spiritual voices and visions. Jackson's affiliation with the Shakers appears to be directly related to their openness to the "female" realm of mystical gifts and to the circles of female fellowship their communities supported.[20] In addition, their gender-inclusive god imagery appeals to her. Jackson specifically refers to the offer of a spiritual mother through Shakerism during one of her early visits to a Shaker community. When a female Believer asks her, "Don't you wish you had a mother?" (162), she smiles in response. After receiving her first vision of "a Mother in the Deity," she comments, "Was I not glad when I found that I had a Mother!" (154). On another occasion Jackson describes that she was "filled with love" and felt "like one moving in the waves of the sea" when she received a "Mother's look" during a Shaker meeting (168). Jackson understood spiritual mothering in Shakerism in light of Ann Lee stories read through the lenses of her experiences in Philadelphia.

Whether Jackson learned of Lee by reading Shaker texts or by orally transmitted stories Shakers are known to have shared, the ecstatic visionary experiences, celibacy, itinerant preaching without her husband, and persecution by unbelievers imply Jackson's awareness of Lee's life. More specifically, Jackson describes her abilities to heal people by the laying on of hands, or touch, accompanied by prayer (132, 164), to see into a person's heart (150), and to inspire people to confess their sins (164, 186). As for her suffering and persecution, she describes how she had been accused of being a witch (160), and at one point she makes an explicit connection between her suffering and that of Mother Ann and Jesus (275–76). Further, Jackson's vision of her biological mother in the spirit world echoes Mother Ann's vision of her deceased mother (*Testimonies* [1816], 42).

In addition to these implicit allusions to Lee, other explicit references to mother figures reveal the importance of the Shakers' gender-inclusive god imagery to Jackson. Describing one of her first Shaker meetings in 1842, for example, Jackson writes:

I saw the head and wings of their blessed Mother in the center of the ceiling over their heads. She appeared in glorious color. Her face was round like a full moon, with the glory of the sun reflecting from it in streams which formed a glorious crown. And her face in the midst. And she was beautiful to look upon. Her wings was gold. She being in the center, she extended her golden wings across the room over the children, with her face toward me and said, "These are all mine," though she spoke not a word. And what a Mother's look she gave me. And at that look, my soul was filled with love and a motion was in my body, like one moving in the waves of the sea. (168)

The depiction of Holy Mother Wisdom with her gathering, sheltering wings marks the passage as analogous to several references to Lee in the *Testimonies* and to biblical passages regarding Jesus and Jehovah (Matthew 23:37; Malachi 4:2), possible sources for Jackson's creative imagination. In addition, however, the verbal description mimics visual details of Holy Mother Wisdom in spirit drawings of the period, another possible source. Jackson's depiction of Holy Mother Wisdom demonstrates not only the importance of mother imagery and feminist theology to her but also the physicality and specificity typical of her early visions.[21] Although verbal instructions usually accompany them, these depictions in her early writings are often visually dramatic and descriptive. The physical, bodily image of Holy Mother Wisdom, for example, speaks without speaking: "she said, 'These are all mine,' though she spoke not a word." Although not a complete portrait, the depiction does re-create her bodily presence. This body, though a spiritual one, appears tangible; Holy Mother Wisdom, to Jackson, is not merely a "felt sense" or a metaphor for interior, mental peace. Perhaps reminiscent of Jackson's physical relationship with her mother, the images of sheltering wings and rocking in the waves impart a sense of comfort and physicality that goes beyond words.

Jackson later describes a vision of an unnamed woman, while "under the instruction of my heavenly Father and Mother":

I looked out in the elements and saw a woman in the air. . . . She wore a white garment, and a crimson scarf which was brought over her right shoulder and loosely tied under her left arm, and the two ends hung down to near the bottom of her garment. She was bare headed, bare footed, and bare handed. Her hair was black, loosely falling over shoulders, and she was beautiful to look upon. She appeared pensive and looked upon this city like one bemoaning her only child. (203)

Two images dominate this vision—the silent woman appearing to mourn her lost child, perhaps again reflecting Jackson's unresolved emotions about her mother-daughter relationship, and the women's physical beauty, evidence of the pictoral and emotional force of the narrative.

As her life progresses, however, Jackson's writing and the appearance of mother figures become less physical and more abstract. The women continue to offer instruction, but it is often only verbal; Jackson hears the Mother's instructive voice rather than sees her authoritative presence and comforting body. For example, she wrote on her fifty-seventh birthday: "I have spent the day in prayer and thanksgiving to my Heavenly Parents for their kind dealings with me, and in reading *Holy Mother Wisdom's Book,* from which I received understanding in the work of God, and in reading *The Sacred Roll*" (232). A year later, turning fifty-eight, she writes: "A day wherein my Heavenly Parents have looked upon and instructed me in mercy, concerning the two continents, the eastern and the western, which are a representation of two in the spirit world—one for those who are in the work of regeneration, and the other for souls that leave the body, wholly in a natural state" (232). This passage continues, heavily saturated with the language of Shaker doctrinal texts and lacking the physical description of earlier visions.

The shift from visual to verbal instruction is understandable—Jackson's reading has increased. She frequently refers to her reading of Shaker texts, often accompanied by spiritual instruction. Undoubtedly one reason for Jackson's increased reading is her new position of authority among the Philadelphia Shakers. When she eventually receives a blessing from the leaders at Watervliet in 1858 to oversee the Philadelphia community, she requests two doctrinal works. The request implies that she did not have personal copies before—which implies that her reading of them was limited—and that as an official leader she may sense a responsibility to do more "book learning," since in general during this period Shaker leaders, including women, were allowed more reading time. Jackson's reading of inscribed texts may also increase because she is growing old and her health is failing. Once extremely active physically, but now less capable of such activity, she has more time for books. One vision, which occurs during an illness in 1858 when Jackson was about sixty-two, depicts Mother Ann comforting her by assuring her that in the spirit world she will be able to continue her work of spreading salvation; thus she should not feel guilty for relinquishing some of her ministry in this world.[22] Jackson's ministry among "her people" in the Philadelphia area, a task she has borne since the 1830s, has been physically demanding, as she traveled and delivered orally to them the messages she received from the spirit, rather than writing tracts and publishing essays as Alonzo Hollister did.

"But a voice above my head told me to sit still. . . . And this was the way I sat all the time he was amangling my body—"

Jackson's writing even in the early years demonstrates an awareness of her body's presence. She knows others read her body racially and she fears how they will treat it subsequently. An account of her "Dream of Slaughter" presents these sensibilities perhaps the most vividly. In this chilling vision, a burglar flays her face and eviscerates her while "a voice above [her]" directs her to sit still (95). The dream, as Humez has suggested, most likely reveals Jackson's subconscious concerns for her bodily vulnerability as an African-American woman in Philadelphia during the racial riots of the 1830s (*Gifts of Power,* 14). In addition to its feminist theology, then, Shakerism probably attracted Jackson for reasons associated with race.

One reason among these might have been that the communal sect as an established institution offered a haven; life in a rural Shaker community would have been safer physically for her than the racial turmoil of Philadelphia. As well, Shaker concern for the salvation of ethnic minorities could have attracted her. The 1816 *Testimonies* records Lee visualizing the salvation of "negroes": "She mentioned the names of some that she had seen rise from the dead. . . . She further said, 'I have seen the poor negroes, who are so much despised, redeemed from their loss, with crowns on their heads'" (42–43). These depictions probably instituted visions of salvation that flourished during the Era of Manifestations, the period in which Jackson came in contact with the Shakers. During the revival embodied spirits of ethnic minorities such as Indians, Arabs, Africans, and Asians appeared in living Shaker mediums or "instruments" and testified of their conversions to Shakerism while in the spirit world.[23] However, the conversions in the spirit world could not counterweigh the physical imbalance of racial representation in Shaker communities, where few ethnic minorities lived at the time of Jackson's initial contact with them. In spite of teachings and practices Jackson initially might have thought would allow her literacies and leadership to grow, a conflict that appears to be affiliated with race as well as with manifestations of spirituality and literacy emerged between Jackson and Shaker leaders. As Bassard has argued, Jackson's "race," a socially constructed category, comes to problematize the Shakers' dualistic view of the universe as composed of "natural" and "spiritual" realms. Bassard believes Jackson's presence causes Shakers, because they read celibacy as a unifying sign, to "categorically jettison" race (153–54). Yet Jackson's writing reveals that she and they continue to recognize her as representing a bracketed category, albeit one that may exist among them.

The primary Believer with whom Jackson disagreed was Paulina Bates, author of the anthology of spiritually revealed writings *The Divine Book of Holy and Eternal Wisdom* (1849), which Jackson eventually reads and upholds. Perhaps looking through the lenses of mainstream white culture, Bates may have viewed Jackson, in spite of her proclaimed celibacy, as a sexually aggressive or loose woman who could threaten the "union" of the family at Watervliet. Or Bates may have seen Jackson, as many whites viewed "free" blacks and slaves, as potentially savage and inherently rebellious. White Shakers exhibited, like many of their counterparts "in the world," an imperialistic attitude and belief in manifest destiny. They described the embodied spirits of ethnic minorities who appeared as "exotic" and "savage."[24] Their hymnals of the revival period also demonstrate these stereotypes. Spirit "instruments" received "Indian" and "Negro" songs, which Believers sang in dialect during worship. For example, this "'Negro' song in an unknown tongue" was recorded at Enfield, New Hampshire, in 1838:

E ne me ne mo del e
Sanc to luro lu ral lee
Lu ral lan do me ne see
Pa ri an dor hoo sa me.
(Andrews, *Gift to Be Simple,* 75)

The Church Family at Shirley recorded the following "Indian song," replete with condescending racial stereotypes, in 1845:

Me love come meety learn to tand,
Like whities trait & fold de hand,
Me tink dat dey look so pretty
Dat me like dem want be goody.

Me like learn toot toot on de trump
Me seen dem try how high dey jump;
Now me want learny singy too,
Me like learn dant as shiney do.
(Andrews, *Gift to Be Simple,* 71)

Some critics have interpreted Shaker interest in minorities as a vicarious shared suffering with African-Americans and Native Americans as oppressed, marginal groups within mainstream American society, but the discourse of the predominantly white Shakers also reveals their desire to civilize these "savages," to assimilate them into their "white man's" religion.[25] Jackson's writings—especially her readings of her dreams and visions—underscore racial difference and, quite often, racial tension or conflict not only outside Shakerism but within the "haven" of the community at Watervliet.

    In a vision of 1843, for example, Jackson sees a group of "colored people" rise from beds of "dirt" with "cover" of "dry sod," only to be teased by "an Irish girl about ten years old" in "a baiting house for the poor." As is typical in her descriptions of these dreams, Jackson bears the burden of comforting the people as prophet or spokesperson. She records:

I comforted them with the words that was given to me for them. . . . and they heard me gladly. . . . Then I woke and found the burden of my people heavy upon me. I had borne a burden of my people for twelve years, but now it was double, and I cried unto the Lord . . . . 'Oh, my Father and my God, make me faithful in this Thy work and give me wisdom that I may comply with Thy whole will.' (179–82)

As Humez suggests, the vision alludes to conflicts between black and recently immigrated Irish as W.E.B. Du Bois describes them in *Philadelphia Negro (Gifts of Power,* 179, n. 42); however, Jackson's description also illustrates her concern, even before officially joining the community at Watervliet, with lifting her people from the "dirt" and "dry sod."

Five years later, while living in the Watervliet community (March 1848), Jackson receives a message from Ann Lee's brother, "Father William," in the spirit world: "the Lord has called thee for a great work to thy people, both on earth and in the world of Spirits" (212). He refers to her as a "chosen vessel" who must be "fit" for this great work "by honestly confessing thy sins to God, in the presence of the Elders that stand here in Zion" (212). She glosses the recorded message with its revelance to her at the time: "A word in season, for it was given when I underwent great temptation, and deep affliction on account of a change in our Elders" (212). This passage refers not only to Jackson's belief that she was to serve "her people," but also to her conflict with Bates, who was not in leadership when Jackson first committed to live with the Shakers (Humez, *Gifts of Power,* 212, n. 15). Perhaps the sins she had not confessed were negative feelings toward white Shakers who, isolated from the conflicts of urban areas, displaced concern for the physical oppression of blacks with concern for conversions in the spirit world. Thus they could appear to Jackson to reinforce a distinction between spirit and body. These kinds of messages recur frequently from 1848 until Jackson leaves Watervliet in 1851.

In July 1848, for example, she dreams of a lion who attacks her as she "was going south to feed the people." When her prayers to God "weakened the lion's hold," her "prayer increased" until the lion "fell back" and left her. When she arises, she commands James Ostrander, her friend and spiritual brother, to shoot the lion. The responding dialogue suggests Jackson's frustration with the Shakers and her view of herself as separate from them: "He said, 'There is not a gun.' 'What?' said I, 'Have not the Shakers got a gun?' He said, 'Nay.' 'Well,' said I, 'He will return'"(213). By referring to the Shakers by name rather than using the third-person plural "we," Jackson here and elsewhere distinguishes herself from them, although she has lived with them for four years. She does not view herself as entirely within the circle of Shakerism, though she is empowered by its tenets. With this and many of the recorded visions, Jackson provides no interpretation, perhaps because she, like Harriet Jacobs, hopes not to offend possible white readers, but the vision's concerns with racial difference are clear.[26] The lion, like the burglar in the "Dream of Slaughter," reflects a latent fear of physical harm. The dream suggests that the Shakers' lack of a gun, symbolic of their unwillingness to bear arms in the face of serious physical dangers in the world and to acknowledge the reality of the physical abuse blacks face and endure, perturbs her.

A March 1849 dream of an eagle that seems capable of destroying her echoes the fears of the dream of the lion. In this case, however, Jackson bravely faces her aggressor. She writes, "Yet I watched it, for I felt that if I took my eyes off from it, it would have power to hurt me" (215). As a result the eagle flies away. Once again her approach to the problem differs from the family of Shakers, who "made signs" to her to leave her work and enter the safety of the Dwellinghouse.

In another vision of 1849 Jackson sees "hundreds" of "East Indians," including a chief and a high priest, who gaze "steadfastly" at her before entering the Second House at Watervliet. Perhaps they look at her as a role model or for answers to questions about life within Shaker communities: How are ethnic minorities treated? Does the faith offer what it promises? Her failure to respond to the "Indians" reveals her ambivalence about racial issues during this period, but Jackson's stance becomes increasingly clear when she writes that after two years of secret prayer, she witnesses the leaders advocate "the salvation of the souls of the children of men" (216). She records her happiness and sense of "union" with the Shaker family: "When I stood in the congregation and heard our beloved Elders tell us that we must all remember the world in our prayers, my heart leapt for joy, and I gave glory to God in the highest heaven" (216). In spite or because of this message, which should provide a reprieve from her internal struggles about how to act with regard to "her people," Jackson's racial visions soon return. In winter 1850, only a few months after her vision of East Indians and less than a year after the leadership's announcement of "labor" for the world, Jackson dreams of herself in Philadelphia, mothering a young child and a "family of spiritual children" (218). Two days later, she records, "I received an encouraging word in confirmation to the word of God which He gave to me concerning my people, which work He has called me to do. And when the time arrives, no man can hinder me from doing it through the help of God" (219). The "man" who wants to "hinder" her is Paulina Bates. In an entry that soon follows, about the Rochester "rappings" of 1848, Jackson asserts after the fact that she had accurately predicted the "knockings" would soon be heard at Watervliet, whereas Bates said they would not. Less than a month after receiving the "encouraging word," Jackson enters a lengthy retrospective account, reflective of her thoughts at the time as well as in the past:

After I came to Watervliet, in the year 1847, and saw how Believers seemed to be gathered to themselves, in praying for themselves and not for the world, which lay in midnight darkness, I wondered how the world was to be saved, if Shakers were the only people of God on the earth, and they seemed to be busy in their own concerns, which were mostly temporal. . . . Then seeing these at ease in Zion, I cried to God in the name of Christ and Mother that He in mercy would do something for the helpless world. At that time, it seemed as if the whole world rested upon me. I cried to the Lord both day and night, for many months, that God would make a way that the world might hear the Gospel—that God would send spirits and angels to administer to their understanding, that they might be saved in the present tense, for I knew by revelation, that it was God's will that they should be. (220–21)

Jackson's entries continue to exhibit this distinction between the Shakers ("them") and "her people" until she leaves for Philadelphia in 1851.

In a dream of March 1850, for example, Jackson sees herself and her spiritual sister and companion Rebecca Perot "in a garden." She writes, "In a moment I understood that the people designed to kill us. I wanted Rebecca to make haste, and we would fly to Philadelphia, but she hindered me a long time. At last we went. And as we went, we met the people. The men had killed all the women and children, and were dragging them like dogs through the street" (223). This part of the vision suggests several interpretations. Humez sees explicit "female fear of male violence" but is uncertain "whether there is covert racial fear as well" (*Gifts of Power,* 223, n. 39). She believes "the violence . . . may very well be associated with living among whites at a time when the Fugitive Slave Law justified whites" in treating black women and children in such a manner. But the vision could also represent the spiritual death Jackson fears will result from her continuing to live a cloistered life at Watervliet. As the dream continues, Jackson and Perot escape to Philadelphia, but they are entrapped and escape three other times. In the last of these escapes, a lion and a bulldog sit as "gatekeepers" by a door Jackson "was agoing to pass out into the street." In a miraculous act echoing Lee's movements among mobs in New England, Jackson writes that she "prayed, and passed through, and they had not power to touch" her (223). The violence of the dream could represent Jackson's fears of racial abuse in the city. She could see herself in a "no win" situation: Life in Watervliet may be physically safe but spiritually stifling; life in Philadelphia promises possibilities of physical abuse but also spiritual struggles and growth. Throughout the first part of 1851 Jackson continues to record dreams of herself and Perot in Philadelphia, probably working through the turmoil surrounding her decision to leave and minister to "her people" in July of that year.

Jackson's most powerful and creative reading of Ann Lee occurs when she interprets these visions to justify her decision to leave the predominantly white community without the blessing and authority of the leaders there. She probably draws from Lee's itinerancy during the "opening of the gospel" in New England; she was an aggressive missionary who did not confine herself within the (metaphorical) fences of a Shaker commune. Jackson may also have read a second time the image of Lee visualizing "negroes" being receptive to the Gospel, creatively rereading the passage with herself as the evangelist rather than as one of the converted. Jackson's spiritual literacy, like Lee's, directs her and gives her agency. Many visions and passages in Jackson's writing demonstrate that her concerns with her racial self and her physical and spiritual persecution do not disappear when she leaves Philadelphia, even after she lives with the Shakers at Watervliet in the 1840s and 1850s. Her spiritual literacy assists her in moving between separate racial spheres, just as it allows her to transgress gender boundaries; she moves her body away from one established Shaker home and creates a new one.

Because Jackson found her way to Shakerism as a result of her spiritual literacy—because uninscribed texts as well as inscribed ones instructed her in and validated the resurrection life that Lee similarly had received and taught—she represents for Paulina Bates, Alonzo Hollister, and other white Shakers the possibilities of the future: "improvement" of uneducated ethnic minorities in the world at large as well as conversion of new members.

ALONZO HOLLISTER: LONGING FOR LITERACIES OF THE PAST

Images of Jackson, like images of Lee, provided Hollister spiritual sustenance during the years he was editing Jackson's text and writing about it in his "Reminiscences." Their examples of spiritual literacy sustained him in a period of personal and communal change. In addition to copying works by Believers such as Jackson, Hollister had assisted in the compilation of the first bibliography of Shaker literature and what has come to be the largest collection of documentary materials by and about the Shakers.[27] Yet Hollister was never an official scribe nor a church leader in the ways McNemar and Dunlavy were; nor was he a charismatic leader like Lee or Jackson. His narrative, then, provides insights into the perceptions of a male Shaker steeped in textual traditions but without communal authority. Unlike Jackson's narrative, Hollister's narrative has received little attention from scholars.[28]

Hollister writes that he arrived at the New Lebanon community with his family in 1838, just before his eighth birthday, and in the midst of the mystical activities of the Era of Manifestations. Besides his entrance into Shakerism as a child and his near lifetime involvement with the sect, Hollister's narrative describes his physical labors within the community—working in the shoeshop, the garden, the herb industry, and the extract business. In addition, throughout the narrative Hollister continually refers to his work as a writer and editor, work he took upon himself "after hours" and initially without official sanction by Shaker leaders. Writing and reading are important to him. He opens his narrative with a preface explaining why he writes; he mentions receiving a blank book as a Shaker child; he describes his offense at being inappropriately edited by Shakers responsible for publishing his work in their periodicals; he lists the numbers of works he has written and published; and he quotes from letters received as positive responses to his writing.

His narrative exudes the discourses he has absorbed from nineteenth-century physical and social sciences as well as travel literature. In one instance he refers to Ralph Waldo Emerson's birthday, casually exhibiting his familiarity with the poet philospher and theologian. In another he refers to visits to bookstores during his travels and instructions from Shaker leaders, much to his dismay, not to buy more books. Sasson has noted, and I echo, Hollister's role as a Shaker person-of-the-book. Examining his "redaction" of one Believer's autobiography, she notes Hollister wanted to correct the time sequence, clarify the point of view, and find an organizing metaphor. Of this narrative as a whole, she explains that it is drawn "from written sources rather than personal experience" (*Shaker Spiritual,* 85). For Hollister, though, the personal experiences *are* largely the experiences of written sources. Further, the experiences apart from inscribed texts, expressed on paper late in his life, have been shaped significantly by his high level of alphabetic literacy.

In 1859 he lost the fingers of his left hand in an accident with a cutting machine (Sasson, "19th Century Case Study," 159), a physical blow that influenced his work within the community. Sasson proposes that the accident moved him from the herb shop into the extract business, and I suggest that it may have initiated for him a sense of loss and may have situated him more deeply in the realm of letters. Hollister's increasing sense of loss and productivity with texts coincide temporally with three changes within Shakerism other studies have noted: a declining membership, a shift from a male-dominated to a female-dominated sect, and a decline in the mysticism that had prevailed during the first generation of the church and was revived during the Era of Manifestations.[29] In combination these aspects of Hollister's experience influence his reading and writing of mother figures Lee and Jackson and the emphasis on spiritual literacies and home within his narrative.

Hollister's spiritual narrative, in relation to Jackson's, is almost without mother imagery. Hollister implicitly alludes to Lee's life as he briefly comments on his temptations, his suffering, and his longing to know God's will for his life (175–77). Less than a half-dozen explicit references to her appear in his 100-page narrative and none refers to Holy Mother Wisdom. Readings of these few references, enriched by an awareness of his numerous other writings and his experiences as a white male Shaker suggest first, that whereas Jackson most often reads herself in parallel relation to both black and white mother figures, Hollister's readings of mother figures are in stark contrast to his own experiences; they are "others" he admires, not necessarily because of gender but because of their authority and their mystical power. Second, his readings reveal that the manifestation of this latent admiration increases as he ages, as numerical loss and encouraged rationalism increase within the sect, and as progressive voices emerge in Shaker publications.

Shaker mother imagery may have first appealed to Hollister as it came to replace his biological mother in a community where explicit devotion to a divine mother figure—though not bodily relation—was acceptable and encouraged. Visitations by Holy Mother Wisdom occurred frequently during the early years he was separated from his biological mother and living in the "Children's Order" under the guidance of a male caretaker. But in later years Mother Ann and, in her shadow, Mother Rebecca, contributed to his security, stability, and sense of home. Yet Hollister's two explicit references to Mother Ann in his "Reminiscences" (other than those where he associates her with Jackson) depict her as an authority figure rather than as a nurturing woman. First, in a recorded conversation with Brother Abram Whitney of the Shirley community, recipient of the Shaker's musical notation system, which differed from the world's by using the first eight letters of the alphabet rather than round or shaped notes, Hollister notes that Whitney explained that "Mother Ann was the author of that system. He received it from her" (164–65).

In the second passage referring to Lee, Hollister glosses a discussion regarding the value of sermons directed to outsiders at Shaker meetings. A Shaker "preacher" has explained that they help bridge the gap between Shakers and the world by increasing outsiders' understanding of Shakerism. Hollister assents, borrowing Lee's words for support: "As Mother [Ann] said on this subject, 'I say it does good.

If the living will not hear the word of God, the ded [*sic*] will. There is not a word of God lost, that ever was spoken.' When the Gospel is preacht in this world, it is heard in both worlds at once" (179–80). Again, the Lee image here is not a nurturing woman but a wise instructor and authority figure. In addition, in neither of the two references does Hollister "see" Mother Ann. Her physicality seems to have been repressed; she has been translated into a bodiless "other," much more easily known and acceptably described by a celibate male Shaker than the physically beautiful type of woman Jackson described. The description underscores his belief in the power of language and alphabetic literacy; he recognizes this Shaker woman for what she said—words of wisdom she spoke—rather than her physical beauty.[30] It is possible that he does not refer to nurturing aspects of Mother Ann because he had the comfort of male caregivers as a child, but he needs her authority now because leaders who knew her in the flesh have died and other living Shakers are suggesting changes in doctrine and practice.[31] As an authority figure Lee is an "other" Hollister admires, for she possesses the acknowledged power within the community that he does not.

In addition to acknowledging Mother Ann's authority, the passage demonstrates Hollister's belief in the spirit world. Like Jackson and other Shakers, Hollister believes that the physically dead as well as the living may be converted. Given Hollister's strong belief in the spirit world, we should conclude, as Humez has noted, that when copying and editing Jackson's text, he "respected his author" and "believed absolutely in the authenticity of her visions" (67). In fact, Hollister's other references to Mother Ann appear as he discusses Mother Rebecca, bringing the two together as significant figures for him. Why would Hollister make this connection? The possible answers emerge through analysis of these references.

He reiterates in his "Reminiscences" two intertwined characteristics embedded in Jackson's narrative—her race and her spiritually informed literacy. In the midst of his hundred-page manuscript, he devotes nine pages to Jackson's writing. Hollister first describes his trip in 1878 to visit the Philadelphia Shakers where he reads his edition of Jackson's autobiography to them to have its accuracy confirmed. Next he perfunctorily gives her dates of birth and death. Then Hollister turns to Jackson's literacy, noting that "she was taught by the spirit to read and write" (188). Although her writing and spelling are "of inferior grade," they are "intelligible," he explains. The two sections that follow are lengthy excerpts from her writing, describing her conversion and sanctification experiences, respectively. The first restates Jackson's description of being guided by two voices in the midst of a thunderstorm. She discerns the voice of God from the voice of Satan and follows God's instruction to pray for deliverance rather than run for safety as the other voice advises. She is delivered. The "sanctification" excerpt marks Jackson's understanding, through a spiritual vision, of sexual relationships as "works of the flesh" that must be left behind when living a regenerate life. In both passages Hollister highlights Jackson's reliance on the directions of the spiritual voice.

This emphasis on her spiritual literacy continues as he next explains her being "constrain'd *by the spirit* to go abroad and preach the gospel that was taught her *by the spirit*" (192, emphasis mine); this itinerancy, of course, is what leads to her first contact with the Shakers and her receipt of a doctrinal book. Significant first for Jackson and now for Hollister is her preaching of Shaker doctrine before she read the book; the doctrine came to be known extratextually, apart from the written word, beyond the sacred page. She was accused, by some who heard her during her itinerancy, of preaching from the Shaker text; she did not. "At least," Hollister notes, "such is the impression I retain from a recent reading of her story" (193). In his eyes her literacy, like Lee's, drawn from many sources, informed her doctrine and provided a sense of agency that allowed her to blur racial and gendered boundaries as she preached to primarily white audiences and to men as well as women. The power of these literacies also moves Hollister as he reads her text.

Evidence of his desire to validate her spiritually informed literacy follows the passage, when he summarizes Jackson's fragmented physical interaction with the community at Watervliet. Although somewhat incoherent in its chronology, the summary verifies her life as a Shaker and the spiritual authority she possessed. He culminates the passage with a forthright statement: "I regard her as a true Prophet of Jehovah—and as a second and independent Witness to the Second Appearing of Christ" (193). He reinforces the statement with her first appearance at Watervliet "on the 100th anniversary of Mother Ann's natural birth," a numerological reading of events typical of millennialist groups' apologies for their faiths. He continues his association of Lee with Jackson, noting especially their alphabetic illiteracy: "It is remarkable that both Mother Ann and Mother Rebecca, were destitute of book learning—& were educated in the common duties of life by practice & the Spirit of God. They were Divinely illuminated, and commissioned proficient in all the duties of life, and became Leaders and Teachers of Men, examples of Righteousness blameless in action, and wise in things spiritual, beyond all others in their day and generation" (193–94).

The passage demonstrates Hollister's racial biases as well as his acceptance of her spiritual powers. His attitude toward the "uneducated negro" appears not unlike what he expresses about native "spirits" as he recalls visitations of ethnic minorities during the Era of Manifestations:

I was deeply interested in watching the strange acting of brethren and sisters under the influence of native Indian spirits, negroes and others, who came to us for a number of months in 1842. They exhibited some awkwardness and ignorance of the ways of white people, at first, but were soon and easily tamed and brot into a degree of order and conformity to our customs. . . . After they had learn'd their lesson, they exprest great thankfulness both in word and song for their privilege and the instruction that had been given them. . . . When one tribe had learn'd, it withdrew, and another came. (174)

His ethnocentrism appears also in a passage describing the observation of a mystical experience at Watervliet, where an "Indian spirit" testifies that Hollister is capable of "thinking work." He glosses the spirit's message: "Part was spoken in broken English, and part in deep seriousness and good proper English as any of *us* do" (187, emphasis mine). His attitude toward these natives as "other" than himself and white Shakers ("us") appears also in his descriptions of Jackson. He twice refers to the Philadelphia community in which she lives not simply as Shaker Sisters but as "the colord Sisters" (188–89). Later, he lists seven members by name, followed by the gloss "all colord." The community also included, according to his record, Hattie Walton, "a Jewess" (194).

Hollister's fascination with Jackson as an African-American Shaker centers upon her authority as a mother figure, which is intertwined with her literacy. This literacy includes learning rationally and mystically from both uninscribed and inscribed texts. Thus Hollister privileges spiritual vitality and agency apart from texts. Hollister's fascination with Jackson's literacy and the spirit world may be read as a regressive fantasy, his desire for a part of the female realm, associated with the mother from whom he had been detached since childhood; yet the narrative gestures toward much more than that loss. His narrative contains only one reference to his biological mother, in a brief summary of his pre-Shaker life, although she continued to live at New Lebanon until her death in 1874, two years before he began copying Jackson's work. However, Hollister writes with high regard for Philemon Stewart, who cared for him during his first summer at New Lebanon. Known as the inspired author of *A Holy, Sacred and Divine Roll and Book,* which Jackson read and admired, Stewart may have served as a role model for Hollister in later years as he increased his writing, editing, and interest in mystical activities of the past. Although the narrative suggests that Hollister was able to transfer his need for relationships from his biological mother to male caretakers and to female god imagery, it also suggests latent unresolved anxieties about other losses.

Hollister's losses at this point in his life included continuity, stability, and mysticism—ironically, a mysticism that allowed for change. Shaker writings from the Era of Manifestations and afterward note a concern over the loss of members who knew Mother Ann in the flesh and a concern for the loss of "true Shakerism" of the earlier periods. Discussions or debates over theological changes exhibit Hollister as a more conservative Shaker, as Sasson has noted ("19th Century Case Study," 163–70). Several of the doctrinal tracts Hollister wrote, which concern themselves with women's roles in light of Shaker theology, appear "progressive" by title but are implicitly conservative. In addition to "Divine Motherhood" (1887), "Heaven Annointed Woman" (1887), "The Free Woman" (1904), and "Brief Sketch of Ann Lee, the First Anointed [*sic*], Emancipated, New Woman" (1905) discuss Ann Lee as founder and exemplar of Shaker faith.[32] These tracts testify to Hollister's fascination with this Shaker mother figure and his attempt to rekindle Shakerism of the past by focusing on Lee while appealing to readers in the world—possible converts—who are concerned with the changing status of women. Thus Hollister hopes for the future of the sect, but he also values its traditions of spiritual agency, exemplified by Ann Lee and Rebecca Jackson. However, his "evangelism" is carried out by inscribed texts to be read privately rather than through face-to-face confrontation.

Hollister's concern for maintaining the traditions of Shakerism is manifest in his explicit references to the crumbling sense of "home" in the Shaker communities. Of the period when a New Dwelling House was being built within his community, he writes, "I felt the absence of a home feeling—that is, as if without home" (181). He continues a little later on the same page: "Reading the paragraf of the home feeling, reminds me that bringing hired men to board in our kitchen was a great detriment to the union of the family, and to the home feeling" (181). Readers familiar with psychoanalysis may want to gloss these entries with Hollister's subconscious desire for the comfort and stability associated with the mother, the womb, and death. The passages demonstrate that unlike African-Americans Jackson and Frederick Douglass, who present themselves as both within and without the circles of their pasts, Hollister situates himself firmly within. He favors a "closed circle," except for potential converts, and vicariously recalls his momentary trips without.

Hollister's attitude toward home has perhaps not so much to do with being gendered masculine or feminine as it has to do with becoming accustomed to moving in his childhood. Although Hollister lived almost his entire life in one Shaker community, he writes in the opening of his narrative that in his childhood his family "moved so often that I think it gave me a roving disposition, so that when we came [to the New Lebanon Shaker community] I was ready and glad to move. It opened to me a new field of discovery" (158). He claims that he liked to move, travel, explore, and read maps. Indeed, his narrative substantiates this love of travel.

References to trips punctuate Hollister's text. These travel descriptions, which are of two kinds—events he participates in at other Shaker communities and observations of the world outside Shakerism—follow the pattern of nineteenth-century travel narratives. As Dennis Porter has written, "In their writings travelers put their fantasies on display often in spite of themselves. In one way or another, they are always writing about lives they want or do not want to live, the lost objects of their desire or the phobias that threaten to disable them" (13). Hollister depicts himself as a fragmented subject positing himself through his gaze over and upon the sites he observes, generally devoting energy to the different and the "other"— topography, vegetation, terrain, soil, and architecture.[33] In addition to describing his physical surroundings, Hollister records spiritual conversations both with people of the "world" and with fellow Shakers that reveal his desires for "home" and the familiar. He twice refers to his interactions in other Shaker communities as "ecstacies," apparently for the fresh spiritual companionship and the intellectual discussion they provide. Describing a trip to Harvard, Shirley, and Enfield in 1872, he writes, "Like the visit to Watervliet and Groveland, in 1857, it was one continued ecstasy. A feast of reason and flow of soul" (183). He also describes a trip to Watervliet as "an exstacy" [sic] but gives no explicit reason. One possible reason is that there were many young people to talk with about "interesting matters."[34] These fresh though familiar interactions—not the contacts with people of the world—titillate him.

The interactions with outsiders most often cause anxiety and fear, though they also demonstrate his dependence on mystical forces. Having reached the end of his initial train travel to Boston, where he is to catch a ferry to Portland, he finds himself amidst city chaos—a parade has brought about extreme crowds, blocked streets, and "idle" cars. Hollister feels insecure and trapped. He writes, "Feeling some uncertain[ty] as to my future chances, I exclaim'd in *thot* 'Thou O God can'st Deliver me out of this.'" The result, "soon after," is that "*something seemd* to say, 'Get out of here.'" He placed himself near a policeman, "of whom I might ask any question tending to relieve the the [*sic*] situation." He recalls, "All at once *I felt as tho* help might come from there" (200, emphasis mine). This event, which causes anxiety and fear, also leads to an increase in his reliance upon the spirit for knowledge and guidance. Another recorded experience similar in its production of anxiety and Hollister's dependence upon the spirit is a nightmare that precedes a sales trip to Connecticut with Skeen's Biblical Chart. After an encounter with some "ruffons" who feigned interest in the chart and drew him into a bar or club, Hollister remembers a dream of wolves wanting to devour him. He writes of the humiliating and frightening situation away from home, "I believe it was a Divine Power that saved me" (243). Both experiences, where the chaos of the city and the brutality of the bar overwhelm him, cause him to depend upon his spiritual literacy in the ways Jackson and Lee frequently did. However, his phrasing about his assistance in both situations reveals his lack of certainty or conviction about the spirit's aid. In the first case, the phrasing "Something seemd to say" and "I felt as tho" indicates not that the guidance comes from the spirit, Lee, Holy Mother Wisdom, or the Almighty Father but from "something"; in the second passage, he refers to a "Divine Power" but does not use gendered terms to describe it.

Unlike Jackson and Lee, who use dislocation to grow spiritually by reading uninscribed texts and who speak confidently about their visions, Hollister draws from his travels a stronger yearning for home, for other Shakers, and for the comfort of his inscribed texts. These trips into the world reinforce the stability, comfort, and correctness of the home on which he depends. In one passage, he writes of another trip, "I don't know that I ever felt a more contented, happy, *satisfied* home feeling, than during a few weeks previous to this journey and after" (215). Hollister manifests his desire for a stable, continuing home in his travel accounts—his "ecstacy" when in the surroundings of his extended "home" (other Shaker communities) and his fear when in the face of the "other"—and in his explicit references to a "home feeling." Lee's and Jackson's mysticism and actions in the realm of bodily presence and orality mark them as ideals. With the increasing bodily absence in the Shaker communities, and placing himself more and more in the isolated world of texts, he looks to them as he creates the embodied Shaker spirits that fill the voids of his nontextual experiences.

Alonzo Hollister, like Jackson and Lee, fulfills his spiritual needs by, among other venues, reading and writing creatively. As a complex writing and reading subject influenced by Shaker literacies, Hollister fails to remain consistently fixed in either a "masculine" or "feminine" domain. Hollister's literacy at the close of the nineteenth century and the opening of the twentieth century illustrates the shifting strategies Shakers employ to carry on their traditions of embodied spirituality. His reliance on the spiritual presence of inscribed texts—especially narratives such as Jackson's—counters the physical losses of the Shaker family at New Lebanon and parallels the literacies of Shakers at other communities.

NOTES

1. I choose the phrase "spiritual narrative" to label their works, since the primary concerns of the lives have been spiritual. For definitions of the genre in the larger scope of Christendom, see Peter A. Dorsey's *Sacred Estrangement: The Rhetoric of Conversion in Modern American Autobiography*. For distinctions between the Shaker genres "testimony," "autobiography," and "spiritual narrative," see Sasson (*Shaker Spiritual*, 67–83) and Mercadante (128, 192, n. 43). Sasson describes "Shaker authors' modifications and innovations in response to the changing concerns of the community of Believers" (*Shaker Spiritual*, x). She notes that whereas "testimonies" written prior to mid-century reflect little difference from each other, the "autobiographies" written after mid-century exhibit variety.

2. Although their comments instigated this analysis, neither Humez (*Gifts of Power*, 65–68) nor Sasson (*Shaker Spiritual*, 84–89) elaborates on literacy or the role of mother imagery in the narratives. I have also been influenced by Robert Stepto's study of the editorial framing devices and publications of slave narratives, "Narration, Authentication, and Authorial Control in Frederick Douglass's *Narrative of 1845*."

3. I draw concepts such as "wholeness" and "otherness" from Lacanian psychoanalytic and linguistic theory. See the introduction to Jacques Lacan's *Feminine Sexuality*.

4. With regard to Shaker narratives, Sasson notes that narratives of men tend to be concerned with externals such as natural surroundings and to be outwardly directed, whereas the writing of women tends to be more internally focused, that is, personal and directed primarily to the self (*Shaker Spiritual*, xii). Mercadante explains that Shaker women are "more self-abnegating and servile" in descriptions of their inadequacies than Shaker men (136). See also Cheryl Glenn's "Author, Audience, and Autobiography."

5. See also Bynum's introduction to *Gender and Religion: On the Complexity of Symbols* (1–20).

6. Priscilla Brewer writes, "In 1840, e.g., census enumerators found only thirty-four blacks (some still slaves) living in Shaker villages, or less than 1 percent of the Society's total population" ("'Tho' of the Weaker Sex,'" 627, n. 92). She draws from Bainbridge (355–56).

7. The most in-depth analysis of Jackson's life and writing as a mystic, an African-American, a female, and a Shaker is Humez's introduction to *Gifts of Power*. All references to Jackson's writings refer to this edition of her manuscripts. Sasson analyzes the text in the context of other Shaker works, suggesting that AME pulpit rhetoric contributed to the lyrical and oral qualities of Jackson's prose (*Shaker Spiritual*, 158–88). Brewer discusses Jackson's conflicts with Shaker authorities, noting her mystical power, her attempt to "exercise . . . executive authority," and her view of racial oppression within the predominantly white communities ("'Tho' of the Weaker Sex,'" 627–28). Richard Williams in *Called and Chosen* focuses on Jackson's life and work with the Philadelphia community of Shakers.

William Andrews, Nellie McKay, Joanne Braxton, Candis A. LaPrade, and Katherine Clay Bassard discuss Jackson's work in the light of other nineteenth-century African-American spiritual autobiographies. McKay emphasizes the importance of female "supportive communities" for both Jackson and Jarena Lee and argues that each woman demonstrates her "connectedness" to "collective human experience" through the genre (140, 150). Braxton notes the fragmented form of Jackson's narrative and argues that Jackson distanced herself from her oppressive surroundings through her writing, thus carving a space in which she could "create" her "self" (51, 61). Andrews comments only briefly on Jackson's writing (3). LaPrade emphasizes the African influences upon Jackson's work, especially with regard to time and space, and the influences of these elements upon twentieth-century works by African-American women. Bassard points to differences between Jackson and Jarena Lee, noting that African-American sisterhood includes a diversity of theologies ("Spiritual Interrogations," 136–62). Alice Walker comments on Jackson in a review of Humez's book (*In Search of Our Mothers' Gardens*, 71–82).

8. Humez comments on the influence of Lee's example and the Shakers' "feminist theology" upon Jackson (24, 37–39). She writes, for example, "Shakerism was to provide a feminist theology, useful when she came to the decision to create and lead her own, predominantly black, Shaker sisterhood in Philadelphia" (*Gifts of Power*, 24). However, she does not elaborate on Jackson's response to Shaker attitudes toward literacy.

9. She also aptly argues that the texts available present writers "in varying stages of literacy and with multiple positions vis-à-vis ideologies of literacy and education" ("Gender and Genre," 128). That is, their attitudes toward literacy as associated with freedom and economic advancement vary according to how each "writer perceives her/himself in the social order," and this perception influences the autobiography's form (119).

10. According to Humez, the second is "a short booklet containing several . . . accounts of [Rebecca Perot's] dreams, as dictated to Jackson, along with a few of Jackson's own." Hollister's "anthology" was later "edited and rearranged . . . by another Shaker hand" (*Gifts of Power*, 65–66).

11. See, for example, Gates, *The Signifying Monkey* (Chapter 4) and *Figures in Black* (Chapter 1); William L. Andrews, *To Tell a Free Story;* and Robert Stepto, *From Behind the Veil*.

12. Jane Tompkins writes of Ellen Montgomery's reading, for example, that it helps her "stay put and submit" (161).

13. Jackson elaborates: "I can now understand why it was that I was not to read. It was because the time had not yet come for me to read anything else. . . . He intended that I should believe what I saw and heard, without the help of man. . . . If I had read those writings which are so common among men, they would have darkened my understanding, so that when the time came for me to read the truth, I would not have been able to have received it" (141–43).

14. Vygotsky defines the "zone of proximal development" as "the distance between the actual developmental level as determined by independent problem solving [i.e., the decoding of the alphabet or specific words] and the level of potential development as determined through problem solving under adult guidance or in collaboration with more capable peers" [Shaker leaders or the spirit] (86). For a more complete discussion of the implications of this "zone" and its place in the acquistion of higher order thinking skills, see *Mind in Society* (84–91).

15. On Harriet Jacobs's resistant reading and writing see Hazel Carby, Valerie Smith, Jean Fagan Yellin, Annette Niemtzow, and Frances Smith Foster.

16. Nellie McKay elaborates on the support of and empowerment by these women's groups. Jacqueline Jones, though dealing primarily with slaves and former slaves in the South, discusses the significance of work and family for black women.

17. Another dream suggests that even as a young child Jackson was given responsibility as a caretaker: "I dreamt that my mother was out, and I had to take care of my younger sister, and brother, who was but a few months old" (234).

18. This is the second complaint of this nature. See also (82).

19. This post-Freudian reading of Jackson's relationships to women and men is suggested by psychoanalytic theory as articulated by Nancy Chodorow. Although her early work, *The Reproduction of Mothering*, has fallen in disregard for attempting to create a mythic structure that transcends temporal and cultural bounds, Chodorow qualifies and revises her theories in her more recent work, *Feminism and Psychoanalytic Theory* (4–6). Her discussion here of the influence of historical context, cultural specificity, and individual's gender identities upon their relationships, along with her earlier work,

illuminates Jackson's relationship to nineteenth-century Shakerism.

The central argument I draw from is her reworking of the Freudian Oedipal complex: Daughters, unlike sons, maintain a feeling of connection with their mothers throughout their lives. This connection between women emerges not necessarily because of bodily similarities but because daughters become gendered as women by their mothers. As a result of this continued connection with their mothers, women also sometimes experience latent anger, hostility, and frustration if they feel unable to create a sense of "self" separate from that of their mothers. Through a desire to separate themselves, daughters turn to heterosexual relationships. Experiences varying from "the norm" may be explained by deviations from the typical mother-daughter bonding during infancy. She explains, for example, that "girls from father-absent homes were uncomfortable and insecure with men and boys" and were "slightly more dependent on adult women"; however, both "father-absent" and "father-present" girls maintain a sense of connection to their mothers (and other women) even while desiring autonomy and separation, which is manifest in their relationships with men (*Reproduction*, 139).

20. Rosemary Gooden, drawing from letters and poetry, has elaborated upon the fellowship and bonds among female Shakers in "The Language of Devotion."

21. For reprints of the spirit drawings, which include sketches of Holy Mother Wisdom's wings, see Edward Deming and Faith Andrews's *Visions of the Heavenly Sphere* and Sally J. Promey's *Spiritual Spectacles*. Sasson has argued that the writings of female visionary Shaker Minerva Hill have "a specificity of image, a concreteness of detail" that make them "more akin to spiritual drawings than linear, written narratives. Shape and color predominate" ("Individual Experience," 31). She suggests that this characteristic is gender-based, since the writings of William Leonard are more "linear." Jackson's writing in some ways supports Sasson's theory, but more importantly, it demonstrates the fluidity of the gender boundaries among the Shakers.

22. Jackson writes, "I felt that I must be a wandering spirit in the spirit world, and have no place of rest, until I had suffered enough in the spirit world [to compensate for] the work that I had not done in time" (274). She visualizes not only herself in the spirit world but Mother Ann "waiting for" her. She concludes, "This brought a ray of hope to my fainting soul, that it would be better for me in the spirit world" (274).

23. For descriptions of the deceased spirits who visited the Shakers during this period, see two accounts by anonymous non-Shakers: *A Return of Departed Spirits of the Highest Characters of Distinctions, as well as the Indiscriminate of all Nations, into the Bodies of the "Shakers," or "United Society of Believers in the Second Advent of the Messiah"* (1843) and *A Revelation of the Extraordinary Visitation of Departed Spirits of Distinguished Men and Women of All Nations* (1869). Eldress Catherine Allen wrote of the former, "The spirit of the writer was fair and statements approximately correct" (Richmond, II, 100–101).

24. In the first chapter of *Black Women Novelists* (1–34), Barbara Christian delineates several images that appear in American literature: the "sexually aggressive" female who "sometimes mated with orangutan males" (6); the mammy (8); the sexually loose woman (14); and the rebellious and savage woman (24–25). See also George M. Frederickson's *Black Image in the White Mind* and Elizabeth Fox-Genovese's *Within the Plantation Household* for a discussion of these stereotypes. Lawrence Foster has written that the Shakers in this period "shared much of the cultural baggage of their contemporaries. . . . [T]he figures from whom the Shakers received revelations were strikingly similar to the heroes and heroines of the school textbooks of the period" (*Women*, 257, n.18).

25. Humez notes in reference to the frequent appearance of ethnic minorities during the Era of Manifestations, "Believers intensely identified with oppressed races and nationalities throughout history and across cultures. Viewing themselves as descendants of an oppressed

religious minority, they saw much of Christian and European history as taking place in the 'reign of Antichrist.'" (*Gifts of Power*, 217–18, n. 28).

26. On Jacobs's sensitivity to white readers see, for example, Carby, Smith, Fagan Yellin, Niemtzow, and Foster.

27. Sasson writes of Hollister in her "19th Century Case Study": "He recorded hymns during the Era of Manifestations. He kept records of the extract business. He copied visions, narratives and poems of other Shakers. And he himself authored and published over 25 pamphlets and monographs in addition to innumerable periodical contributions" (155). She also writes of Hollister's correspondence with John Patterson MacLean, early historian and bibliographer of Shaker materials, responsible for the beginnings of the Western Reserve Historical Society Shaker Collection (170–72, 188–89).

28. The most extensive work with Hollister's narrative is Sasson's "19th Century Case Study," primarily a biographical essay.

29. See Brewer ("'Tho' of the Weaker Sex,'" 628–35) and Stein (*Shaker Experience*, 256–72).

30. This lack of pictoral qualities also corresponds with the "masculine" nature of William Leonard's narrative that Sasson describes ("Individual Experience," 31). Sasson implies in her analysis of Minerva Hill's and Leonard's writings that the female's is more empowering than the male's because of its visual imagery, whose "meanings cannot be fixed." The interpretation of visual imagery is perhaps more open to varied interpretation than verbal imagery, but *all* words are images whose meanings cannot be fixed. Although Hollister's writing is similar to Leonard's in its lack of pictoral qualities, my point is to demonstrate how *both* Jackson and Hollister are empowered through their narratives.

31. For discussions of the "progressive" and "conservative" factions within Shakerism, see Sasson ("19th Century Case Study," 164–70); Stein (*Shaker Experience*, 205, 207, 213, 227–28, 236, 266, 304); Deignan (Chapter 4); and Brewer (*Shaker Communities*, 190–95).

32. "Brief Sketch of Ann Lee" is one among several subtitles for "Prophesy Unseal'd." "The Free Woman" is printed in the twenty-six-page collection entitled "Calvin's Confession." The title page blurb "Dawn of Woman's Era" refers to the article "The Free Woman."

33. While highlighting the desire for alterity common to travel writings, James Buzard argues that the tourist is looking for the "peculiar"; he asks, "Who goes abroad to encounter what is near at hand?" ("A Continent of Pictures," 30–31). In *The Tourist Gaze* John Urry similarly discusses the "difference" necessarily seen in the object of the tourist's gaze.

34. Another possible pleasure is a group outing to a bridge, which he details in size and structure and explains that it was burned down and rebuilt.

Chapter 6

Preserving the Body in Poetry: The Canterbury *Obituary Journal* and Funeral Rituals

> Soon Mother the last of her first born will gather
> Home, home to her mansion of peace;
> Shall Zion then falter, the tender buds wither?
> Or shall they still grow and increase?
>
> Lavinia Clifford, *ca.* 1856

The Canterbury, New Hampshire, community's *Obituary Journal,* much as Alonzo Hollister's "Reminiscences," recollects and preserves the past as it looks into an uncertain future. The three-volume manuscript record preserves more than 400 signed and unsigned poems, collectively embodying in written form the Shaker community of that locale. The poems memorialize Shakers of Canterbury, from its first "gathering" in 1792 until 1977. The *Journal*'s primary compositor, Emeline Kimball, was more like Alonzo Hollister than Rebecca Jackson in that she lived within one community for most of her life. Born in 1810 in Canterbury, she began to live with the Shakers' Second Family as a child and was officially "received into the Church" at the age of seventeen. She continued to live in the Canterbury Shaker Village until her death in 1876. Kimball served as caretaker of the little girls for a year or two in her early thirties, and then in 1846 she began work in the Infirmary. When she began keeping the *Journal* ten years later, she was about forty-five years old and had lived as a Shaker for almost thirty years. She continued her efforts with the *Journal* and other tasks of the Infirmary until near her death at age sixty-five, winning respect though no formal leadership positions. Canterbury Elder and historian Henry Blinn refers to her as "a most efficient nurse" in his reflective narrative of the community (I, 256), and the published obituary in the March 1876 issue of *The Shaker* memorializes her as "a physician, nurse, and dear good Sister" (24). Harriot Hunt, known as a "physician" by the New England Shakers with whom she interacted, in spite of being denied entrance to Harvard Medical School in 1847 and 1850, wrote of Kimball, "I went to Canterbury, and visited the Shaker society; taking a severe cold I was there nearly a week, and tested the kindness, skill, and care of Dr. Emeline" (*Glances and Glimpses,* 275). The references to a Shaker woman as both physician and nurse, not atypical near mid-century, reflect the blurred gender boundaries in the sect's "scientific" realm of medicine. Kimball, like some women in other Shaker communities' infirmaries, was responsible for more than washing patients and changing bed linens.[1]

Refracted through the sect's theology and practice, Emeline Kimball's work in the Infirmary, including her oversight of the *Obituary Journal,* challenges the world's patterns of "masculine" or "heroic" medicine and feminine health care; more specifically, though, the *Journal* serves as a repository of Shaker literacies at Canterbury, much as Hollister's bibliographic work does for Shakerism at large, by including samples of many Believers' writings. Kimball's project codified in 1856 a writing, reading, and funerary ritual that blended the scientific and the sentimental, or the reasonable and the emotional elements of spirituality. Each entry in the *Journal* includes, in addition to a poem, an introduction that gives such scientific information as birth and death dates and causes of death—equally important as the sentimental verses. In contrast to much of the sentimental writing of non-Shaker women, the *Obituary Journal* conjoins intellect and contemporary "scientific" thought with mysticism and the emotionalism of sentimental verses.

Yet the verses themselves illustrate much of the power of these diverse Shaker literacies. Ann Douglas has argued that nineteenth-century Protestant women and ministers gained power and "feminized" American culture by writing poems about death and biographical sketches.[2] Similarly, poems within the *Journal* reflect the increasing "feminization" of Shakerism after mid-century, a period during which historians Stephen Stein and Priscilla Brewer have found a decrease in male membership and an increase of power for female leaders.[3] In the sect's literary realm, the "feminization" includes an increase in the production of "feminine" genres (such as occasional verse) and an increase in the numbers of published and unpublished texts written by women. The tradition Kimball initiated at Canterbury, then, empowered other male and female Shakers in that it gave them a means of personal expression.

These poems also reflect the blurred communal and individual values and beliefs of Shakers in the face of personal and communal changes over a period of 120 years. The lines of Lavinia Clifford's poetic memorial tribute to her spiritual brother James Daniels, who died in 1851, typifies others in form and theme. Driven by Daniels's death, Clifford inquires of the sect's future: "Shall Zion falter, the tender buds wither?" She does not answer the questions directly within the poem, but the poem's preservation suggests a means Believers—individual "buds"—used to "grow and increase" spiritually rather than "falter" and "wither." This poem and others follow Victorian America's elegies in purpose and format, yet they veer from traditional patterns to embody Shaker theology and experience. At times the poems ironically contradict overt Shaker teachings about personal relationships, individual identity, and the immaterial afterlife in the spirit world. Like the gift drawings that

Sally Promey has recently described as materializations of the immaterial spirit, these poems also simultaneously exhibit Shaker characteristics of the artist or poet as well as his or her unique signatures or style.[4] The writer verbally depicts the deceased as she or he views him or her. In some cases, the writer and the deceased were good friends; in others, they were acquaintances; in still others, especially those written by young poets about early Canterbury leaders, the writer knew the deceased only verbally and imaginatively, through orally transmitted stories about or documentary references to him or her. Thus the readings of the poems that follow point to Shaker variations in the typical poetic movement of the elegy, revisions of nineteenth-century images of church and family, ironic representations of bodies of the deceased, and shifts in poetic representations of those who died around and after mid-century. Two topics—the relationship between Shaker elegies and funerals, and the composition of the *Journal* within its historical context—are foundational to understanding the motivations, form, and content of the poets and recorders; thus explorations of these two topics precede the discussion of elegies as a significant genre of Shaker literacies.

In sum, for Shakers at Canterbury in 1856 and later, the poems mark not just the loss of an individual that the speaker confronts but the shrinking of the church body as well.[5] Kimball and others who followed her as compositors exemplify the Shakers' spiritual literacies as they work through progress and change within the sect at large as well as at Canterbury. The poems within the *Journal* and the poets who wrote them reflect the increasing sense of individualism, fragmentation, and loss within Shaker communities after the mid-nineteenth century. Kimball and, by extension, other poets and compositors were empowered by the act of gathering the community of deceased Believers into the *Obituary Journal* in 1856. In the late eighteenth century Mother Ann had gathered living Believers and, she claimed, some spirits of the dead; the Canterbury Believers are likewise embodied and gathered, albeit in textual form. The collection demonstrates the Shakers' paradoxical attitudes toward the physical body and its role in spiritual life, as they use images of physical bodies and the physicality of pen and paper to embody the spirits of deceased Shakers. They also demonstrate their awareness of the world's literacies and funerary literature as they mimic popular nineteenth-century elegies. These volumes, then, at once record what persists as distinctive Shaker literacies even as they record the community's adoption of the world's literary practices. By binding these poems into volumes, the poets and compositors of the *Obituary Journal* demonstrate the Shakers' strategy and ability to unify and strengthen individuals within the community through writing and reading rituals.

SHAKER FUNERAL RITUALS

What shall we do with our bodies when we have done with our bodies?
Frederick Evans, *Shaker Sermon*, 1886[6]

When Emeline Kimball began the *Obituary Journal* in 1856, she was following a tradition not only well known in the world but also already established at Canterbury. As early as 1831, the date of Canterbury Elder Job Bishop's death, the members of the community were writing poetry to memorialize the deceased. Through this writing and the later *Journal,* the Shakers mirrored the world's literary practices. Historians of Victorian America have written about the apparent nineteenth-century obsession with death and dying manifest in the heavy, ornate, and extensive materialization of funerary rituals of the period: the appearance of suburban "rural" cemeteries serving cities, the enlargement of tombstones into monuments and sepulchers, the fashion industry's involvement in the development of mourning clothes and mores, and the fashioning of seemingly insignificant gewgaws such as bracelets of braided hair from the deceased. Professional and amateur artists and photographers created portraits, and women of the period wrote and collected poems about death, organizing and preserving them in scrapbooks dedicated to the topic. When Mark Twain creates his maudlin Emmeline Grangerford in *The Adventures of Huckleberry Finn* (1884), only coincidently of the same name as the Shakers' *Journal* compositor, he parodies a well-established tradition.[7]

The four-page *Poetry and other writings at the time of Elder Job Bishop's Death,* created by Canterbury Believers, typifies this tradition. The piece "includes two poems, a copy of Bishop's obituary notice from the *New Hampshire Patriot,* and a description of communication between Bishop and Elder Elisha in the spirit world" (McKinstry, 232). In addition to being a *bricolage* of mortuary literature like the scrapbooks mid-nineteenth-century women of the world compiled, the piece indicates not only that the Shakers wrote poetry to memorialize the deceased but also that the "deceased" continued to live and communicate "in the spirit world" after leaving their bodily forms on the earth.[8]

Even before Bishop's death in 1831 the Shakers, as other Christian sects had and did, participated in funerary rituals and struggled with the theology—especially concerning the resurrection and the spirit world—to support them. Barbara Rotundo describes Shaker funerary practices as following the patterns of other Protestants in rural New England during the eighteenth and nineteenth centuries. Because the Shakers claimed not to believe in a physical resurrection, they considered elaborate gravesites and services unnecessary. In 1784 Believers buried Lee in a grave with only a small marker. Yet records indicate the sect did hold services to commemorate early leaders soon after their deaths and before the burials. After communal ownership of property had been established in the late eighteenth century, Shaker cemeteries with simple headstones soon followed, indicating a need for lasting symbols of a gathered community of Believers. Further shifts in attitudes toward preservation of bodies of the deceased were manifested in 1835, when Lee's body was exumed and reinterred. Then in 1880 the Shakers followed the pattern of Victorian American cemeteries, though on a reduced scale, by replacing "small stones" with larger and more ornate "marble tablets" (37). Some communities used cast-iron "lollipop" markers, which were less expensive and more easily produced than marble markers (44).

In spite of following the world's funerary practices of the nineteenth century in part, some Shakers resisted these practices for their material emphasis on the body after physical death. For example, the "progressive" Shaker Elder Frederick Evans, who asked the public in print, "What shall we do with our bodies when we have done with our bodies?" offered a simple answer. He suggested that "it would be a great relief to the poor and middle classes to have Shaker funerals become as popular as Shaker brooms and garden-seeds" because they devoted so little money to the rituals ("Rational Funerals," 130). Apparently drawing from John Dunlavy's theological description of the nature of resurrection in *The Manifesto,* Evans explains Shaker mortuary practices as "Rational Funerals": "The doctrine of the resurrection of the body is the foundation of the honors paid to the body after the soul has left it. Spiritualism, which proves that the soul exists in spirit-life independent of the body, annihilates the doctrine of a physical resurrection. Shakers being Spiritualists repudiate the physical resurrection, and dispose of 'remains' in accordance with the idea of 'dust to dust;' hence their strictly Rational Funerals" (131). This article, "Rational Funerals," is a summary reprint of his first on the subject, in which he describes the spiritual—rather than physical—emphasis of the Shaker funeral service. Presenting what appears to be a dichotomized view of body and spirit, he writes, "The Shakers do not, for a moment, think of being put into a grave, nor of putting their friends into the cold, cold ground. Once out of the body, they are gone whence no traveler ever returns, into the gross elements of an earthly body." Yet the passage continues, revealing the fundamental Shaker belief of spiritual presence—the spirits of the deceased intermingle with their embodied counterparts in community. Evans writes, "Time and again, disembodied spirits attend and officiate at their own obsequies, to the edification and comfort of the survivors—thus, settling anew the ever ocurring question—'If a man die, shall he live again?'" These spirits validate the Shaker life as they reveal the tension between spiritualism and materialism and Evans's irrational approach to funerals.

In spite of Evans's and Dunlavy's writings, which counter to many nineteenth-century mainstream Christian teachings of "golden streets" and "mansions above" denied a material afterlife, the Shakers' attention to the body in the funerary ritual and in the memorial poems emerges nonetheless, a manifestation of the Believers' inability to divorce completely spirit from embodied forms. Two journals from Canterbury illustrate this synthesis as they provide information about Shaker funerary rituals at the community during the period preceding the initiation of the *Obituary Journal.* Francis Winkley's *Journal* (1784–1845) includes early examples of what become the poetic rituals of the 1856 *Obituary Journal.* Winkley's objective record of Shaker events resembles those kept by leaders at other communities, but he personalizes his communal journal with entries marking the deaths of Believers. First, he uses the traditional method of verbal record to trace perfunctorily the facts of the death; in addition, though, he highlights these entries with marginal emblems—usually a sketch of a simple coffin, sometimes including a body. This marginalia permits readers to skim the record for Winkley's comments about the deaths and the deceased. Another element that distinguishes these entries from those in other communal journals is the memorial poetry Winkley records, which mimics the verse of epitaphs. For the August 27, 1816, entry, for example, marked in the margin by a black coffin, Winkley perfunctorily notes: "Elijah Wiles Came here and Bro,t word that Mother Hannah at Harvard Died on Sabath Evening the 18th Day of this Month." His more emotional, personal, and poetic response follows immediately: "Oh! Good Mother Hannah, is in the Clod- / The riteous fill there day and go to God—" (59). Less than a month later, for the September 12 entry, again marked by a marginal black coffin, Winkley writes, "Elder Emund Lougee Dies (10 Oc, Evening) of a Consumption being aged 57 years and Since the 25th of May last." The verse immediately follows:

> A fathfull Minister he*s* been
> He*s* gone where Natural eyes han,t seen
> He*s* gone to have his Bles,t reward
> With Saint, and A,ngles in the Lord (59)

Although these entries are a part of an official, communal record of the Society at Canterbury, the poems, in contrast to the statistics about death, appear to be Winkley's emotional and more personal responses.

John Whitcher's journal description of the events surrounding Bishop's death fifteen years later indicates that the composition of memorial lyrics was not unique to Winkley during the first half of the nineteenth century. The personal compositions were often shared in the ritual of Shaker mourning. Whitcher, Elder of the Church Family at the time, describes in detail the death and the events following it. Whitcher writes in his "official" journal that on the evening of December 5, 1831, "Father Job" having "just retired to rest and being greatly pressed for the want of breath, soon rose up again & expired within a few minutes" (151). He tells readers that this event within the Church Family, "though long anticipated, . . . was sudden & unexpected at the time"—some 15 minutes before 11 P.M. that chilly December evening. The journal implies that almost immediately the community responded to the loss. Messages were dispatched to the Ministry at Canterbury's sister community at Enfield, New Hampshire, some sixty-five miles away, so that "four of the elders *vis*. Elder Br. John Beck, Elder John Lyon, Achsa Huntington & Elder Sister Phebe Kidder" were able to arrive on December 7, within forty-eight hours of the death, in time for the funeral service on December 8.

If "Father Job" had not been in the Infirmary at the time of his death, his body would have been moved there soon after by his spiritual brothers in the faith. Thomas Corbett, the resident Shaker physician, possibly accompanied by a physician from the world, determined the cause of death as "dropsy of the heart," perhaps hastened by Bishop's trip to Enfield the previous week, and by his "feeble" and aged body of seventy-one years. The deceased was "laid out" by his spiritual sisters who worked in the Infirmary. Those who had not heard the news of the death during the night would have learned of it the next morning. Canterbury's carpenters would have been instructed to build or have ready a simple pine or fir coffin for the burial.[9] The announcement would have motivated Believers to take time within their labors to labor in love for Bishop and the community by composing prose addresses, personal testimonies, and hymns to be shared at the upcoming funeral service.

Whitcher's journal provides an overview of the 2 P.M. service in the Shaker meeting house. His seven-paragraph record refers to the attendants and their bodily carriage, the addresses delivered, the hymns sung, the viewing of the corpse, and the burial. "Some of the world, among whom were two ministers" attended. Though he refers to those of the world twice later as "spectators," he also indicates their participatory role in the service.[10] Elder John Lyon directs his address to all; the Believers, however, participate more fully in the funerary ritual. Whitcher's comment that the "brethren and sisters arose . . . and took their ranks" indicates that they took the positions usually used for the animated dances that gave the Shakers their name and drew spectators to their services. Instead of dancing they "arose with a cautious stiffness" to stand in their "ranks" for what appears to be the duration of the service; in the sect's funeral services, linguistic action displaces bodily action in expressing emotion and bolstering spirituality.

Participants at Bishop's funeral heard five prose addresses, a combination of personal testimony about the deceased, and exhortation to live likewise, from five Elders. Micajah Tucker's own "tender feelings" and "sympathy," his attention to "the characteristic virtues" of the deceased, and his attempt to elicit "a feeling sense" among his audience so that they might be prepared for "the accountability that awaited each," marks his address as similar to those in funeral services of the world. In contrast to the "address," the "testimony" of Elder Benjamin Whitcher, Father Job's "immediate companion . . . in labor, for more than 20 years," re-established, maintained, and solidified Bishop's image within the community in a more spontaneous fashion. Elder Elisha Pote, who arrived from Alfred, Maine, after the meeting had been "closed," was allowed to make "some remarks concerning their former acquaintance & friendship," an event that suggests that almost anyone who wished to speak could have done so.[11] The meeting was thus a time of public but personal expression, emerging from years of intimate relationship and reflecting several private, verbal acts that had been prepared in the two days prior to the shared communal ritual.

Some of these synthesized personal and public verbal expressions are almost buried among Whitcher's references to the prose testimonies. Whitcher notes the singing of three hymns, one of which, "the funeral song," "closed the meeting."[12] He also writes: "We sung a hymn composed for the occasion." The quick composition (here within three days) of a hymn for this specific occasion marks a unique element of the Shaker funeral service. Hymn writing—both lyrics and music—was an important ritual for Shakers throughout the nineteenth century, allowing personal expression through the writing and communal unification through the voicing of shared images.[13] The funeral hymn created by one Believer to memorialize another Believer, not unlike the memorial poem, exemplifies the solidarity of community that was strengthened through the mourning ritual.

The memorial poems mimic the hymns in their rhythm, their imagery, their authorship, and their use in worship. Rosemary Gooden, who has analyzed Shaker poetry memorializing women, asserts the unifying relationship between inscription of texts—the private, personal expression of writing—and their oral, communal performative readings during memorial services.[14] As she notes, hymns and elegies had been a common part of funerals in rural America since Puritans circulated published elegies at burials in the late seventeenth century. The poetic funerary rituals of the world often included favorite hymns or poems selected by the deceased prior to death and, sometimes, the composition of a hymn for the occasion. Thus the Shaker ritual is not unlike its counterparts in the world in its use of testimonies, addresses, hymns, and poetry. In what ways is it unique? How do any differences contribute to our understanding of Shaker literacies?

One difference between Shaker memorials in verse and those in the world emerges from the relationships between poets and deceased Shakers. Even in the services of the world where a friend or family member composed a poem, the relationship between deceased and what Peter Sacks calls the "cast of mourners" differed significantly.[15] William Dean Howells's description of a Shaker funeral for Sister Julia at the Shirley, Massachusetts, community underscores the sect's revision of the biological family central to Victorian American culture. Howells's account, in an *Atlantic Monthly* article of 1876, affirms the general funeral format Whitcher describes but it also captures this difference:

There was no prayer, or any set discourse, but the elders and eldresses, and many others spoke in commemoration of Sister Julia's duteous and faithful life, and in expression of their love for her. Their voices trembled, and the younger sisters, who had been most about her at the last, freely gave way to their tears. Each one who spoke had some special tribute to pay to her faithfulness, or some tender little testimony to bear to her goodness of heart; several read verses which they had written in memory of her, and amongst these was the leader of the Church Family, who conducted the ceremonies. *What was most observable in it all was the familiar character; it was as if these were brothers and sisters by the ties of nature, who spoke of the dead.* (702, emphasis mine)

Howells's depiction emphasizes not only "the familiar character" among these Believers but also the spontaneity that Whitcher's account of the 1831 service suggests.[16]

In addition to the sometimes spontaneously created hymns, memorial poems, and testimonies that reflect the Shakers' differences from the world is the ritual viewing of the corpse at the service's close, which exemplifies the paradoxical role the body plays in Shaker spirituality and literacies. The language of Whitcher's journal, for example, emphasizes his attempt to relinquish the deceased person's body: Before "both believers & spectators" was "the corpse," which he refers to also as "a personage." Whitcher adds parenthetically "(though lifeless)" as if to remind himself that Bishop's spirit was no longer housed there. Although Evans refers boldly to "the never-again-to-be-animated form and features" of deceased Shakers ("Shaker Burials," 60), Whitcher describes Bishop's corpse as "a personage . . . who seemed to exhibit a pleasant and expressive appearance of animation"—an indication that the outward signs of the body may be read as representations of the inner "animation," or spirit.

After the service and the viewing of Bishop's body the closed coffin was carried up the hill to the Shaker cemetery for interment in a a previously designated and charted plot. These cemeteries were distorted imitations of the world's family plots, which signified social bonds and affirmed the continuity of these kinship bonds in the afterlife.[17] For the Shakers these plots emphasized the bonds and already resurrected condition of the living Shaker family. The cemetery charting and recording, a rigorously and meticulously upheld responsibility of the nurses and the teachers, attests, like the headstones and the coffins, to the importance of bodies of the deceased to those still living physically.[18]

The *Obituary Journal* shifted the mourning and preservation away from the site of the physical body in the cemetery to the verbal and less material preservation of the spirit. Also charted and plotted by the community's nurses and teachers, the *Journal* is an inscribed and bound graveyard, containing poems that served as covert epitaphs. It extends the funerary ritual from the bodily rites and performances of the meeting house and the cemetery to the private sites where the volumes were composed, shelved, and retrieved over the years. Reading the poems at any time could invoke the spirits of the deceased and continue the communication between the community of mourners and the spirit world.

THE CANTERBURY CONTEXT

Writing a poem memorializing a recently deceased spiritual brother or sister and recording it in the *Obituary Journal* appears to have been a fairly routine task. The routine itself may have eased the emotional burden of mourning or the writing process somewhat. However, the routine of *compiling* the *Journal*—more than sixty years after the first Canterbury Shakers began to leave their physical bodies—was a task of another scope. A comparison of the dates of the deceased who are memorialized with the dates of the physical and spiritual births of the poets whose names are assigned reveals the immense task of collecting "factual" information from written and unwritten Canterbury history to compose poems dedicated to Shakers who died prior to 1857. The third poem within the *Journal* (the first signed piece), for example, memorializes a Shaker who died in 1784. The poet Zillah Randlett, who did not come to Canterbury until 1808, would not have known the deceased other than through orally conveyed images, inscribed texts, or visions. Another example is the poem devoted to "Father" Job Bishop and written by John Kaime. Kaime came to Canterbury in 1841, ten years after Bishop's death. A few exceptions to this pattern demonstrate that some poems had been written earlier and preserved, transcribed into the official volume around 1856. For example, records indicate that Lydia Kaime left the community in 1854, two years prior to Kimball's initiation of the *Journal*. However, the *Journal* preserves poems she wrote memorializing those who died in 1846, 1847, and 1848. Kaime's poems were respected and considered worthy of inclusion in this verbal gathering of community, although the author herself had apostatized.

The names of the approximately eighty poets whose works are included reflect a primarily female body of writers.[19] Among the five Shaker males whose poems are transcribed, James V. Chase, a teacher, was the major contributor. His poems mark themselves as different from those by women in that he memorialized only Shaker Brothers, whereas the female writers portrayed with pen both male and female Believers. The other male writers, with the exception of Henry Campbell (also a teacher, who contributed a handful of poems), James Kaime, John Kaime, and Abraham Perkins, contributed one each. These men held leadership positions, indicative of the extra time available to them for writing and the higher level of alphabetic literacy among those in these roles. Several of the female poets served in the Infirmary, and a large number of them were also teachers. It is not clear whether their work as teachers influenced their poetic abilities or that their verbal prolixity, as demonstrated in the poems, contributed to their selection by the Canterbury Ministry to serve in the Shaker school. Whichever the case, the survey of the *Journal*'s poets indicates two realms within the village at Canterbury where "book knowledge" predominated—the Infirmary and the schoolhouse. These two realms, the *Journal* suggests, were ruled quantitatively by women, reflecting the "feminization" of Shakerism and the role of female Believers in the sect's literary endeavors during this period.

This survey of the poets represented in the *Obituary Journal* and their respective gendered realms provides part of the framework in which we may consider Kimball's work. None of the poems bears her name. Several unsigned works within the volume could be attributed to her, but since she inscribed her name so clearly on the title pages, it seems unlikely that she would have hestitated (because of modesty, for example) to sign her name to a particular leaf. Two poems bear the initials E. H. K. and E. K., respectively; however, because Kimball's middle initial was L., at most one of these could be attributed to her. Kimball's role, then, was primarily that of transcriber and compositor.

More compositor and transcriptionist than a poet, Kimball performed writing and reading acts that were as much mechanical as mental and as much ritualized as rationalized. Her work keeping the *Obituary Journal,* as well as her work in the Infirmary as both "nurse" and "physician," reflect Shakerism's support of both rational and irrational reading and writing acts and somewhat fluid gender boundaries, respectively. Perhaps performed "after hours" in the Infirmary or between caring for patients, the *Journal* fulfilled an emotional need and a scientific need in accordance with the Shaker unity of the two in spirituality and literacy. Kimball's recordkeeping, one example of the Shaker insistence on order, provided her a means of ordering and "composing" herself and her community as she spent her life among the dying.[20]

This union of science and sentiment becomes apparent on the *Journal*'s title pages as well as in its structure. Each volume contains an index, organized alphabetically by the last name of the deceased, and entries are arranged chronolog-ically by death date. The orderly format not only reveals the acceptance and appreciation of booklearning and recordkeeping by the Shakers at this point in their history; it also balances the emotional or sentimental element of each entry—the poetry. The title pages indicate the same balance. Volume I opens: "An Obituary Journal of Members connected with this society since the first opening of the gospel AD 1782; ten years before the gathering of the Church. Embracing the date of birth: the time of death, the age at that time; the disease; also a passing notice to each one." The scientific import of the *Journal* lies in the fascination with the cause of death and in the statistical details the nurses provided. The phrase "a passing notice to each one" becomes on the Volume II title page, "a memorial tribute to each one." The former indicates that the survivors communicate through emotional verse with the deceased in the spirit world; the latter marks with the "memorial" a shift toward an audience of Believers remaining in the physical community. The ongoing emotional and spiritual bonds between the deceased and the community remain present in later years, but the description of communication is more guarded. As Shakers such as Frederick Evans argue, this communication with spirits is rational and scientific.

This community, concerned with rationality and spirituality, is the one in which Emeline Kimball initiates the *Obituary Journal* in 1856, a key year for her as well as for the community as a whole. The year's recorded events reflect the aftermath of the revival years. Some Shaker historians imply that by 1856 the Era of Manifestations had passed; however, limits of the era are not so easily delineated, and documents from Canterbury reveal that the interests and concerns of the revival had not dissipated completely.[21] Correspondence of the period, for example, refers to Canterbury as "Holy Ground," the community's spiritual name adopted during the era. The turmoil at Canterbury around 1856 included continued tensions between those keenly interested in spiritualist activities and those concerned with maintaining Shaker traditions and the teachings of Mother Ann, as they had been known apart from and prior to recent revelations by spiritualists. Several changes in communal leadership during the period reflect these conflicts.[22] The leadership of Henry Blinn and Dorothy Durgin, who first took positions as Elder and Eldress in 1852, contributed to significant changes. According to Nicholas Briggs, Blinn and Durgin ushered in an increasing emphasis upon literacy and science: "Both of them had been teachers of the school, were highly intelligent and progressive in their ideas, and they stimulated reading and study, and we now began to have *The Scientific American*, *Phrenological Journal* and *Life Illustrated*" (59).

In addition to changes in leadership, the turmoil included numerous illnesses and deaths of older Believers. Phrases in letters of the period indicate concern over the loss of the last generation that had known Lee and the first Elders. Of the few known extant letters written by the Canterbury Ministry during 1856, one dated March 17 to the ministry at "Lovely Vineyard" (Harvard) lists specifically the illnesses and debilities of four brothers and one sister before concluding: "Others of the aged still keep about but the lamp of life in them evidently grows dim and will in all probability, before many years, be extinguished and those of us, of a later call be kept to keep the gospel and administer it to the rising generation as it has been administered to us or fall short of the blessing promised to the faithful." A January 1858 letter to the "Beloved Elders" at "Chosen Vale" (Enfield, New Hampshire) includes two pages (half the letter's length) extracted from a December 29, 1857, letter from "Holy Mount" (New Lebanon, New York). The letter responds to the death of Mother Asenath, who "has fled the shores of time, and gone to that far happy land to rest with her dearest companions, where peace and quietness reign." Not unlike memorial pieces Shakers published for the world and themselves later in the century, the letter gives details of the Shaker woman's illness, death, and funeral services, and of her life as "a Mother in Israel indeed." But the letter's closing editorial comments, directed only to Believers, overtly state the sense of loss within the communities: "So one after another of our parents drop away; not long, before it will be said, all of those saints that ever saw Mother Ann and the first Elders in the body will be gone, but we hope and earnestly pray that a large portion of their power and unflinching courage may rest upon us, and enable us to keep the way of God in its purity." [23] The Canterbury *Church Record,* similar to the correspondence in tone, records spiritual hardship as a result of physical disabilities in the year-end review of 1856: "The Year closes with seemingly unusual cares and anxieties on account of the great amount of sickness prevailing in the church, consisting of measles, of which we have had over 30 cases, with heavy influenza's and cough, besides two cases of insanity and the increasing helplessness of several of the aged" (258–59).

As well as having these health problems, the *Record* indicates, the community had participated in several "missionary trips" in 1856. Most had been to Providence, Rhode Island, and had succeeded in bringing back converts or seekers to the North Family, Canterbury's novitiate clan. The year-end review summarizes: "We have had some addition to the Society the past year. Several families of the Spiritualists gathered from Providence, bringing their own and other children with them" (258–59). Two references to the Canterbury-Providence pipeline and the spiritualists appear among the notes recorded prior to the review. On October 26, a Sunday, "The church marched to the North Family door yard to hold a meeting with both families and some of the Providence spiritualists" (256). The November 6 entry records: "Sally Ceeley and Eldress Betsey Hastings return from Providence, accompanied by one man two women and six children. Spiritualists" (257). Described as "spiritualists"—a term that suggests their affinity for Shakerism—the seekers did not all remain and may even have contributed to communal conflict. Blinn writes of the interaction with the Providence spiritualists: "This was our introduction among the Spiritualists and since the above date [July 24, 1856], have been introduced to nearly every phase of spiritualism and but little benefit has been derived" (115).[24]

Information on the Providence spiritualists and the illnesses—the only two areas mentioned in the year's official review—indicate that the Canterbury Shakers struggled in 1856 to maintain their spiritual fervor amidst communal changes, including losses of loved ones. Who would better know the struggles with illnesses than one such as Emeline Kimball, who worked in the Infirmary? Certainly Kimball was not the only Shaker to maintain such meticulous records as the *Obituary Journal,* but during this period she would want to temper the excessive and destabilizing changes with the orderly and explanatory record of Shaker losses.[25] Most significant among these losses driving her to initiate the *Journal* is that of the mentor Kimball has worked with for several years.

One of the 1856 letters lists Brother Thomas Corbett, primary physician at Canterbury, as recently impaired. According to the letter, "Corbett experienced a paralytic shock a few weeks since which has greatly impaired his mental and physical capacity. He is unable to perform any labor or even to dress himself without help, but can walk about some, yet requires constant attention." Kimball's relationship to Corbett and her capacities and abilities as a writer emerge in a signed piece following the close of a letter from Corbett to Brother Cha[u]ncy at Wisdom's Valley (Watervliet, New York). This document, one of the only records of Kimball's verbal work, other than the *Obituary Journal,* suggests that she was esteemed enough by leaders to have traveled away from Canterbury and was asked to write for Corbett during his illness. She begins her postscript to Corbett's dictation: "As I copied the above for brother Thomas, and seeing a blank left, I feel very earnest, (though I would not be burdensome,) to fill it up." Kimball's desire to fill the page may be ascribed to Shaker thrift (but using paper frugally was common in the world as well); it may mark merely a desire to write, which she also fulfills in the act of keeping the *Obituary Journal.* Her use of the humility *topos* ("though I would not be burdensome") may be attributed to Shaker spirituality or to nineteenth-century "True Womanhood," but the writing *is* a self-assertive act. Kimball gives her motivation in the phrases that follow. She desires to fill the page, for according to her, "so great is my love, attachment and gratitude for all in Wisdom's Valley, that I am pleased with every opportunity to speak with them." Her love and gratitude for Believers in another community emerges in part from her visits there, just as Hollister experienced "ecstacy" among Believers of other communities. But she also reaches out to "Brother David and the beloved physicianses [*sic*] sisters," to whom she sends her "love and blessing" in order to compensate for the dislocation she feels among the losses at Canterbury.

Kimball's extant writing—the letter and the *Obituary Journal*—blur the boundaries between public and private; they are both communal expressions and personal expressions. Especially in the *Obituary Journal,* we see glimpses of a Shaker writer deeply embedded in the work of maintaining the communal identity of Shakerism during a period of change. Kimball's writing act grounded her position during years of transition and change at Canterbury. For Kimball the ritualized, mechanical copying—rather than the creative, expressive composition of memorial verses—grounded her physically and contributed to her spirituality. Her stance was one planted in scientific as well as spiritual realms, which for the Shakers were open to males and females. Kimball's stance depended upon the physical demands of the present, yet she acted in the present by looking to the past and hoping in the future.

THE ELEGIAC TRADITION AND THE VERSES AT CANTERBURY

Emeline Kimball's movement from the present struggles into the past and, through the writing act, into a vision of the future mimics the pattern of the Shakers' elegiac verses and of elegies in general. The Shaker poetry of the *Obituary Journal* differs little from popular poetry of the period; its sentimental, hackneyed images and regular rhyme and rhythm may distract contemporary readers from the emotional impact of the ritual of which it is a part. Undoubtedly the rather predictable style lead William Dean Howells to write in an *Atlantic Monthly* article of 1876 that Shaker poetry is "hardly up to our literary standard," using "our" to refer to his audience of elite readers. Placing the poetry within its communal context, however, we grasp a literary standard that differs from the one Howells applies to Shaker verse.

My reading of the Canterbury manuscript verses as ritualized writing and reading acts that provide consolation and unity necessarily draws from studies of the elegiac tradition. Peter Sacks explains that elegies since the Classical period have tended to maintain a ceremonial or ritualized structure that emphasizes performance—that is, the present moment—and "draws attention to the mourners or cast of mourners," otherwise known as the "speaker" and the "audience." Elegies demonstrate a movement on the part of the speaker from confusion, denial, and grief that focuses on the past to acceptance and consolation through a vision of the future. In Christian elegies, the consolation is often marked by a vision of the deceased in heaven. The performative element and movement emerge from pre-Christian "rituals associated with the death and rebirth of vegetation gods," which mimic the natural cycle of death and rebirth. The speaker's descent into a figurative or literal dark and mysterious underworld is followed by an ascent from the crisis into light and revelation. The speaker moves from submission to natural forces to psychological or spiritual mastery of them.

The mourning speaker of elegiac verse achieves mastery through several poetic tropes, such as questions, repetition, and manipulation of images of vegetation, water, dark, and light. Questions, for example, may express the speaker's ignorance or protest and, most importantly, channel the emotional energy of grief or rage outwardly. If directed away from the speaker or the Deity to a community, they signify an attempted resocialization from the isolation often brought about by mourning. Repetition of a phrase, a name, or even a sound contributes to a poem's ritual effect, providing continuity and stability to counter the discontinuities and instabilities confronted in death. The repetition (or even the singular calling) of a name also invokes the spirit of the deceased from the grave. Through stating the name and, on the larger level, voicing the poem, the speaker asserts his or her power and ability to fill the void left by death with a materialization in verbal form. The elegy becomes a sign of the speaker's ability to continue life. In sum, through the poetic action of the speaker's voice, substituting language for the material body, the poem achieves its consolation. The poem represents the deceased immortalized in an idealized state that provides a point of inspiration and imitation to the living individual and the larger community of mourners who are unified and strengthened through this shared, idealized image.[26] For example, Lavinia Clifford's poem to James Daniels, whose opening serves as the epigraph to this chapter, begins with questions in traditional elegiac fashion, and the poet achieves consolation through direct address to the deceased in the final lines, sending him away to the spirit world. Clifford begins with general questions (probably instigated by the loss of James Daniels) about the community and the future of Shakerism. With the direct address "Such art thou, Dear Brother" (l. 9), she turns from the general to the specific, creating a personalized portrait with details such as Daniels's office ("Deacon") and his role as a builder ("To every building thou didst lay the foundation / And framed them in order complete"). The poet has a consciousness of the withdrawal of the founding members who leave behind not only their own bodies but also the body of the community—the infrastructure of the physical community they have helped to build (literally, in the case of Daniels) and support. The questions Clifford raises are very significant ones about the ability of the physical community to live on earth if founding souls such as Daniels are gone. The direct address of the poem's close ("enjoy sweet communion / With those who have gone on before") moves from the specifics of Daniels's life to place him in the Shaker community of deceased Believers in the spirit world.

Thus Shaker elegies of the *Obituary Journal* adhere to the characteristics Sacks describes in many ways; however, they also veer from the patterns. The elegies in the *Journal* dedicated to those who died a decade or so before Kimball initiated the project adhere to the pattern of visualizing the deceased in a transcendent realm, but they tend to lack expressions of anger, questions, and grief. These absences may be attributed to the belief in the continued life of the deceased in the spirit world. The Shaker understanding of the interaction between those living in the spirit world and those living physically on earth means that the deceased, who has simply been "translated" to join the "gospel family" there, continues to be present in the Canterbury community. Grief, when expressed in the poems, does not last long.

The lack of emotional expression of anger or grief also results from the Shakers' deconstruction of the mainstream notions of family. For the Shakers the "community of mourners" provides a strong support system for the speaker, who is never so isolated in grief as her mainstream counterpart might be. The speaker quite often does not distinguish herself from the larger Shaker body. These Shaker elegies thus tend to emphasize collectivity rather than isolation. Clifford's poem, as well as many others similar to it, not only follows the convention of invoking the spirit of the deceased from the grave but also reinforces Shaker teachings about the afterlife. Communication between those of the spirit world and those still entrapped on earth in their physical bodies was not merely an imagined event of the poetic realm—a poetic convention—but a daily reality. Clifford's poem emphasizes continuity between the deceased and the living and in so doing, in addition to illustrating characteristics Sacks delineates as typical to elegies, suggests a pattern described in recent analyses of elegies written by women and other "marginalized" individuals, written since Sacks's book appeared. According to Celeste M. Schenck and Margot Gayle Backus, for example, these elegies have deconstructed and revised the genre by resisting consolation through the masculine mode of transcendence, or an illusory attempt to rise above material reality. The speakers of these elegies deconstruct the patriarchal tradition and resist resolution of grief by refusing to relinquish the bodies of the deceased through displacement of the body into "heaven" by means of poetic language. Quite often these poems make overt political statements about the patriarchal forces that govern society, and the speakers fill the voids created by the losses with openly and often hostily unresolved anger. Shaker elegies do not go to this extreme, although they may be said to refuse to relinquish the deceased by placing them in a spirit world that continues to interact with those physically living on earth.

In these two critical traditions, described by Sacks and Schenck, respectively, an elegy is either patriarchal and traditional or feminist and innovative; it either reinforces the patriarchal mode of the genre or deconstructs it. This "overly rigid distinction," according to Jahan Ramazani, "obscures the relational work in men's elegies and the dissociative impulse in women's" (1143). He requests, through his reading of the "harsh ambivalence" of Sylvia Plath's elegies, both a resistance to essentializing two oppositional categories in the reading of any elegies and an embracing of an "enlargement of the elegy's affective parameters beyond the traditional pathos, love, reverence, and competitive camaraderie" (1143). My reading of Shaker elegies finds such ambivalence in their discourse of death; the *Journal* and the poems within it echo the unity of masculine and feminine categories of their theology and their literacies. Rather than categorizing these elegies as masculine or feminine, I will demonstrate ways in which they echo and revise patterns common to the world in the mid-nineteenth century and ways in which the *Journal* entries change stylistically as the community moves forward in time.

The deconstructive features appear increasingly in poems dedicated to those who died after 1856, as they speak more specifically of the deceased, defying the anonymity and uniformity we often think inherent in Shakerism, and as they occasionally voice unanswered questions, frustration, and grief. The supportive Shaker family at Canterbury had begun to feel the effects of multiple losses by mid-century, when the *Journal* was initiated. The poets had lived, worked, and worshipped with the deceased rather than merely imagined them when hearing orally conveyed remembrances or encountering them in the spirit world. Thus the poems become more specific in their depictions of the deceased and the speakers, and they also reflect more intimate relationships between the two. Quite often these poems express more grief as a result of experiencing the physical loss firsthand. Gooden, writing about the sect's published memorials, which tended to honor leaders and serve as evangelical tools to the outside world, accurately explains that the memorial poetry "reveal[s] something about the quality of Shaker spirituality during the late-nineteenth century and, also, the relationships between the ministry and the common members" (134). Shaker memorial poems, "songs and tributes . . . gave Believers the opportunity to express, personally as well as communally, gospel affection for the deceased Believer while affirming union with one another and commitment to the Shaker Way through renewal of the Shaker covenant. The ritual of covenant renewal was necessary for maintaining or restoring gospel union among Believers" (133).[27] The introductions to the published pieces overtly state that they hope to win converts by means of the exemplary lives of the deceased, yet as Gooden explains, they also reflect personal relationships, gospel union, and covenant renewal among the community of Believers.[28] The unpublished poetry recorded in the *Obituary Journal,* even more than published pieces, reflects this spirituality and these relationships as it embodies shifts in Shaker literacies. In my readings of several of the later poems, in particular, I will continue to underline Shaker discourse, but I will also note how the materializations in them indicate unique elements of the deceased and of the poet. These poems exhibit more deconstructive tendencies and reflect the increasing feminization of the community. That is, in traditional or patriarchal elegies the idealized institution (i.e., the church or the state) provides support to the speaker as he or she reimmerses himself or herself in it; in the elegies of marginalized figures, uncertainties about or discontent with the support community cause the speaker to cling to the deceased. In the later elegies of Canterbury, the Believers who write them struggle not only with personal loss but also with uncertainties about their idealized institution.

A brief consideration of the implied audience of Lydia Sigourney's *Weeping Willow* (1847), published just nine years prior to the initiation of the *Obituary Journal,* provides a backdrop against which the dramatizations of Shaker memorial poems play before their community. In particular, the rather generic speakers, memorialized deceased, and support communities of Sigourney's poems highlight the specificity of the Shaker poems that appear increasingly as the *Journal* progresses.

Sigourney's volume enjoyed immense popularity as a gift book, designed especially to be given to the grieving. Her preface to the collection notes that mourning is best done in solitude and silence, that sometimes "the voice of even the dearest, may inadvertently touch some chord, whose vibration is anguish" (v). In contrast, "the sigh of sacred poesy steals without startling" into the solitude, eventually wooing the mourner back into the light. Sigourney emphasizes the solitude and privacy in which these poems are to be read; they console by allowing readers to read themselves and their situations into the generic imagery of the poetry. In *The Weeping Willow,* Sigourney generally erases the specificity associated with the particular deceased loved one, perhaps subconsciously dissolving the deceased into the idealized image as a part of her mourning process, or perhaps consciously considering how to make the poems most readable for her imagined audience of mourners.[29]

Although the poems may appear generic or disconnected from the deaths of particular individuals, Sigourney notes at several places within the volume the specific situation which gave rise to the poem. Below the title "Thou Art Not Him," for example, she explains that the poem was "written on seeing in the garden of a departed friend, a stranger who at a distance, resembled *him*" (83); "Death of the Original Proprietor of Mount Auburn" was "derived from a description of Miss C. F. Orne, herself a descendant of this pious man" (80); and of "The Fated Barque," she notes, "The wreck of the steamer Swallow, on the Husdon river, Monday night, April 7th, 1845." The poems' titles help to illustrate the use of both specific and idealized, or real and ideal, images in the world's elegies: "The Son of the Widow," "Student at College," "Death of a Young Maiden," "Our Oldest Man," "Death of a Lady," "The Young Missionary," "The Pastor," "The Only Daughter," "The Good Son," "Death of an Infant," and "Sister at the Brother's Grave." The indefinite articles "a" and "an" are generic, but the numerous uses of the definite article "the" indicates specificity. The implied distinction, however, does not appear in the poems. In poems with definite articles and those with indefinite ones in the titles, there are no names and few other references to a specific deceased individual. As Nina Baym has written, these poems are designed to reach numerous readers and "to make suffering people feel better" by allowing them to read their situations into the language of the poetry ("Reinventing Lydia Sigourney," 154).

As Sigourney's titles suggest, in these poems the speakers address two generic communities of mourners: the biological family and the church family. The poems "The Young Missionary" and "The Pastor," for example, invoke no specific sect's creed—the missionary and the pastor could belong to almost any nineteenth-century Christian group. In keeping with Sacks's theory of the speaker's isolation and resocialization, in Sigourney's poetry the speaking subject—the "self" of the increasingly industrialized, specialized, and isolating nineteenth-century society—through the use of first-person plural pronouns "we," "our," and "us" becomes a part of a social whole constructed and stabilized through the unifying images of idealized home and idealized church. Perhaps originally written to mark the loss of specific individuals, Sigourney's poems address a generic larger audience—a broad "church" family and a typical "biological" family. Where Sigourney's introductory remarks emphasize the comfort of reading the poetry in solitude, the Shakers perform their poems in a shared, public sphere. The right to speak and to mourn moves from the biological or the generic church family to a specific Shaker family, one physically present at the poem's performance. Family and church for the Shakers are different from those in the world. Given these primary differences, the elegiac images of family, heaven, eternal life, and the like, mean something different to Shakers; Believers hearing memorial poetry at funerals interpret the images differently than their mainstream counterparts would read similar images in Sigourney's poetry. In spite of differences in speakers and audiences and the ways in which they write and read images, the Shakers' poems are like those of Sigourney and mainstream Protestants in that they unify the community through the presentation of idealized images and they broaden the world in which the speaking or writing mourner lives, reincorporating or embracing her or him. In the poems appearing earlier in the *Journal,* the speaker refers to herself as part of the collective "we," buoyed by a stable, supportive community. As the *Journal* proceeds, the generic Shaker elements recede as specific characteristics of the deceased emerge. Likewise, the specific support community Canterbury should provide begins to be replaced by generic images of the world.

The poem to Hannah Goodrich, for example, who died in 1820, thirty-six years before the *Journal*'s initiation, inscribes ideal and typical Shaker characteristics more than images specific to the deceased. The poet Zillah Randlett could not have known the living Goodrich, but she knew the ideal characteristics of Shaker motherhood and drew from them as she wrote the memorial to Mother Hannah. Though the poem opens and closes traditionally with an invocation of the muses and a call to the community of mourners to imitate the deceased, the poem's language and imagery exhibit distinctly Shaker discourse. Ann Lee appears early (l. 9) in a reference to Goodrich's "call" in youth:

When young, by Mother's gospel called,
to leave a vain and wicked world,
She freely did obey the call,
and cheerfully resigned her *all.* (l. 9–12)

Randlett explicitly designates Goodrich a "parent" and "Mother" to "her faithful [Shaker] children":

A parent kind, a Mother dear,
to all her faithful children here.
The aching heart would often soothe
with her parental tender love. (ll. 17–20)

In the lines that follow, Randlett delineates Goodrich's "holy life and precepts," in adherance to the patterns established by Lee. In addition to becoming a spiritual parent, she "resigned her all,"

Her countenance was mild, serene,
altho' her word was sharp and keen
To separate the soul from sin,
that Christ might reign and dwell within. (ll. 25–28)

Goodrich became a "minister" whose "soul was filled with truth divine" (l. 21); and, like Lee, both "her countenance" and "her word" influenced those around her, so that she was able to have others "follow [her] along the way" (l. 32).

In addition to creating an image of the deceased similar to that of the shared, communal imagery of Lee, the poem should create an image of the mourning speaker as well. However, other than her name at the poem's close, Randlett is practically absent from the poem. Her voice is dissolved in the collective voice of the Shaker community she knows so well. In the first line, for example, as Randlett invokes the "heavenly muses" to "lend" their "aid," she displaces both the expected preposition and object of the aid ("to me") from herself to the deceased. She writes: "Ye heavenly muses, your aid here lend / in honor of a worthy Friend" (ll. 1–2). And then, near the poem's close, Randlett chooses the plural "we" to indicate the community that will collectively review Goodrich's "life and precepts": "Her bright example we review, / her holy life and precepts too" (ll. 29–30). The elegiac speaker's turn from isolated self to community or a collective voice is a traditional sign of consolation and emergence from grief, yet in Randlett's poem the mourning "I" never appears. Other than the ineffability *topos* (often associated with expressions of mourning) expressed in ll. 5–6—"No pen of mortals e'er can paint / the worth of this beloved Saint"—the poem lacks any other verbal signs of mourning. Two reasons explain the lack of grief: First, the Shakers have no doubt, as the final lines indicate, that Goodrich is in "that abode . . . Where holy Saints and Angels sing." Second, Randlett wrote the poem thirty-six years after Goodrich's death. Goodrich represents only an ideal being; Randlett's attachment to the deceased is a distanced one.

Other elegies within the *Journal* written for those who died several years prior to 1856 similarly demonstrate a lack of anger, doubt, or grief. For example, B. J. Kaime's poem to Emma Leavitt, who died in 1822, opens with confident imperatives: "Open heaven's portals wide / To receive a soul well tried / Let her sit by Mother's side" (ll. 1–3). One might argue that these imperatives reflect the speaker's need to speak through and over uncertainty or confusion. On the contrary, the poem demonstrates a clear inversion of the elegiac convention of movement from questions to answers and an imperative *envoi*. Another inversion occurs in references to the deceased's body, which usually appear near an elegy's opening. Here they appear in the final stanza: "Tho' the body see decay / Death be written on thy clay" and "As we bear the dust along, / To its bed so lowly" (ll. 17–18, 23–24). But in this final stanza the poet also refers openly to "grief" and "mourn[ing]," only to reason that these emotional expressions should not exist because as the first two stanzas illustrate, Emma Leavitt lives eternally in heaven.

A similar inversion appears in the second stanza where "natural" images of vegetation (falling leaves, a blown rose, a broken branch) do not indicate loss but appear as signs of the deceased's and the mourner's power and control. This stanza also interestingly intertwines elegiac conventions and Shaker imagery:

> Taste my Sister sweet repose,
> Such as in her garden grows;
> Pluck the lily and the rose
> Of delightful flavor.
>
> O'er the hills of gladness skip,
> From the fount of goodness sip;
> Eat that fruit which never yet,
> Had an earthly savor.

Here the imperatives, addressed directly to the deceased, reinforce the traditional pattern of the speaker gaining and revealing mastery of the loss by becoming the actor rather than one acted upon. And the poet-speaker has the deceased consume fruit and flowers at their prime rather than describing vegetation in decay. The imagery of "Gospel family" ("my Sister sweet") is combined with reflections of Shaker interests at mid-century, when Believers gave each other imagined or "spiritual" gifts of fruit and flowers and hiked "o'er the hills" of their communities to the "holy founts" where they had outdoor worship. The poetic speaker has Leavitt continuing the spiritual activities she and other Believers participated in on earth, summarizing in the final stanza, "Dissolution [of the clay] paves the way / To a world of glory" (ll. 19–20).

Even poems written to those who died unexpectedly in accidents during the years prior to mid-century reflect the Shakers' assurance of eternal life; such providential events do not raise doubts as they might in the world. For example, B.J. Kaime's poem memorializing John Rowel, who died in 1822 after being thrown from a wagon, follows the traditional pattern of movement. It begins with specific incidents about the deceased, using the natural image of a bird and its unnatural death brought about by an unheeded fowler, and it closes with the transcendent image of the deceased in heaven, sitting down to "Mother's feast." As in the other poems, the speaker, who refers to herself only with the collective "our," appears to be buoyed both by Shaker theology of a resurrection life that begins with crucifixion of the flesh on earth and by a supportive church family.

The poems dedicated to those who died closer to mid-century begin to break some of these conventions by expressing more emotions and by giving more specific references to the deceased's life. This shift reflects the poets' more personally felt senses of loss and the increasing individualism in Shaker literature at that time. The poem memorializing Deacon Francis Winkley, who died in 1847, for example, breaks the typical patterns. In addition to informing us of Winkley's activities in both the world and the Shaker community, it reveals information about the particular poet, Asenath Stickney.

Stickney employs the rhetorical device *occupatio,* a preoccupation with a topic the speaker claims will be ignored, by implicitly comparing Winkley to three secular successes. She states that he should *not* be likened to Daniel Webster, John Calhoun, and Henry Clay: "To whom shall we like this venerable one / To Webster the Orator to Clay or Calhoun? Not to these, not to these with their high sounding name" (ll. 1–3). Of course, by being a Shaker and not of the world, Winkley was worthy of more honor than these three, his contemporaries involved in the nation's political affairs, since by 1856 the reputations of these men of the world were somewhat tarnished. (Webster and Clay, both orators and statesmen, died in 1852; and Calhoun, lawyer and vice president of the United States under Andrew Jackson, died in 1850.) As a Shaker deacon, Winkley was in a position that allowed and demanded interaction with the world, and from his journal we learn that he, too, was involved in politics and public speaking, as he testified in court. This interaction, filled out by details of Winkley's journal, also appears in the poem's last two stanzas.[30] Stickney depicts Winkley thinking and speaking in court: "In the Courthouse of justice where worldly men ruled / Thy mind was consulted, & thy word oft controlled" (ll. 15–16). Thus, Stickney selects appropriate images to delineate characteristics unique to Winkley; additionally she uses discourse characteristic of the Shakers at mid-century. These images abound in the second, third, and fourth stanzas, where she distinguishes Winkley from Webster, Calhoun, and Clay. The phrases "Zion," "United Body," "worthy parent," and "the fruit of thy labors" and the image of the tree reflect Shaker discourse. "A fountain of love" draws from the Shaker image prevalent during the Era of Manifestations, when trips to holy sites with their imaginary fountains were frequent rites of worship. (At Canterbury, the site was known as Pleasant Grove). In the poem's final stanza Stickney displaces the customs and laws of Webster, Calhoun, Clay, and the secular courts with "Shaker Customs and laws."

Stickney reveals that she knew more of the world than Winkley's interaction with it, possibly gleaned from his journal or from oral tradition. Although the poet lived most of her life as a Shaker (she came to Canterbury at the age of four, in 1830), she also knew something of her nation's politics (seen in the references to Webster, Clay, and Calhoun) and her culture's rhetoric. In addition to using *occupatio,* a technique Stickney may have picked up through oral or written culture rather than overt training in rhetoric, she uses the term "encomium"—referring to a formal expression of praise—at the end of the first stanza. Further, the overall form of this piece demonstrates her grounding in the rhetorical arts. Stickney was one of the Canterbury schoolteachers (she served from 1855 to 1861 and from 1866 to 1880). She may have taught speech or rhetoric, she most likely read a lot of poetry, including occasional and didactic verse, and she probably had her students read and memorize it as well. Thus the poem adheres very closely to traditional elegiac form, seen, for example, in the opening question "To whom shall we liken"; repetition: "Not to these, not to these"; direct address: "Thou wert noble"; an *envoi:* "Go then worthy parent"; and a call for imitation of the deceased: "And be our endeavors, / To copy thy goodness." A poem written by another Shaker might have mentioned Winkley's interaction with the world, but it may not have done so in the same way.

The *Journal* entry devoted to William Dennett, who died in 1858 after falling from a building, also reflects the relationships between poets and deceased. Two poems, by James V. Chase and Asenath Stickney, respectively, both include more specifics about the deceased and more expressions of confusion and grief than poems devoted to those who died earlier. Stickney and Chase follow traditional elegiac patterns of the world and of the Shakers, but their tributes to Dennett exhibit the characteristics that appear increasingly in the poems written for those who died around and after 1856. Both Stickney and Chase employ the ineffability *topos.* Chase begins,

> How feeble are words to portray the emotions
> Which obtain in our midst;—moving every heart
> Consequent on the exit of our brother William
> With whose mortal presence, death calls us to part. (ll. 1–4)

Stickney, after attempting through several lines to praise Dennett, concludes, "Too much cannot be said / In thy praise dear brother; Yet words are / Powerless and unavailing" (ll. 30–32).

In addition to acknowledging the powerlessness of words, Stickney's poem opens with several unanswered questions directed to "Death," that "mysterious messenger": "Why was it? Did we not appreciate / The prize once ours? Did we not know what / Could be lost in losing William?" (ll. 5–7). She also includes references to Dennett's singing voice, which personalize him:

> . . . we no longer list
> To the deep-toned voice, that eloquent in
> Praise of our Heavenly Father was often
> Raised in seasons of divine worship
> And now silent in death! (ll. 16–20)

In this moment of praise, she quickly stops herself from erecting a verbal memorial too ornate or extraordinary:

> . . . Oh devoted brother!
> We need not rear the perishing marble
> To perpetuate thy memory; Worth
> Excellence love and faithfulness combine
> To form a monument Kings & Princes
> Cannot boast. A monument which will
> Resist decay. Ah and outlive the stately
> Obelisk of Darian or Grecian
> Marble; lettered with the most glowing
> Eulogy suggested by mortal man. (ll. 20–29)

This movement suggests her awareness of the Victorian world's patterns of memorializing and the Shakers' conscious decision to resist it—perhaps instigated by biblical verses, and perhaps by secular events such as the opening of the garden cemetery in Concord, New Hampshire, Canterbury's nearest city.

The Shakers' resistance to the world's burial patterns of course emerges from their belief in the eternal life of the spirit world and in the spirits' abilities to communicate with those living physically. These beliefs appear in the poems not only through images of the deceased in the spirit world but also in inscriptions of their voices. These voices may be read as consolations to the living that the spirits are on their side or as a tacit recognition of the growing weakness of the community, who will have to count on the dead rather than the living for help with evangelism and conversions. Zillah Randlett's poem to Nancy Bacon opens with questions about Bacon's early death (at twenty-two years), but by line 6 the speaker confidently sends the deceased off to the spirit world: "Be as it may, in peace repair / Beyond this vale of toil and care" (ll. 6–7). Then Bacon's spirit explains to the living:

> In wisdom I was called away,
>   To leave the transient things of time
> And dwell in fairer worlds sublime;
>   I am not free from wit and care,
> The cross of Christ I still must bear,
>   To find a mansion with the just,
> A treasure free from moth and rust,
>   So farewell friends in purest love
> With you in union I will move.

Bacon's message (inscribed by Randlett) reveals that she continues to work in the spirit world and that her work is "in union" with those still living physically. Randlett's doubt or uncertainty about the help of those in the spirit world emerges nonetheless, even as she works to certify it through the poem, for Bacon's message is preceded by the phrase "*Methinks* the spirit seems to say" (l. 9, emphasis mine).

In Mary Wilson's poetic tribute to Marion Montague, who died in 1879, Wilson completely silences the speaker (the living mourner) and gives voice throughout the poem to the deceased (the living spirit), who addresses the would-be mourners. The poem opens, "Dearest friends, I still am with you, / Working for the heavenly prize" (ll. 1–2). Marion's avowal may be read as a statement that she continues to be with the living, who are "Working for the heavenly prize." She offers them a "blessing / From her spirit store of wealth," and she "speak[s] a word of cheer" to them (ll. 11–12, 14). Or the opening avowal may be read as a reflection of the Shaker belief that the deceased continue to work and to progress to perfection in the spirit world. The latter would especially need to be expressed in Marion's case, since her death at age nineteen prevented her signing of the covenant and allowed her less time than Believers such as Winkley to "progress" while in her physical form.

Several poems written to those who died after 1856 rupture the pattern of less personal memorial poems written to those who died earlier by referring specifically to the relationship between the poet and the deceased. For example, in Mary Whitcher's poem dedicated to poet Lavina Clifford, who died in 1857, Whitcher refers to the speaker (or herself) in the first person rather than with the collective "we" which is typical of the more generic earlier poems:

> My helpful sister, patient friend,
> At length has passed away,
> I've seen her childhood, youth, & all
> Up to the present day. (ll. 1–4)

As the poem continues, Whitcher expresses the love between the two as different from that among herself and other Shakers, a break from the teachings of the Millennial Laws, which discouraged special friendships or relationships:

> I own her mortal, tho my love
> For her was strong; sincere,
> But nothing more than the return
> Of what her heart did bear.
> She loved me too, beyond deserts (ll. 5–9)

Whitcher seeks to justify this unique love by using it as an ideal she hopes to share with all her Shaker family:

> In like may love inspire my soul
> For all my gospel kin,
> To think no ill, but love them all
> Thus their forebearance win. (ll. 13–16)

Yet she returns in the poem's close from this statement of aspired love for all her Shaker family to that unique love between herself and Clifford, which she visualizes continuing in the spirit world:

Take this [poem] enwrapped in purest love
A gem from heaven's store,
Ere long we meet beyond, above,
To love and part no more. (ll. 21–24)

Marcia Hastings's poem dedicated to Emeline Kimball also reveals the close relationship between speaker and deceased. The second stanza concludes: "We've been companions from our youth, / One year, toiled side by side" (ll. 13–14). The "toil" Hastings and Kimball have shared for one year we gather from Canterbury records and the poem's first stanza, where Hastings comments,

How many souls and bodies too
You've nurtured, vivified;
"Beloved Physician" many years,
And true as sun and tide. (ll. 5–8)

Hastings turns from a use of "we," which refers to her relationship with Kimball, to a more collective "we" in the second stanza: "Your helping presence still we ask, / Nor ever would divide" (ll. 15–16). Hastings's plea for Kimball's "helping presence" reflects the belief that those living in the spirit world continue to help the few remaining alive. The plea for Kimball's undivided state could refer to the unity of her spirit to her body, or it could refer to Hastings's unwillingness to divide Kimball's attention or love to share with those in the spirit world.

Asenath Stickney's poem to Mary Acton, who died at age fourteen in 1861, also reveals the relationship between the poet and the deceased by using the singular first person rather than the collective Shaker "we": "A mournful feeling o'er me steals as silently I view / The vacant desk where Mary sat not many months ago" (ll. 1–2). The poem unabashedly opens with sorrow, instigated by Stickney's relationship with the deceased. We understand from words such as "desk" and "my darling little scholar" (l. 9) the relationship to be that between teacher and student. As the poem continues, Stickney speaks of Acton's ability to influence her, the teacher on earth, while the young scholar continues to progress in the spirit world.

Though to thy earthly presence I'm forced to bid farewell
I trust they gentle influence will rest upon me still.
Thy every upward tendency proclaims to me this truth
"Eternal progress thine shall be, no blight shall check thy growth"
Go then and grace the spiritland thou bud of promise rare
E'en as a flower shalt thou expand in life & beauty there. (ll. 11–16)

Like these poems expressing personal relationships between the speaker and the deceased and continued progress in the spirit world, poems dedicated to those who died accidentally or unexpectedly after the *Journal*'s initiation at mid-century mark a point of departure from others in the *Journal*. They express more uncertainties, unanswered questions, and judgments, and they have a more narrative pattern. Though not uncommon in the world in this period (Simonds and

Katz Rothman), the need to make narrative the events of death in a type of ballad form indicates ambivalent feelings about the deed and its consequences. S[usan] Whitcher's lengthy poem memorializing Clarissa Morrison, which includes many more specific physical details and much more emotion than do the earlier poems, exhibits this need to narrate the life and death. It opens with allusions to the specific situations surrounding Morrison's youth and unexpected death.

> When bowed with age, or worn by toil and care
> Our active powers bereft of natural tone;
> We welcome death as a kind messenger
> To call the spirit to its untried home.
> But when it comes an unexpected guest,
> To chill the vitals of a youthful friend
> It brings a sadness one cannot repress
> To see the cords of life so quickly rend.

The date of Morrison's death, 1859, indicates Whitcher wrote out of her own immediate emotions, rather than from a mediated story of a Shaker of an earlier generation. Thus result the self-reference and expression of sadness—she uses "one" rather than "we" to refer to herself (l. 7). However, when the speaker asks in the second stanza, "Ought we to murmur, or repine at this?" (l. 13), she quickly turns the emotion with the rhetoric of a second question of spiritual transcendence: "Or shall we plant our happiness so high / That resignation fills us with such bliss / We can behold a loving Sister die?" (ll. 14–16). Whitcher answers the questions implicitly throughout the remaining three stanzas, where she falls into the traditional pattern of re-creating the deceased's "virtuous traits" and calling the living to "imitate" her.

In these three stanzas that attempt to emphasize a transcendent spirit, however, Whitcher continually refers to the deceased's body, its significance to the community, and the significance of other Believers' bodies to the spiritual community. The third stanza opens,

> Not on a bed of sickness was she laid,
> Wasting away as heavy hours rolled on—
> but walked among us with familiar tread . . .
> Until the purple current issued forth. (ll. 17–19, 20)

The poem's closing states: "May we be mindful of the 'outer man' / Preserve it in good health as stewards wise." The emphasis on preserving the physical body emerges from a concern for the immaterial, spiritual body, but the elegy under-scores the integral relationship between the two. Whitcher first suggests the importance of the physical body in the second stanza, where she refers to Morrison, at the time of death, as "just in the strength and bloom of womanhood / When every faculty we might deem ripe / To honor God and do the greatest good" (ll. 10–12). In Shakerism, of course, the "bloom of womanhood" does not include a woman's "ripeness" for bearing children and mothering biological offspring. Yet her physical loss would be felt more acutely in a community beginning to worry about the proportion of able-bodied adults—essential to the community's necessary labor—to children and aged members.

Another example of the need to make narrative appears in the poem devoted to the fourteen-year-old Henry Mead, who drowned after testing the ice. The poem implies Mead unnecessarily hastened the movement to "the other side." The community probably would have been ambivalent about Mead's eternal life, since he was neither a child nor a covenanted Believer. Because of the scandals and accusations surrounding the deaths of their charges at Enfield and Canterbury, Shakers might also have been conflicted about their responsibilities for the death.[31]

Two other poems to those who died unexpectedly also mark confusion. Brownson's poem devoted to Achsah Gross breaks the patterns of those within the *Journal* even in its physical appearance on the page. The section that should give the "reason for death" in 1849 is notably absent; the poem, however, suggests suicide. In the first half of the sixteen-line poem, the speaker raises four questions that remain unanswered in the second half:

> What are we poor feeble worms
> Of mental powers bereft
> O why should souls in human form
> To such rash deeds be left?
> . . .
> What was the cause alas? why should
> She to this deed be moved? (ll. 1–4, 7–8)

The questions do not ask merely why death, but why this particular kind of death? In the poem's second half, "this deed" becomes a "rash act" that Achsah committed. The Canterbury *Historical Record* fleshes out the unwritten narrative suggested in the poem. Henry Blinn notes that Achsah Gross was appointed Eld[er]. S[iste]r. of the Second Family on February 28, 1838 (260), and then "removed on account of ill health" less than a year later, December 22, 1838 (261). She remained in the Second Family until her death eleven years later, at the age of seventy-four. In another record, he includes a transcription of the "Coroner's Inquisition," which states that

> those charged to inquire for the state, when, how and by what means the said Achsah Gross came to her death, upon their oaths do say that on the morning of the 5th day of September, 1849 between the hours of one and two o'clock the said Achsah Gross left her place of residence and proceeding eastward about one fourth of a mile to a mill pond owned by the Shakers in said Canterbury, then and there voluntarily and feloniously did kill and murder herself against the peace and dignity of the state. (*Church Record,* 86)

Drowning was not an uncommon means of suicide used by females in the nineteenth century. However, in addition to revealing a similarity between Shaker Sisters and the world's women, the transcription's mere appearance in Blinn's work much later in the century bills the event as an anomaly at Canterbury. (Written records indicate only one other suicide in the community, Henry Hathaway's, in 1908.)

Although the state's legal language, recorded in Blinn's work, clearly labels Gross's death a crime against the state, the Shaker stance toward suicide is not so clear. Remarkably, John Whitcher's official Church Journal, which was a day-to-day account rather than a retrospective history like Blinn's, does not comment in 1849 on Gross's death. Perhaps he refrains from recording the suicide because his record is primarily concerned with the Church Family rather than with the Second Family of which Gross was a part. However, the families were so close physically, it seems more likely that Whitcher consciously decided not to inscribe her death in the record because he had conflicted responses to it. "Normal" Shaker apostasy perhaps could be accepted more easily than suicide. Willfully turning away from the Shaker life to win worldly possessions such as spouse and children was an action that made some sense; willfully leaving life on earth was another matter. The Shaker attitude, as reflected in the poem surrounding Gross's death, appears to revolve around the good use of what had been given individuals. The speaker softens the "deed" she describes as the "rash act"—namely, Gross's responsibility for her own death—in several spots. She presents Achsah as victim, as acted upon rather than primary actress. Although the acting agency is left unstated, the speaker explains, "She to this deed [was] moved" and "to this rash act was led" (ll. 8, 11). The speaker also says that Gross was "left" to the "deed," which occurred in an "unguarded hour" (ll. 4, 12), phrases that implicitly place responsibility on Gross's caregiver. References to Gross's mental state—"of mental powers bereft" and "Twas when that slender mental thread / had failed and lost its power" (ll. 2, 9)—also soften the act. Brownson shifts the focus from questions about suicide to questions about insanity and free will, which culminate in the speaker's closing prayer,

> O may I keep . . .
> My mental faculty,
> that I may ever sense and know
> What God requires of me. (ll. 13–16)

Gross's life and its end serve as motivators to the speaker, as is common in other memorial poems. However, the deceased is not depicted in the spirit world. Perhaps the writer had problems imagining her living eternally.

The poem written after the second Canterbury suicide, almost sixty years later, presents slightly different treatment of the deceased's act. S. F. Wilson's poem dedicated to Henry Hathaway in 1908 gives no glimpses of the reasons for his death. As Wilson begins the poem, the questions rise to the surface and float unanswered throughout:

> Sometimes the darlings of our God,
> Seem past our finding out
> Ofttimes His great and wondrous works
> Encompass us about.

We plan for long and happy life,
With household friends most dear
We ponder not the coming days,
Our hearts have ne'er a fear.

We wake, to find our loved ones gone,
They're passing on before,
We failed to hear the Angel call,
Unto the other shore.

Here the deceased and his death are presented in a much more positive light than in Brownson's poem to Gross. An implication of the first line is that Hathaway was a "darling"—a favorite or a loved one—of God, perhaps because he's been called to the spirit world rather than left behind. The closing two lines' references to "the Angel call" and "the other shore" imply that Hathaway's spirit lives there with the Angels. His death and departure are considered, according to the first stanza, "great and wondrous works" of God. God is clearly the agent; any blame for Hathaway's death is displaced from him or his support community to God. The overall emphasis of the poem is on the loss of loved ones through death in general rather than on the suicide of a specific individual. The penultimate line, "We failed to hear the Angel call," may be read as the speaker's small sense of blame, since the living Believers "failed to hear" the deceased's interactions with the spirit world. However, the overall thrust is not one of guilt for the death and doubt about the deceased's eternal state but one of loss and general uncertainty about the future of Shaker's living physically at Canterbury.

A primary reason for the differences in the two poems pointing to suicides is the historical context of each; these poems reflect the shift in the *Obituary Journal*'s ritualized work as it moves from its initiation in the mid-nineteenth century through the numerical decline of the twentieth century. Wilson's poem, typical of the poems of Volume III, contains few references that might be called uniquely Shaker, a mark of the Canterbury Shaker's increasing interaction with the world's literature and theology. God in this poem is masculine, and the angel who calls from "the other shore" could be beckoning one from any Christian sect. Volume III includes transcribed poems by secular poets such as Henry Wadsworth Longfellow and Harriet Beecher Stowe, demonstrating the increasing blur in the boundaries between the world and the sect. (Poems about death that appear in *Cedar Boughs* also reflect this more ecumenical vision.) Gooden provides another explanation for these shifts. She suggests that in poems where deceased and poet knew each other more intimately, which would have been the case in the twentieth century, the covenant renewal "is expressed less ritualistically, less formally, and less didactically" (167).[32] Certainly Volume III breaks the prior ritualized format in many ways. Sometimes old Shaker hymns are transcribed instead of a new poem, and on one occasion an "old" poem is used—the Shaker poet whose name was given with the piece had been deceased for several years. Prose pieces, rather than poems, begin to be written and included. Also, miscellaneous notes appear as epigraphs, postscripts, and marginalia much more frequently than in the earlier pieces: "Casket taken to Blossom Hill, Rev. Lamb, Concord, until May 18th" (27); "Funeral service conducted by Rev. Mr. Fitzpatrick" (35); or "Second Alto in Qui Vive Quartette, she had a rare voice" (38).

The description of the work, as noted on the volumes' title pages, also indicates the changes within the Society and the accompanying changes in attitude toward the *Journal.* Volumes I and II describe the poetry as "a passing notice to each [deceased] one." In Volume III the reference becomes a "Memorial Tribute to Each." The former more openly suggests direct address to the deceased, indicating that spirit communications were more popular at mid-century than they were in later years (although the belief in spirit communications continued, by 1856 at Canterbury they had slowed considerably). The former, written during what some have called the peak of Shakerism, indicates no overt need to memorialize (though of course, the need existed); whereas the latter, written in the midst of years of numerical decline, does. These twentieth-century Shakers seem to have accepted the numerical decline and to be more willing to overtly memorialize the deceased with poems from the world.

The works individually and as a collection mark, in typical elegiac fashion, the rising generation taking the torch from the older generation, attempting to seize power and master forces otherwise overwhelming and disheartening. In the early years of the *Journal's* compilation, the ritualized composition and transcription fulfilled an immediate need to counter losses and uncertainties. As years progressed, the *Journal's* use continued to be of importance as a ritual or habit that stabilized living mourners in the face of a particular death. However, it and the other funerary rituals it accompanied reflected the Canterbury Shakers' embracing of the Christ Spirit at large. By imagining the world as full of believers in Christ's Second Appearing, and by incorporating the world's funeral and literary rituals, Canterbury Shakers sustained themselves and their community in the face of individual and private losses.

NOTES

1. For information on Kimball, see Henry Blinn's *Church Record,* Vol. I (1784–1879), (256). The "Physicians' Journal" kept by Susan Myrick at the Harvard community beginning in 1843 shows that both men and women served in the "Physicians' Order" through the 1820s, and only Sisters served in the "order" until 1843 (OClWHi V-B:41). Hunt also wrote in *Glances and Glimpses,* "In each of their societies a woman is set apart as a physician, because they believe she has a peculiar gift in that direction" (230). Suzanne Thurman discusses Shaker women's progressive uses of medicine at the Harvard and Shirley, Massachusetts, communities as illustrative of the sect's interaction with the world's intellectual debates as well as their blurred gender boundaries ("The Order of Nature, the Order of Grace," 160–65).

2. Ann Douglas writes that "the authors of consolation literature were intent on claiming death as their peculiar property . . . a place where they would dominate rather than be dominated. . . . [I]t was crucial to the rationalization and exploitation of their status that they inflate the significance of death, dilate heavenly time and compress earthly calendars,

stake out a property in territory where claims were by definition untestable" ("Heaven Our Home," 68). Mid-nineteenth-century mourning "is still intended clearly to foster spiritual development, but a curious kind of exhibitionism seems to be doing the work formerly expected of the rituals of self-scrutiny"; it is a "therapeutic self-indulgence" ("Heaven Our Home," 57). She also writes that clerical-feminine biographies mark a celebration of the individual rather than an acknowledgment of human limitations as earlier spiritual biographies and other social histories do. Social historians "were always concerned with the individual, but they refused to sever him from the context of historical change which both created and overcame his heroism" (*Feminization,* 189). In contrast, the clerical-feminine works "contain a therapeutic indulgence in the power of the individual" (*Feminization,* 189–90). They are dislocated from history or time.

3. See Brewer ("'Tho' of the Weaker Sex,'" 628–35) and Stein (*Shaker Experience,* 256–72).

4. See especially her first two chapters (17–43).

5. Brewer calculates that at Canterbury in 1840 there were 103 males and 157 females; in 1850, 85 males and 163 females; in 1860, 82 males and 159 females; by 1870, the numbers had decreased significantly to 54 males and 123 females. In 1840, 62 of the 258 Believers were sixty years or older; in 1850, 37 of the 248 Believers were sixty years or older. In 1840 there were 72 Believers age fifteen through twenty-nine; in 1850 there were 76; in 1860, 68; in 1870, 51; and in 1880, only 38 (*Shaker Communities,* 235).

6. Evans raises this question at the opening of the fourth section, "Funeral Reform," of a fifteen-page pamphlet entitled "Shaker Sermon: He is Not Here" (Richmond, 637). No publication date appears on the piece, but the title pages refer to the "sermon" being delivered in 1886 at the funeral of John Greves of the North Family, Mount Lebanon. This final section of the pamphlet appears to be a revision of his "Shaker Burials" (1877) and his "Rational Funerals" (1878).

7. A thorough social history of death in nineteenth-century England is John Morley's *Death, Heaven and the Victorians.* He examines the "theatricality and drama" surrounding death, which follows from the tradition of the execution sermon; the material objects, such as gloves, candles, and tea sets, associated with mourning; graveyards and rural cemeteries; debates over disposal methods; and the influence of scientific progress and spiritualism upon funerary rituals. On death in American culture, see Jessica Mitford's *American Way of Death;* Martha V. Pike and Janice Gray Armstrong's *Time to Mourn;* and David E. Stannard's *Death in America,* which includes a bibliographic overview as well as eight essays. Lewis Saum suggests that "intimacy" with death because of high mortality rates and lack of institutional services for preparing the dead was a primary reason for the nineteenth-century preoccupation with death. He explores letters, diaries, and journals in an attempt to re-create "Death in the Popular Mind" (Stannard, 30–48). On the rural cemetery movement see Stanley French, "The Cemetery as Cultural Institution" (Stannard, 69–91); Donald Simon, "The Worldly Side of Paradise" (Pike and Armstrong, 51–66); and John F. Sears, *Sacred Places* (99–115). On mourning portraiture see Phoebe Lloyd, "Posthumous Mourning Portraiture" (Pike and Armstrong, 71–87). On mourning costume, see Barbara Dodd Hillerman, "Chrysallis of Gloom" (Pike and Armstrong, 91–106).

For discussions of scrapbooks and the literary traditions surrounding mourning rituals, see Norma Johnsen, "'Our Children Who Are in Heaven'"; Barton Levi St. Armand, *Emily Dickinson and Her Culture;* Ann Douglas, "Heaven Our Home"; and Wendy Simonds and Barbara Katz Rothman, *Centuries of Solace.* Twain's Emmeline Grangerford appears in Chapter 17 (137–41). In his introduction and first chapter St. Armand describes the scrapbook and the quilt as domestic "art[s] of assemblage" that influenced Dickinson's poetry.

8. In his bibliography of the Winterthur collection of Shaker documents, Richard McKinstry describes several that sound similar to the *Obituary Journal*. For example, between 1856 and 1860, Isaac Newton Youngs kept a record (W 861) that contains a list of "Casualties among Believers," including deaths, fires, drownings, suicides, floods, and what are called "woundings." These casualties occurred at many Shaker communities between 1797 and 1853 (206). Angeline Brown's sixty-page volume of essays and poetry (W991) contains "many . . . pages [that] carry recollections of Shaker funerals.—probably maintained by more than one person" (233). An eight-page bound manuscript hymnal from Hancock, *ca.* 1835 (W 885), contains "Elder Nathaniel's funeral hymns" and "Mother Dana's funeral hymns" (212); the South Union, Kentucky, community preserved "Eldress Molly's funeral hymn" (W 971) from 1835 (228). Of a thirteen-page bound hymnal, *ca.* 1876 (W 919), McKinstry writes, "Most of the hymns in this manuscript were written for or sung at Shaker funerals, 1813–1876" (218). McKinstry also describes several manuscripts (W 1055, 1056, 1060, and 1068) of funeral addresses and sermons (253–55).

The Shaker periodicals—*The Shaker, The Manifesto,* and *The Shaker Manifesto*—published obituaries and memorial poems from the 1870s through the 1890s. These appear with increasing frequency and length as the century progresses, marking the sect's concern with the losses.

A collection of poems called "Facts and Gems" by Edith Green, written ca. 1898–1912, reflect the continued tradition. Among the eighteen entries, two are memorial poems. One of these is dedicated "To Eldress Dorothy [Durgin] and Eldress Joanna [Kaime]," who died in 1898. Green also records "Lines received from Eldress Joanna / March 16, 1901," where Kaime's voice addresses those physically living. The poem manifests Shaker belief in communiciation between the spirit world and the physical world, even after the turn of the century.

9. I extrapolate this section from Rotundo's essay, which describes not only funerals and cemeteries but also "laying out" of the deceased.

10. Job Bishop's funeral is described in Whitcher's *History,* 151–54. Henry Blinn writes that Bishop's funeral, "contrary to the usual custom of Believers, was made public" (*Shaker Manifesto,* May 1882, 103).

11. Notably, the speakers—Elder Micajah Tucker, Elder Benjamin Whitcher, Elder John Whitcher, Elder John Lyon, and Elder Elisha Pote—were all male. This phenomenon could reflect a backlash of male authority after Mother Lucy Wright's death in 1821, or it could signify the male-to-male friendship bonds within the community. Since friends spoke on behalf of friends, it is not surprising that male communal leaders would speak about Bishop.

12. For an example of a funeral hymn, see Andrews (*Gift,* 102).

13. Daniel Patterson's *Shaker Spiritual* is the comprehensive text on Shaker hymns. Thurman describes the importance of the hymn writing of Eunice Wyeth in "The Order of Nature" (157–60). See also Stephen Marini (*Radical Sects,* 156–71).

14. Although Gooden makes these points about late-nineteenth-century Shaker memorial poems in Chapter 6 of her dissertation (132–72), analyzing the phrase "Mother in Israel" as a unifying concept for female Believers, the poetic ritual unifies male Believers as well. She writes, "The memorial service was also the ritual whereby a female Shaker was symbolically transformed, through poetic tributes, eulogies, and songs, from Eldress to 'a mother in Israel'" (133). She also explains that "the Shaker practice of printing memorials as broadsides and including memorials in letters was common during the seventeenth and eighteenth centuries in New England." Like the Puritan funeral elegy, the Shaker memorial "combines portraiture and exhortation in honoring a departed Believer or 'saint'" (134).

15. In some funerals of the world, a poem that speaks about death in general terms rather than with specific references to the death, such as William Cullen Bryant's "Thanatopsis," might be read. For example, several of the journal-keeping attendees of Emily Dickinson's funeral in the rural, western Massachusetts town of Amherst in 1886 noted Colonel T. W. Higginson's reading of "Immortality" by Emily Bronte (Leyda, 474–76).

In his analysis of elegies, Sacks emphasizes the dramatic and performative work of the genre. Thus he refers to the community in which the speaking mourner eventually reimmerses him or herself as the "cast of mourners." His first chapter, "Interpreting the Genre: The Elegy and the Work of Mourning" (1–37), sketches the dramatic conventions.

16. The Shaker funerary ritual, like other communal practices, could have changed drastically over the years. The "feminization" of Shakerism after mid-century and the longstanding "feminist" cast of the Shirley community (Thurman, "Order of Nature") could be said to contribute to the open sharing and spontaneity of this particular service. But because Howells's description affirms accounts of other services, I would argue that the spontaneity, openness, and affection has changed only in intensity.

17. A pamphlet documenting the consecration of the opening of the Blossom Hill Cemetery in Concord, New Hampshire, very near to Canterbury, records William L. Foster speaking of such marked family bonds in 1860: "Here then, to-day, we found this City of the Dead. . . . Behold already the lines and boundaries of its sacral homesteads marked out upon the turf—household sanctuaries, wherein, one by one, day after day, the broken families of yonder living city shall be gathered together" ("Religious Services and Address of William L. Foster"). The 1860 establishment and consecration (Lyford, 456) corresponds closely with Kimball's initiation of the *Journal*.

18. Robert P. Emlen notes that charts and maps of Shaker villages were generally kept by males who were teachers and elders, whereas females created spirit drawings (16–19); he does not refer specifically to cemetery charts.

19. Some of the *Journal's* poems are unsigned, some are marked only by initials I have not been able to attribute to particular Shakers, and some are by poets "of the world." Poems by the latter (Harriet Beecher Stowe, Henry Wadsworth Longfellow, and James Russell Lowell, for example) are dedicated to those who died in the twentieth century.

20. Kimball's role among the sick, dying, and deceased was a common female role of the nineteenth century. Cynthia Griffin Woolf's biography of Emily Dickinson explains that women were expected to become "trained" watchers at the death and sickbed (Chapter 1).

21. Shaker Henry Blinn gives dates to the era with the title of his *Manifestation of Spiritualism among the Shakers, 1837–1847*. White and Taylor write in one instance that the era spanned 1837–1844 (163). On another occasion they write that the manifestations lasted about ten years (222). Yet they emphasize that spiritualism has always been a significant part of Shakerism (219–52). Andrews implies that the period ends in 1850 by closing his chapter on "Mother Ann's Work" (152–76) with an 1850 quotation from Youngs, who wrote, "We are satisfied that this form of communion with the spirit world is not for Believers in our faith" (175). Sasson avoids discussing closure dates by focusing on the 1840s, when the era "culminated . . . with the appearance of Holy Mother Wisdom" ("Individual Experience," 45). Stein delineates the period loosely as "beginning in the late 1830s and extending into the 1850s" (*Shaker Experience,* 165), but he cites "the standard account of the period [which] begins with the report of some extraordinary behavior among 'a class of young girls, ten to fourteen years old,' in the Gathering Order at Watervliet, New York" who began to manifest unusual "trancelike activities" (165). "No single event," he writes, "marked the close of the revival period. . . . The commitment to spiritualism, in fact, never disappeared completely" (183). He cites Andrews's *People Called Shakers* (152) as unnecessarily "heighten[ing] the distinctiveness of the revival period" rather than

recognizing the continuities it has with earlier Shakerism. Flo Morse describes the period loosely as "during the late 1830s and . . . into the 1850s" (173).

22. For a thorough discussion of the concerns and conflicts of the revival throughout Shaker communities, see Stein, *Shaker Experience*, 165–84. At Canterbury, Durgin and Blinn took over as "second" Elder and Eldress in 1852. Durgin became first Eldress in 1857 and James Kaime became first Elder the same year.

23. Canterbury correspondence for 1850–1859 included in the Western Reserve Historical Society collection consists of 111 items, but only three letters from 1856 (IV A 3–8, Reel 17). Other "health" reports follow in this letter, including the gory, bodily details of Elder Sister E. Sharp's recovery from a compound fracture of the lower leg.

24. Blinn's 135-page "Diary of the ministry's journey to New Lebanon and Groveland via Worcester, Pittsfield and Hancock, and return via New York City, Providence and Boston" from 1856 could provide interesting insights to the leadership's attitude toward these spiritualists. Blinn's notes on Peter Ayers suggest the conflicts as well. Ayers "had a full acquaintance with Mother Ann and all the Elders, and was an active minister among the evangelists" (I, 143). Blinn writes later, "It was surprising to many that Peter could make such a radical change. Among the lighthearted, he was the lightest hearted. At feasts and at parties he was always at home and could dance till nearly all had left the floor. As a boxer he would be obliged to go far to find his equal, and even after he embraced the faith, it was not safe to offer him or his gospel friends an insult" (200, 219). Blinn also describes him as "a great reader [who] obtained a fund of information" and the founder of "the hatter's trade" at Canterbury—perhaps he was a "mad hatter." In the *Report of the Examination of the Shakers of Canterbury and Enfield, before the New Hampshire Legislature* (1849), which resulted from accusations that the Shakers beat the boy George Emory to death, several witnesses testify that Ayers was gagged and beaten by other Believers, instruments to native spirits, because he did not agree fully with them; he lived by himself on the margins of the community; and he "tried to express his opinion" (17, 25, 57–58). These records suggest the conflicting views Believers at Canterbury had during the 1840s and 1850s as they worked through the world's spiritualism and concerns of the sect.

25. From 1853 to 1855 at Canterbury, for example, just prior to the initiation of the *Journal,* someone kept a "Record of the Quantity of Fluid Drawn from Mary Jane Thurston who had a Tumor" (OClWHi, V:B-5).

26. On nineteenth-century verses, Norma Johnsen has argued, drawing from "simple psychology," that journals and scrapbooks about death, and in particular the numerous poems that depict the deceased in a comfortable heaven, provide consolation by "mak[ing] what is feared into something attractive" (80). Though focusing specifically on poetry written by grieving mothers (published in *Godey's* and other popular nineteenth-century periodicals) that deals with the loss of infants, Simonds and Katz Rothman have also argued that the primary role of this type of literature is consolation, regardless of any larger cultural impact or role it had or played (21). Sacks also draws from psychoanalysis but adds to it linguistic theory and the history of the genre to provide a thorough structural and "dramatic" analysis. See especially his first chapter.

27. The "gospel union" she is most interested in is that of female Shakers during the late nineteenth century. As she writes, "Memorials help to provide a clearer understanding of Sisters' relationships with one another, and the meaning of spiritual motherhood as demonstrated by the female leadership and denoted by the phrase, 'a Mother in Israel'" (134). She summarizes: "The ritual of symbolically transforming an Eldress to 'a Mother in Israel' offers some sense of spiritual security to aged female leaders who have dedicated their entire lives to the Society and, perhaps, need some reassurance in the sect's declining years that the Shaker Way and the principles of 'Mother' will continue. The memorial highlights a cult of

devotion surrounding Mother Ann, Mother Lucy, and all subsequent Mothers in Israel" (170).

28. On published poems as evangelical tools, see also the introduction to *Mount Lebanon Cedar Boughs*.

29. My approach to these poems differs from Nina Baym's, who classifies Sigourney's elegiac verse into three types: "reflective memento mori poems deriving from some general observation in nature or the world"; "generic, or situational, elegies, whose subject is denoted as a member of a class rather than an individual"; and "elegies for named persons—memorial, or obituary poems" ("Reinventing Lydia Sigourney," 153). I appreciate the distinction Baym makes between types of verses about death, yet her most important point, with which I agree, is about the ways in which Sigourney's poems were read. As Baym summarizes, "The memorial poem that forms part of the public occasion of the funeral and is then used, reused, and adapted by successive groups of mourners who find it pertinent implies" active readers, rather than antebellum women readers as the "isolated and passive consumers" Richard Brodhead has described (154).

30. Winkley records in his journal entry for October 4, 1810: "Fisher Lyon & I (*viz.*) Francis Winkley went to Enfield—the 8*th* we went with Deacon Nath'—& others to Haverhill to attend Court in a Case against John Heath who Wished to Brake our Covenant, But did not succeed. the Law Suit cost us besides our time $71.00" (51). And according to Henry Blinn's *Church Record,* Winkley spoke "in behalf of the Society" before the New Hampshire legislature in 1828 when "a bill was introduced praying that the Shakers might be forced to do military duty" (79).

31. See note 23 above.

32. In her discussion of memorials to Dorothy Durgin and Joanna Kaime, "special companions" and leaders at Canterbury, she writes, "The differences in structure and style in the two memorials highlight the difference in the status of the two Eldresses" (166). Sister Joanna's lacks a description of the service and poetic tributes, and the prose tributes included, except for one, were written by Sisters. "Compared to the Lead Eldress, an associate Eldress was more intimately involved with the family in various situations in their daily lives" (168).

Chapter 7

Private Acts and Possible Worlds: Shaker Literacies at the Turn of the Century

The noblest conceptions in literature, art and music are yet to come,
from intellects clarified by spirituality . . .

Anna White and Leila Taylor,
Shakerism: Its Meaning and Message, 1904

In 1904 the Shakers published Anna White and Leila Taylor's *Shakerism: Its Meaning and Message* (1904). White and Taylor's work, like that of Emeline Kimball, Alonzo Hollister, Rebecca Jackson, Richard McNemar, and John Dunlavy, demonstrates that the authors favor "improvement" and "progress" in the intellectual and literary realms even while they believe in the presence of an active, living spirit. Thus analysis of their text in this concluding chapter offers views of consistent elements of the Shakers' literacies while it exemplifies the ever-present differences among individual Shakers, whose personal experiences and interests contribute to quite diverse writing and reading styles and abilities. White and Taylor's high levels of alphabetic literacy and their highly self-conscious attempts to preserve Shakerism through written records address this book's central questions and mark the changes in Shaker literary practices since the sect's inception by an "illiterate" female more than a century earlier. In their text these Eldresses of the North Family at Mount Lebanon, New York, point to the importance of ecstatic gifts and the spirit's interpretive and creative work while they illustrate the importance of reason, of education, and of alphabetic literacy. They do so by describing the past to fit the present—providing a revisionist history—and by imagining a positive future. They present, in spite of fragmented or individualized practices present among Shakers and in communities elsewhere, a vision of a world whose inhabitants are unified by desire to achieve higher spiritual planes.

The work's full title does not indicate the women's futuristic vision, which emerges in the final chapters, but it does suggest the text's historical slant: *Shakerism: Its Meaning and Message*; *Embracing an Historical Account,*

Statement of Belief and Spiritual Experience of the Church from Its Rise to the Present Day. In addition, it indicates that White and Taylor view "spiritual experience" as having been a consistent element among Believers since their earliest days. This consistent element marks the progressivism of Shakerism that recurs throughout the text—in the retrospective accounts of Ann Lee and the Shakers' early years, as a credo of the present, and, finally, as a rhetorical tool that could win converts in this "new age" of religious beliefs and biblical criticism. Roughly the first half of the 417 pages provides a chronological history, with sections on the founders and brief sketches of each communal site. In these chapters White and Taylor prepare the ground for their final exhortation by emphasizing the Shakers' progressivism. In an aptly titled chapter, "Yesterday and Today (1865–1904)," White and Taylor create a narrative bridge to the remaining chapters that, organized topically, focus on theology and spiritual gifts. The Shakers' theology of the spirit will allow for their future growth.

Critics who have discussed the work in any detail—Stephen Stein, Priscilla Brewer, and Kathleen Deignan—emphasize the influence of the world and the physiological changes (such as numerical decline and feminization) occurring within the communal body upon the text's evangelical thrust. Stein describes the outward directedness of the text as largely due to the concerns of its authors, who are part of a line of female leaders (in the latter part of the nineteenth century) who turned their concerns from "the needs and concerns of their own sex within the society." Unlike their forebears of earlier years, they "took seriously the social and political implications of the Believers' religious views" (*Shaker Experience,* 263). They were involved with vegetarianism and other dietary and social reforms, believed in the new sciences and their compatibility with religion, and explored the spiritualism of the world. Brewer describes the women as "ideological heirs of Elder Frederick Evans" and believers that the sect "had a vital contribution to make to twentieth century America" (*Shaker Communities,* 200). According to her their "progressive departure from traditional beliefs and practices" was necessary for continuance of the sect. "Stressing Shaker success in communalism over its evangelical, Christian roots, they pointed to a long list of accomplishments that demonstrated Shaker relevance to the twentieth-century world, including: brotherhood of man, communism, rights of labor, sexual equality, protection of animals and children, pacifism, temperance, health food and sanitation, and personal freedom. They felt that this shift in emphasis was necessary if Shaker influence in the world was to continue" (*Shaker Communities,* 201). Deignan emphasizes spiritual life and theological changes rather than other sociological impacts upon these women: The "radical changes in the intellectual climate of America . . . introduced by the new sciences of psychology, sociology, and evolutionism, and the newly developing critical study of both the Bible and comparative religions . . . posed serious problems for the churches, challenging as they did the previous assumptions about, and modes of understanding, the Christian faith" (208). As Deignan points out, White and Taylor's emphasis on the spirit's work, a reaction to contemporary forces, plays a crucial part in the traditional and innovative aspects of their text. They reach back to Shakerism's past to describe their pneumatology, yet their descriptions allow them to provide a new vision of the Church.[1]

The first pages of White and Taylor's work attempt to bring together the oral and the written as elements of spirituality. The volume's epigraph, for example, sets the tone by emphasizing reading: "Let him that readeth understand." Following Lee's example, White and Taylor innovatively rework Scripture with this epigraph. Jesus prefaces his teachings on many occasions with an emphasis on orality and aurality: "Let him who hath ears hear" (Matthew 11:15, 13:9, 13:43, Mark 4:9, 4:23, 7:16, Luke 8:8, 14:35). This book's epigraph, like Jesus' remark, suggests that not all who receive the text will understand, yet it also marks the move in Shakerism from Lee's aurally received teachings to the predominance of inscribed texts.

The authors begin their revision of Shaker history in the opening as they retell the story of Ann Lee, underscoring her illiteracy and her spirituality: "There is something here worthy of consideration. Ann could not read and the sermons, the whole body of divinity, as well as the philosophy, religious and infidel, of her time, were of no use to her; she knew not even their names. Church and clergy helped her not. She turned from them, for they lacked the knowledge and power of salvation" (18). The passage demonstrates White and Taylor's belief in personal knowledge of and relationship with the divine in a period when organized religion had been taking a beating by "enlightened" thinkers. They continue: "The conditions of her problem were few and simple. She, an unlettered woman, burdened with her sins, was one of a lost race; God, the Creator, was on high and to Him she went. There was no doubt, apparently, of His being, nor of His power to grant her requests" (18).

White and Taylor clearly want to debunk the myth that Shakers are behind the times, repressed and limited in their thinking. They summarize at one point, "Shaker[ism] . . . is but another name for 'advanced Christianity'" (379). Through their history and discussion of Shakerism in the present, White and Taylor want to counter the argument that Shakerism attracts only people with severe personal "deprivations," people who can neither think independently nor support themselves financially. Of the "deprivations," they write:

The conclusion arrived at by a well-known writer, that communism is successful only among people whose misery is so extreme that any change is for the better, and therefore the hard straits of communistic life are agreeable because they have known so much worse, can hardly be accepted by Shakers, a large proportion of whose members come from homes of comfort or luxury and who, in most cases, are quite equal to holding their own in the competitive ranks of the world's industrial army. (297)[2]

White and Taylor partially counterbalance Lee's economic and educational deprivations, discussed in their first chapter, by devoting a good bit of the remaining text to defending the importance of intellectual endeavors, education, and reading and writing of inscribed texts within Shakerism.

In a section on Shaker schools, for example, they describe Lee's stance toward education in a positive light: "Mother Ann Lee, although unschooled, recognized, as does everyone who is taught of God, the necessity of training and developing the higher intellectual and spiritual faculties. Her famous maxim, 'Hands to work and hearts to God,' has always meant to her people work of the brain as well as the fingers" (132–33). No such explicit interpretation of Lee's quote appears in the *Testimonies* or elsewhere in Shaker documents that I have seen. Throughout this section they similarly exonerate the sect's educational practices in the years after Lee's death.

White and Taylor attempt to revise Shakerism of the past with attention to the religious, political, and intellectual concerns of the world at the turn of the century. Discussing the sect's hermeneutic, they argue that their attitude toward Scripture corresponds with and even preceded the present popular "Higher Criticism." As they do so, they contradict their comments about Lee's emphasis on the "work of the brain": "While not, as a people, learned or scholarly; while, with individual exceptions, unversed in ancient languages and in laws of historic and literary criticism, they have, from early times, held nearly the same ground, in general principles, that the world of scholars is slowly attaining through the long upward climb of critical investigation known as the Higher Criticism" (329). White and Taylor conclude with references to revelation existing apart from Scripture, an age-old Shaker teaching: "Shakers have always distinguished between the Bible and the Word of God. To them, the Word of God is not a book, but the Christ Spirit, ever uttering, ever revealing God,—the Invisible, the Unknown, and to the finite being the Unknowable, save as the Christ Spirit, Son and Daughter, who is in the bosom of the Father-Mother, has declared and manifested, God" (329).[3]

As another sign of their progressiveness in the realm of literacy and literature, these women draw from their own experiences in the Mount Lebanon, New York, community to describe such educational activities as the "Self-Improvement Society," created in 1891 among the "young sisters." According to its records as White and Taylor restate them, the Self-Improvement Society's aim was "harmonious development of being, physical, intellectual and spiritual, unity of sentiment and individuality of expression." The Society was also to "establish a radical improvement in habits and manner, address and conversation and the cultivation of the mind in substantial, beautiful and interesting things" (212–13). Although these aims were stated as the goals of one particular group—the Sisters at the North Family at Mount Lebanon rather than all Shakers everywhere—they provide an articulation of ideas the writers believe Shakers had exemplified from their earliest years and which influenced their writing and reading practices.

The method for achieving these aims within the Self-Improvement Society was adhering to a set of rules, which included avoiding the use of "all manner of slang, by-words, extravagant expressions . . . and encouraged the use of grammatical language and correct pronunciation" (212–13). These sorts of external controls—here expressed only with regard to linguistics—may seem to work against one of the Society's aims: "unity of sentiment and individuality of expression." White and Taylor's statements contain elements unique to this historical period of

Shakerism; though "individualized self-expression" was practiced during much earlier periods, it was not a frequently expressed goal. How could individuals express themselves freely when constricted by such societal limitations? Without explaining how, White and Taylor summarize the success of their group, "*original* work of a superior stamp resulted from this earnest effort at self-education. The efforts of this society have been very apparent in the manner, thought, address *and writing* of the class engaged in it" (212–13, emphasis mine). The Self-Improvement Society's emphasis on "substantial, beautiful and interesting" subjects also marks a turn in direction from earlier years of Lee's leadership and Seth Young Wells's oversight of Shaker schools, when "usefulness" was the determining standard for judging the appropriateness of literary and educational activities.

White and Taylor's revisionary remarks about their literary practices make Shakers appear little different from the rest of the world at the turn of the century. But the authors are well aware that, in the world's eyes, "Shakers have sometimes been regarded as averse to literary and artistic efforts" (319). Rather than ignore accusations outsiders have made about textual repression within the sect, White and Taylor, like many Shakers before them, rise to a defense, asserting "this estimate is hardly a correct one" (319). In a chapter entitled "Literature—Worship," they explain reasons for shifts in writing and reading practices. Because Shakers of earlier days were occupied with temporal concerns and devotional exercises, for example, they did not have time to "engage in literary or artistic enterprises" (319).

White and Taylor's revision of the past and description of the present with regard to literary endeavors inevitably turns to the spirit's role, the element that distinguished their literacies from "the world's." They write, for example, "In seeking the highest possible spiritual development, Shakers have left behind much in art and literature commonly regarded as of value, yet, in this very renunciation, in attaining purity of life and thought, they have developed a pure, refined, spiritual taste, eminently fitting them for the appreciation of the highest in art and literature" (319). Although the women imply that spiritual development is the Shakers' ultimate goal, they never explicitly define the spirit or spirituality. They obliquely suggest some definitions, however, through other discussions in their text. In the description of the Self-Improvement Society, for example, they divide "being" into "physical, intellectual and spiritual" parts. They distinguish the being's physical nature from its mind, or intellect, but this is more than a simple reiteration of the mind-body split, for they provide a third term—the spirit. Distinct from both mind and body, the spirit is an integral third part of a being. The spirit for them is not, as it was for John Dunlavy, the mind or the reason, which makes "man" like the divine. Nor do White and Taylor place the spirit and the intellect above the body. Rather, according to them, Shakers seek and sought a "harmonious development" of the three. "Harmonious development," White and Taylor explain, could be achieved through "improvement in habits and manner," which include "address and conversation." That is, attention to the body's activities—its habits—would contribute to development of both mind and spirit.

The authors also delineate what they mean by "spiritual" in their continued attempt to show themselves familiar with (and as knowledgeable as) the world as well as distinct from it. They write, for example, "While Shakers have little sympathy or affiliation with those coarser phenomena characterized as spiritism, seldom visit seances and have held themselves aloof from the spiritualistic development of the times, they have watched with full sympathy the unfolding of a purer, higher type of manifestation and recognize with hope and pleasure the gradual evolution of a portion of mankind to whom the world of spirit is a living reality" (249). This "higher type of manifestation" they refer to as "Higher Christian Spiritualism" (250), perhaps an outgrowth of Emersonian transcendentalism. They later conclude that "the widening vistas of the modern spiritualistic philosophy are outgoings from the life that started in spirit manifestation in 1758" (387). The Shakers' openness to ecstatic or mystical spiritual gifts, established by Lee and her generation of followers, allowed such Believers as Rebecca Jackson and those at Canterbury to experiment with the spiritualism of the world in mid-nineteenth-century America. White and Taylor's stance in 1904 marks a movement away from ecstatic gifts toward a philosophical belief, such as that of transcendentalism, in a universal spirit.

Throughout their work the authors attempt, as did the early doctrinal writers, to build a bridge between the unlearned and the learned, which the world might classify as spiritual and secular, respectively. But for White and Taylor the bridge is the active and living spirit, which involves itself in learning and in literary endeavors. In their closing exhortation to possible converts, they propose a question potential Believers might ask: "What of literature, art, music—must I abandon these?" Their eloquent answer, from the Shaker perspective, underscores individual freedom as well as responsibility. Those who desire spiritual heights will read and create artistic pieces that emanate beauty, truth, and harmony:

Here is the most noble freedom of all. What do you desire, license to roam through every miasmatic swamp or deadly fen of putrid imaginations? Then will you find true love for your soul's health forbidding. But do you want to breathe pure airs of lofty ideals? Do you want the breadth and height of God-enkindled thought? Is it the expression of absolute harmony for which your soul yearns? Then, with those whose lives are attuned to God and truth, will you find freedom and encouragement, not only to enjoy the works of masters, but yourself to create, if touched by the *creative spirit* of beauty, truth and harmony. (388, emphasis mine)

Finally, they conclude with an emphasis on progress and future development: "The noblest conceptions in literature, art and music are yet to come, from *intellects clarified by spirituality,* from lives attuned to purity, holiness and love. In this development of the aesthetic, as well as the intellectual nature, the principles of Shakerism open the noblest of opportunities and invite to the grandest efforts" (388, emphasis mine). With closing exhortations such as this one, the women's text exudes a positive perspective and hope for the future.

In their final two chapters, "A Look into the Future" and "A Message to Shakers," they continually emphasize the immense possibilities and unknown future of Shakerism, calling Believers to action and prospective converts to open themselves to the progressive work of the spirit. Using the imagery of contemporary geology and Darwinian thought, for example, they explain and exhort: "Nor from the accomplishments of Shakerism in its primal epoch, its era of foundation laying, can its later evolutions be foreseen. Sufficient to know that it holds the great substratal principles of truth—purity, harmony, eternal growth. Then, from the knowledge of what God has wrought in nature, enter into intelligent, sympathetic and responsive receptivity, and place yourself in the line of highest ultimate development"(388–89). For White and Taylor, this line of development depends upon spiritual reading and writing. Although their intellectual pursuits differ significantly from Lee's—they are open to the numbers and kinds of texts people may read and write—like Lee and many other Believers, they continue to uphold the spirit's role in interpretive and expressive acts.

The polished prose of White and Taylor's published volume, like the methodical poetry of the *Obituary Journal* and Alonzo Hollister's rambling, reflective "Reminiscences," emphasizes the spirit's work. As Hollister and Canterbury poets look back, they gather and preserve the "presence" of former Shakers such as Rebecca Jackson and Philemon Stewart. These female authors, however, go beyond retrospection to look forward, prophesying with force an impending "new age" of Shakerism. Rather than turning merely inward to the Shaker collective body, these women turn outward, wanting to embrace the world and share their understanding of spirituality with it. Their public gesture, describing Shakerism at the turn of the century, transfers the bodily work of Lee to textual form. Yet there exists another story about the personalities that created the book's concluding positivism. Taylor provides another perspective of the final chapter in her *Memorial to Eldress Anna White & Elder Daniel Offord.* She writes that White, apparently disturbed by the text's extreme optimism, felt "the whole truth had not been told. The cause of its [Shakerism's] temporary failures had not been portrayed. She seized the pen in hand and in a trenchant, but terrible indictment, declared the tale of unfaithfulness, blight, mistake, and wrong. These passages, the strongest in the book, embodied in the last chapter can be readily recognized" (qtd. in Richmond, I, 209). In spite of Taylor's perspective, to outsiders this chapter has the voice of a jeremiad, calling Shakers to change and be more outwardly focused; it does not appear as scathing as Taylor sees it.

Taylor's comments, however, remind us of the answers to the questions that initially drove this study. What role did reading and writing play in each one's spirituality? In what ways was each influenced by the sect's female leadership? And what impact did the bodily experiences of these Believers have on them? These two women, well read and highly literate, had distinct opinions and personalities, yet they undertook a collaborative venture, unified by their belief in the ideals of the institution. Because White and Taylor similarly viewed Lee's embodied spirituality, they were able to read and write in ways that upheld Shakerism. Certainly their collaboration must not have been too different from the 1816 *Testimonies,* compiled by several men with diverse personalities. Undoubtedly brothers-in-law John Dunlavy and Richard McNemar, producers of a dense theological tract and a narrative history, respectively, did not completely agree on the types of texts most suitable for potential converts to Shakerism. Dunlavy chose to appeal to reason and draw heavily from Scripture, whereas McNemar decided to provide an "eye witness" account. Most likely their opinions of Lee herself were not in total accord. Yet these men, like Rebecca Jackson and Emeline Kimball at mid-century and Alonzo Hollister in later years, found in Lee's example stories of spiritually informed literacy that drove them as they produced their own texts and faith stories. The Shakers' openness to multiple kinds of literacy, informed by spirituality associated with neither minds nor bodies exclusively, allowed them to develop spiritually as they reached out to others—those close at hand, those reached by traveling, or those who might encounter published texts.

This study closes with White and Taylor's published text, not because spiritual literacies ceased supporting the Shakers but because the most drastic changes in literary practices seem to have occured during the sect's first century of existence. The collecting, cataloging, and describing of the sect's material artifacts, including their vast literary productions, by such admiring outsiders as John MacLean and Edward Deming Andrews pointed to the question of the sect's continuance even while it attested to White and Taylor's optimistic belief that Shakerism would continue to be manifested, though perhaps in new forms. In spite of the continued numerical decline and the closing of several villages throughout at least the first half of the twentieth century, Shakerism *has* continued in new forms; I trust the study of Shaker literature and literacies similarly will continue, especially with an emphasis on the past century. The archives are ripe with as yet under evaluated materials of this period.

One example is *The Shaker Quarterly,* which began in the early 1960s as the sect began to manifest signs of another revival period. The periodical, like the periodical publications of the late nineteenth century, became an outlet for personal expressions and a communal voice. The publication, which continues today, consists of articles on contemporary concerns and events, scholarly histories, and reprints of nineteenth-century imprints and manuscripts. Thus it serves the community as well as those outside the sect. Initiated in 1961 by Theodore Johnson, the publication of *The Shaker Quarterly* also reflects the sect's continual conflicted attitudes toward tradition and innovation, or progress. Johnson, a graduate of Colby College and Harvard Theological Seminary, became an active part of the community at Sabbathday Lake, Maine, just prior to the death of Delmer Wilson, the only other male Believer at the time. Johnson helped establish the library as a working archive for researchers, and he pushed for continued literary development. Johnson's thrusts (and perhaps the social climate of America in the 1960s) brought in new Believers, but they caused some older ones to distinguish themselves as "true Shakers," part of a communal movement that had come to a close.[4] Following Johnson's lead, however, more recently converted Believers at Sabbathday Lake continue to practice the Shaker lifestyle.

Undoubtedly the entrance of radio, television, and most recently the Internet have contributed to new forms of Shaker literacies in the twentieth century. Believers carry on the literary traditions discussed in this book; they continue to read, write, and publish inscribed texts for themselves and for the world, and they deserve to be examined in their own right for what they may teach us about the relationships between technology and literacy in religious communities at the beginning of a new century. White and Taylor's *Shakerism: Its Meaning and Message* manifests the spirit's work within and around both human bodies and inscribed texts at the end of the last century. My prediction is that Shaker literature and literacies of the twentieth century will demonstrate a continued belief in embodied spirituality like that of Ann Lee, which will make Believers' bodies and lives among the most important texts anyone may read.

NOTES

1. Stein describes the text as both "history and theology" (*Shaker Experience,* 266) and "an exercise in apologetics" (267). He writes that the history section "celebrated in detail the accomplishments of the Believers" (266) and is "the most comprehensive historical statement ever written by members of the society" (267). See also (268, 306, 322–23). Brewer writes that the text was "the last major Shaker public statement" and "was a substantially progressive manifesto" (*Shaker Communities,* 200). Stein, Brewer, and Deignan recognize the text's generic function as a history—it gathers the past to serve the present's concerns. Stein writes, for example, that the text "was one with the missionary effort launched by the Society in the 1860s and 1870s because it attempted to extend the influence of Shakerism outside the boundaries of the community" (*Shaker Experience,* 267). Deignan also attributes the revision to "the undeniable pattern of diminishment" within the sect. Although the numerical decline "provoked pessimism among some Believers, it also provoked the characteristic spirit of Shaker optimism among others. . . . To these, decline was seen as heralding a greater rebirth of spiritual life in the world at large, in which Shakers were to play a critical and essential role. Indeed, these Believers would insist that the new spiritual life of the larger world, seen as evidence of the ever increasing eschaton, might require their own near extinction. From this liberal perspective a reinterpretation of Shakerism's role in the eschatological designs of God would emerge, orienting their vision all the more in the direction of pneumatology" (199).

2. The "well-known writer" to whom they refer is probably Charles Nordhoff, whose *Communistic Societies of the United States* appeared in 1875 with a lengthy section on the Shakers.

3. They quote from progressive Shaker Elder Frederick Evans to reiterate their point: "Said Elder Evans:—'Bibles are records of the utterances of Divinity—records of God's word. . . . All Scripture records of Divine inspiration help to reveal the power and wisdom of God to mankind; and they should be preserved, studied and interpreted by the light of a present, living revelation, as that includes the whole focal light of all former revelations'" (329).

4. See Stein for details about Johnson and the schism between Believers at Canterbury, New Hampshire, and Sabbathday Lake (*Shaker Experience,* 384–94).

Works Cited

PRIMARY SOURCES

Alcott, Louisa May. *Little Women*. 1868. Franklin Center, PA: Franklin Library, 1982.

Ashbridge, Elizabeth. *Some Account of the Fore Part of the Life of Elizabeth Ashbridge*. *Heath Anthology of American Literature*, 2nd. ed. Vol. I. Ed. Paul Lauter. Lexington, MA: D. C. Heath, 1994. 596–607.

Bates, Paulina. *The Divine Book of Holy and Eternal Wisdom, Revealing the Word of God*. Canterbury, NH: United Society, 1849.

Blair, Hugh. *Lectures on Rhetoric and Belles-Lettres*. Facsimile Imprint. 2 Vols. Ed. Harold F. Harding. Foreword David Potter. Carbondale: Southern Illinois University Press, 1965.

[Blinn, Henry C.]. *Church Record*. Canterbury, 1784–1879. [Vol. II]. NhCa ms. 764.

Blinn, Henry C. *A Historical Record of the Society of Believers in Canterbury, NH. From the time of its organization in 1792 till the year one thousand eight hundred and forty eight . . . East Canterbury, 1892*. Vol. II [Vol. I?]. NhCa ms. 763.

[Blinn, Henry C., et al.]. *Church Record*, [Canterbury], 1872–1889. NhCa ms. 22.

Briggs, Nicholas. "Forty Years a Shaker." *Granite Monthly* 52 (Dec. 1920): 463–474; 53 (Jan. 1921): 19–32; 53 (Feb. 1921): 56–65; 53 (Mar. 1921): 113–121.

Brown, Thomas. *An Account of the People Called Shakers*. Troy, NY: Parker and Bliss, 1812.

Bunyan, John. *The Pilgrim's Progress from This World to That Which Is to Come. The Second Part*. 159–303. New York: Dodd, Mead, & Co., 1968.

Burroughs, Stephen. *Memoirs of Stephen Burroughs*. Hanover: Benjamin True, 1798.

Coffin, John. *Copy Book*. 1823?, 1833. MeSl ms. Box 23.

[Collins, Sarah], comp. "Memorial of Sister Polly C. Lewis." Mt. Lebanon, 1899. R 471.

[Cummings, Ada S.], comp. *In Memoriam, Sister Aurelia G. Mace, 1835–1910*. Portland, ME: 1910.

Douglass, Frederick. *Narrative of the Life of Frederick Douglass, An American Slave, Written by Himself*. Boston: Anti-Slavery Office, 1845.

Dunlavy, John. *The Manifesto, or A Declaration of the Doctrines and Practice of the Church of Christ*. 1818. New York: Edward O. Jenkins, 1847.

Dyer, Joseph. *A compendious Narrative, elucidating the Character, Disposition, and conduct of Mary Dyer, from the Time of her Marriage, in 1799, Till She Left the Society Called Shakers, in 1815*. Concord, NH: Isaac Hill, 1818.

Dyer, Mary Marshall. *A Portraiture of Shakerism*. Printed for the Author, 1822.

Edwards, Jonathan. "A Divine and Supernatural Light." *Heath Anthology of American Literature*, 1st. ed. Vol. I. Ed. Paul Lauter. Lexington, MA: D. C. Heath, 1990. 527–540.

———. "A Faithful Narrative of the Surprising Work of God." *The Works of Jonathan Edwards*. Vol. 4. Ed. Clarence C. Goen, 1972. 144–211.

———. "Treatise Concerning Religious Affections." *The Works of Jonathan Edwards*. Vol. 2. Ed. John E. Smith, 1959. 91–461.

Elkins, Hervey. *Fifteen Years in the Senior Order of Shakers: A Narration of Facts, Concerning that Singular People*. Hanover, NH: Dartmouth Press, 1853.

Evans, Frederick. "Rational Funerals." *Shaker Manifesto* 8 (June 1878), 130–31.

———. "Shaker Burials." *American Socialist* (Oneida Community, New York), 2 (Feb. 22, 1877), 60.

———. *Shaker Sermon*. "He is not Here." Mt. Lebanon, 1886. R 637.

Foster, Hannah Webster. *The Coquette; or, the History of Eliza Wharton*. 1797. Intro. Herbert Ross Brown. New York: Columbia University Press, 1939.

Franklin, Benjamin. *The Autobiography*. 1866. New York: Walter J. Black, 1941.

Fuller, Margaret. "Woman in the Nineteenth Century." 1844. *Heath Anthology of American Literature*, 2nd. ed. Vol. I. Ed. Paul Lauter. Lexington, MA: D. C. Heath, 1994. 1634–55.

The Gospel Monitor. A Little Book of Mother Ann's Word to Those Who are Placed as Instructors & Care-takers of Children; Written by Mother Lucy Wright, and Brought by Her to the Elders of the First Order, on the Holy Mount, March 1, 1841. Canterbury, New Hampshire: 1843.

Green, Calvin. *Biographical Account of the Life, Character, & Ministry of Father Joseph Meacham*. Rpt. from a manuscript copy of the 1827 manuscript, in *Shaker Quarterly* 10 (Spring 1970): 20–32; (Summer 1970): 51–68; (Fall 1970): 92–102.

[Green, Calvin, and Seth Y. Wells]. *A Summary View of the Millennial Church, or United Society of Believers*. Albany, NY: Packard & Van Benthuysen, 1823.

Green, Edith. "Facts and Gems." Manuscript. ca. 1898–1912. NhCa ms.

Hampton, Oliver C. "In Memoriam." Elder William Reynolds. 1881.

———. "Relation of Intellect and Emotion." *Manifesto* 10 (Oct. 1880).

Harper, Frances Ellen Watkins. "The Two Offers." 1859. *Heath Anthology of American Literature*, 2nd. Ed. Vol. I. Ed. Paul Lauter. Lexington, MA: D. C. Heath, 1994. 1973–1980.

Hollister, Alonzo G. "Calvin's Confession." 1904. R 780.

———. "Divine Motherhood." Mt. Lebanon, 1887. R 785.

———. "Heaven Annointed Woman." Mt. Lebanon, 1887. R 789.

———. "Prophesy Unseal'd." Mt. Lebanon, 1905. R 803.

———. "Reminiscences, by a Soldier of the Cross." Lebanon, NY, ms. OClWHi, X:B–31.

Holmes, John. "Short Diary of John Holmes' Work Activities. c. 1804. March 27, 1804–Oct. 19, 1805." MeSl ms.

Holmes, Lucy. "Church Journal Kept by Lucy Holmes, 1834–1850, New Gloucester, ME." MeSl ms.

Howells, William Dean. "A Shaker Village." *Atlantic Monthly* 37 (June 1876): 699–710.

———. *Three Villages*. Boston: J. B. Osgood, 1884.

Hunt, Harriot. *Glances and Glimpses*. Boston: J. P. Jewett & Co., 1856.

Jacobs, Harriet. *Incidents in the Life of a Slave Girl.* 1861. Ed. and intro. Walter Teller. New York: Harcourt Brace, 1973.

Johnson, Theodore E. "The 'Millennial Laws' of 1821." *Shaker Quarterly* 7, 2 (Summer 1967): 35–58.

Kempe, Margery. *The Book of Margery Kempe.* Trans. and intro. Barry Windeatt. New York: Penguin, 1994.

Kimball, Emeline. *Obituary Journal of Members of this Society since the opening of the Gospel AD 1792.* 3 Vols. NhCa ms. 759.

Lamson, David. *Two Years' Experience among the People Called Shakers.* West Boylston, MA: By the author, 1848.

Mather, Cotton. *Bonifacius; or To Do Good.* 1710. Gainesville, FL: Scholars' Facsimiles & Reprints, 1967.

McNemar, Richard. *The Kentucky Revival.* Cincinnati: John W. Browne, 1807.

[Meacham, Joseph]. *A Concise Statement of the Principles of the Only True Church According to the Gospel of the Present Appearance of Christ.* Bennington, VT: Haswell & Russell, 1790.

Meacham, Joseph. *Notes.* Copied by Rufus Bishop, 1850.

Mount Lebanon Cedar Boughs: Original Poems by the North Family of Shakers. Buffalo: Peter Paul Book Company, 1895.

Myrick, Susan. "The Physicians' Journal or an Account of the Sickness in the Society at Harvard." OClWHi, V: B-41.

Nordhoff, Charles. *Communistic Societies of the United States.* New York: Harper & Brothers, 1875.

Poetry and other writings at the time of Elder Job Bishop's Death. DeWint ms. 986.

Rathbun, Daniel. *Letter from Daniel Rathbun.* Springfield, MA: 1785.

Rathbun, Valentine. *An Account of the Matter, Form, and Manner of a New and Strange Religion.* Providence: Bennett Wheeler, 1781.

"Record of the Quantity of Fluid Drawn from Mary Jane Thurston who had a Tumor." OClWHi ms. V: B-5.

"Religious Services and Address of William L. Foster At the Consecration of Blossom Hill Cemetery, Concord, N.H., Friday, July 13, 1860." Concord: McFarland & Jenks, 1860.

Report of the Examination of the Shakers of Canterbury and Enfield, before the New Hampshire Legislature. Concord, NH: Ervin B. Tripp, 1849.

A Return of Departed Spirits of the Highest Characters of Distinctions, as well as the Indiscriminate of all Nations, into the Bodies of the "Shakers," or "United Society of Believers in the Second Advent of the Messiah." Philadelphia: J. R. Conlon, 1843. R 2618.

A Revelation of the Extraordinary Visitation of Departed Spirits of Distinguished Men and Women of All Nations. Philadelphia: L. G. Thomas, 1869. R 2619.

Rowlandson, Mary. *A Narrative of the Captivity and Restauration of Mrs. Mary Rowlandson. Heath Anthology of American Literature,* 2nd. ed. Vol. I. Ed. Paul Lauter. Lexington, MA: D. C. Heath, 1994. 343–66.

Rowson, Susanna. *Charlotte Temple.* 1794. Ed. Cathy Davidson. New York: Oxford University Press, 1986.

Sigourney, Lydia. *The Weeping Willow.* Hartford: Henry S. Parsons, 1847.

"Sketch of the Life and Experience of Issachar Bates." Ed., intro., and rpt. Theodore Johnson, *Shaker Quarterly* 1 (1961): 98–118, 145–63, and 2 (1962): 18–35.

Stewart, Philemon. "A General Statement of the Holy Laws of Zion." 1840. NhCa ms.

———. *Holy, Sacred and Divine Roll and Book.* Canterbury, NH: United Society, 1843.

Stowe, Harriet Beecher. *Uncle Tom's Cabin.* 1852. New York: Penguin, 1966.

Taylor, Amos. *A Narrative of the Strange Principles, Conduct and Character of the People Known by the Name of Shakers*. Worcester: For the author, 1782.

Taylor, Edward. *The Poems of Edward Taylor*. Ed. Donald E. Stanford. New Haven: Yale University Press, 1960.

Taylor, Leila Sarah, ed. *A Memorial to Eldress Anna White & Elder Daniel Offord*. Mt. Lebanon, 1912.

Testimonies Concerning the Character and Ministry of Mother Ann Lee and the First Witnesses of the Gospel of Christ's Second Appearing. Albany, NY: Packard and Van Benthuysen, 1827.

Testimonies Concerning the Life, Character, Revelations, and Doctrines of Our Ever Blessed Mother Ann Lee, and the Elders with Her. Hancock, MA: J. Talcott and J. Deming, Junrs., 1816.

Twain, Mark. *The Adventures of Huckleberry Finn*. 1884. Berkeley: University of California Press, 1988.

Warner, Susan. *The Wide, Wide World*. 1850. New York: Feminist Press, 1987.

Wells, Seth Young. "Remarks on Learning and the Use of Books." (Watervliet, NY, March 10, 1836). DeWint ms.

———. "Letter to the Elders, Deacons, Brethren & Sisters of the Society in Watervliet." (1832). DeWint ms.

Whitcher, John [et al.]. *A Brief History or Record of the Commencement & Progress, of the United Society of Believers, at Canterbury. County of Merrimack. and State of NH. By John Whitcher, A Member of Said Society*. Vol. I. 1782–1871. NhCa ms. 21.

[White, Anna], comp. *Affectionately Inscribed to the Memory of Eldress Antoinette Dolittle, 1887*. R 1434.

White, Anna, and Leila Taylor. *Shakerism: Its Meaning and Message*. Columbus, OH: Fred J. Heer, 1904.

Whitson, Robley, ed. *The Shakers: Two Centuries of Spiritual Reflection*. New York: Paulist Press, 1983.

Winkley, Francis [et al.]. *Journal, [Canterbury], 1784–1845*. NhCa ms. 25.

[Youngs, Benjamin Seth]. *The Testimony of Christ's Second Appearing*. Lebanon, OH: From the Press of John M'Clean, 1808.

SECONDARY SOURCES

Andrews, Edward Deming. *The Gift to Be Simple: Songs, Dances and Rituals of the American Shakers*. New York: Dover Publications, 1940.

———. *The People Called Shakers: A Search for the Perfect Society*. 1953. New York: Dover Publications, 1963.

Andrews, Edward Deming, and Faith Andrews. *Visions of the Heavenly Sphere: A Study in Shaker Religious Art*. Charlottesville: University Press of Virginia, 1969.

Andrews, William L. *Sisters of the Spirit: Three Black Women's Autobiographies of the Nineteenth Century*. Bloomington: Indiana University Press, 1986.

———. *To Tell a Free Story: The First Century of Afro-American Autobiography, 1760–1865*. Urbana: University of Illinois Press, 1986.

Backus, Margot Gayle. "Judy Grahn and the Lesbian Invocational Elegy: Testimonial and Prophetic Responses to Social Death in 'A Woman Is Talking to Death.'" *Signs: A Journal of Women in Culture and Society* (Summer 1993): 815–37.

Bainbridge, William Sims. "Shaker Demographics, 1840–1900: An Example of the Use of U. S. Census Enumeration Schedules." *Journal for the Scientific Study of Religion* 21 (December 1982): 352–65.

Bakhtin, M. M. *The Dialogic Imagination*. Ed. Michael Holquist. Trans. Caryl Emerson and Michael Holquist. Austin: University of Texas Press, 1981.

———. *Rabelais and His World*. Cambridge: Harvard University Press, 1968.

Barthes, Roland. *S/Z*. Trans. Richard Miller. New York: Hill and Wang, 1974.

Bassard, Katherine Clay. "Gender and Genre: Black Women's Autobiography and the Ideology of Literacy." *African American Review* 26, no. 1 (1992): 119–29.

———. "Spiritual Interrogations: Conversion, Community and Authorship in the Writings of Phillis Wheatley, Ann Plato, Jarena Lee, and Rebecca Cox Jackson." Diss., Rutgers University, 1992.

Bauman, Richard. *Let Your Words Be Few: Symbolism of Speaking and Silence among Seventeenth-Century Quakers*. New York: Cambridge University Press, 1983.

Baym, Nina. "Reinventing Lydia Sigourney." In *Feminism and American Literary History: Essays*. Ed. Nina Baym. New Brunswick, NJ: Rutgers University Press, 1992. 151–66.

———. *Woman's Fiction: A Guide to Novels by and about Women in America, 1820–70*. 2nd ed. Urbana: University of Illinois Press, 1993.

Belenky, Mary Field, et al. *Women's Ways of Knowing: The Development of Self, Voice, and Mind*. New York: Basic Books, 1986.

Boone, Joseph Allen. *Tradition Counter Tradition: Love and the Form of Fiction*. Chicago: University of Chicago Press, 1987.

Braxton, Joanne. *Black Women Writing Autobiography: A Tradition within a Tradition*. Philadelphia: Temple University Press, 1989.

Brewer, Priscilla J. *Shaker Communities, Shaker Lives*. Hanover: University Press of New England, 1986.

———. "'Tho' of the Weaker Sex': A Reassessment of Gender Equality among the Shakers." *Signs: A Journal of Women in Culture and Society* 17 (Spring 1992): 609–35.

Brodhead, Richard H. *Cultures of Letters: Scenes of Reading and Writing in Nineteenth-Century America*. Chicago: University of Chicago Press, 1993.

Bruner, Jerome. *Actual Minds, Possible Worlds*. Cambridge: Harvard University Press, 1986.

Buell, Lawrence. *New England Literary Culture: From Revolution through Renaissance*. New York: Cambridge University Press, 1986.

Buzard, James. "A Continent of Pictures: Reflections on the 'Europe' of Nineteenth-Century Tourists." *PMLA* 108 (Jan. 1993): 30–44.

Bynum, Caroline Walker. *Holy Feast and Holy Fast: The Religious Significance of Food to Medieval Women*. Berkeley: University of California Press, 1987.

Bynum, Caroline Walker, Stevan Harrell, and Paula Richman, eds. *Gender and Religion: On the Complexity of Symbols*. Boston: Beacon Press, 1986.

Caldwell, Patricia. "The Antinomian Language Controversy." *Harvard Theological Review* 69, nos. 3–4 (July–Oct. 1976): 345–67.

Calloway, Colin. *North Country Captives: Selected Narratives of Indian Captivity from Vermont and New Hampshire*. Hanover: University Press of New England, 1992.

Carby, Hazel. *Reconstructing Womanhood: The Emergence of the Afro-American Woman Novelist*. New York: Oxford University Press, 1987.

Chiseri-Strater, Elizabeth. *Academic Literacies: The Public & Private Discourse of University Students*. Portsmouth, NH: Boynton Cook, 1991.

Chodorow, Nancy. *Feminism and Psychoanalytic Theory*. New Haven: Yale University Press, 1989.

———. *The Reproduction of Mothering: Psychoanalysis and the Sociology of Gender*. Berkeley: University of California Press, 1978.

Christian, Barbara. *Black Women Novelists: The Development of a Tradition, 1892–1976.* Westport, CT: Greenwood Press, 1980.

Coffin, Margaret M. *Death in Early America.* New York: Elsevier/Nelson Books, 1976.

Connerton, Paul. *How Societies Remember.* New York: Cambridge University Press, 1989.

Cope, Jackson I. "Seventeenth Century Quaker Style." *PMLA* 76:725–54.

Cott, Nancy F. *The Bonds of Womanhood: "Woman's Sphere" in New England, 1780–1835.* New Haven: Yale University Press, 1977.

———. "Passionlessness: An Interpretation of Victorian Sexual Ideology." *Signs: A Journal of Women in Culture and Society* 4 (1978): 219–36.

Crosthwaite, Jane F. "'A White and Seamless Robe': Celibacy and Equality in Shaker Art and Theology." *Colby Library Quarterly* 25, no. 3 (September 1989): 188–98.

Darnton, Robert. *The Great Cat Massacre and Other Episodes in French Cultural History.* New York: Basic Books, 1984.

Davidson, Cathy N. *Revolution and the Word: The Rise of the Novel in America.* New York: Oxford University Press, 1986.

Davidson, James West. *The Logic of Millennial Thought: Eighteenth-Century New England.* New Haven: Yale University Press, 1977.

Deignan, Kathleen. *Christ Spirit: The Eschatology of Shaker Christianity.* Metuchen, NJ: American Theological Library Association, 1992.

Desroche, Henri. *The American Shakers: From Neo-Christianity to Presocialism.* Trans. John K. Savacool. Amherst, MA: University of Massachusetts Press, 1971.

DeWolfe, Elizabeth. "'Erroneous Principles, Base Deceptions, and Pious Frauds': Anti-Shaker Writing, Mary Marshall Dyer, and the Public Theater of Apostasy." Diss., Boston University, 1996.

Dictionary of American Religious Biography. Ed. Henry W. Bowden. Westport, CT: Greenwood Press, 1977.

Dorsey, Peter A. *Sacred Estrangement: The Rhetoric of Conversion in Modern American Autobiography.* University Park: Pennsylvania State University Press, 1993.

Douglas, Ann. *The Feminization of American Culture.* New York: Knopf, 1977.

———. "Heaven Our Home: Consolation Literature in the Northern United States, 1830–1880." *Death in America.* Ed. David E. Stannard. University of Pennsylvania Press, 1975. 49–68.

Douglas, Mary. *Implicit Meanings: Essays in Anthropology.* Boston: Routledge & Keegan Paul, 1978.

Emlen, Robert P. *Shaker Village Views: Illustrated Maps and Landscape Drawings by Shaker Artists of the Nineteenth Century.* Hanover, NH: University Press of New England, 1987.

Fetterly, Judith. *The Resisting Reader: A Feminist Approach to American Fiction.* Bloomington: Indiana University Press, 1978.

Fishman, Andrea. *Amish Literacy: What and How It Means.* Portsmouth, NH: Heinemann, 1986.

Forcey, Blythe. "Charlotte Temple and the End of Epistolarity." *American Literature* 63 (June 1991): 225–41.

Foster, Frances Smith. *Written by Herself: Literary Production by African American Women, 1746–1892.* Bloomington: Indiana University Press, 1993.

Foster, Lawrence. *Religion and Sexuality: The Shakers, the Mormons and the Oneida Community.* Urbana: University of Illinois Press, 1984.

———. *Women, Family, and Utopia: Communal Experiments of the Shakers, the Oneida Community, and the Mormons.* Syracuse: Syracuse University Press, 1991.

Foucault, Michel. *The History of Sexuality: An Introduction. Vol. I. 1976.* Trans. Robert French Hurley. 1978. New York: Random House, 1990.

Fox-Genovese, Elizabeth. *Within the Plantation Household: Black and White Women of the Old South.* Chapel Hill: University of North Carolina Press, 1988.

Frederickson, George M. *The Black Image in the White Mind: The Debate on Afro-American Character and Destiny, 1817–1914.* New York: Harper and Row, 1971.

Garrett, Clarke. *Spirit Possession and Popular Religion: From the Camisards to the Shakers.* Baltimore: Johns Hopkins University Press, 1989.

Gates, Henry Louis, Jr. *Figures in Black: Words, Signs, and the "Racial" Self.* New York: Oxford University Press, 1987.

———. "Introduction." *"Race," Writing and Difference.* Ed. Henry Louis Gates, Jr. Chicago: University of Chicago Press, 1986.

———. *The Signifying Monkey: A Theory of Afro-American Literary Criticism.* New York: Oxford University Press, 1988.

Gee, James Paul. *Social Linguistics and Literacies: Ideology in Discourses.* New York: Falmer Press, 1990.

Geertz, Clifford. *The Interpretation of Cultures: Selected Essays.* New York: Basic Books, 1973.

Gilmore, William J. *Reading Becomes a Necessity of Life: Material and Cultural Life in Rural New England, 1780–1835.* Knoxville: University of Tennessee Press, 1989.

Glenn, Cheryl. "Author, Audience, and Autobiography: Rhetorical Technique in *The Book of Margery Kempe.*" *College English* 54 (1992): 540–53.

Gooden, Rosemary. "The Language of Devotion: Gospel Affection and Gospel Union in the Writings of Shaker Sisters." Diss., University of Michigan, 1987.

Graff, Harvey J. *The Literacy Myth: Literacy and Social Structure in the Nineteenth Century City.* New York: Academic Press, 1979.

Hall, David D., ed. *The Antinomian Controversy, 1636–1638: A Documentary History.* Middletown, CT: Wesleyan University, 1968.

———. *Worlds of Wonder, Days of Judgment: Popular Religious Belief in Early New England.* Cambridge, MA: Harvard University Press, 1990.

Hambrick-Stowe, Charles E. *The Practice of Piety: Puritan Devotional Disciplines in Seventeenth-Century New England.* Chapel Hill: University of North Carolina Press, 1982.

Harpham, Geoffrey. "Conversion and the Language of Autobiography." *Studies in Autobiography.* Ed. James Olney. New York: Oxford University Press, 1988. 42–50.

Harris, Sharon. "Mary White Rowlandson, 1637?–1711." *Heath Anthology of American Literature.* 2nd. ed. Vol. I. Ed. Paul Lauter et al. Lexington, MA: D. C. Heath, 1994. 340–42.

Holifield, E. Brooks. *The Covenant Sealed: The Development of Puritan Sacramental Theology in Old and New England, 1570–1720.* New Haven: Yale University Press, 1974.

Humez, Jean McMahon, ed. *Gifts of Power: The Writings of Rebecca Jackson, Black Visionary, Shaker Eldress.* Boston: University of Massachusetts Press, 1981.

———. *Mother's First-Born Daughters: Early Shaker Writings on Women and Religion.* Bloomington: Indiana University Press, 1993.

———. Weary of Petticoat Government: The Specter of Female Rule in Early Nineteenth-Century Shaker Politics." *Communal Societies* 11 (Spring 1992): 1–17.

———. "'A Woman Mighty to Pull You Down': Married Women's Rights and Female Anger in the Anti-Shaker Narratives of Eunice Chapman and Mary Marshall Dyer." *Journal of Women's History* 6, no. 2 (Summer 1994): 90–110.

————. "'Ye Are My Epistles': The Construction of Ann Lee Imagery in Early Shaker Sacred Literature." *Journal of Feminist Studies in Religion* (Spring 1992): 83–103.

Johnsen, Norma. "'Our Children Who Are in Heaven': Consolation Themes in a Nineteenth-Century Connecticut Journal." *Connecticut Historical Society* 51 (Spring 1986): 77–101.

Jones, Jacqueline. *Labor of Love, Labor of Sorrow: Black Women, Work, and the Family from Slavery to the Present*. New York: Basic Books, 1985.

Juster, Susan. "To Slay the Beast: Visionary Women in the Early Republic." *A Mighty Baptism: Race, Gender, and the Creation of American Protestantism*. Ed. Susan Juster and Lisa MacFarlane. Ithaca: Cornell University Press, 1996. 19–37.

Kamensky, Jane. "Governing the Tongue: Speech and Society in Early New England." Diss., Yale University, 1993.

Karlsen, Carol F. *The Devil in the Shape of a Woman: Witchcraft in Colonial New England*. New York: Norton, 1987.

Kasson, Joy S. "Narratives of the Female Body: The Greek Slave." *The Culture of Sentiment: Race, Gender and Sentimentality in Nineteenth Century America*. Ed. Shirley Samuels. Oxford: Oxford University Press, 1992. 172–90.

Kern, Louis J. *An Ordered Love: Sex Roles and Sexuality in Victorian Utopias—The Shakers, the Mormons, and the Oneida Community*. Chapel Hill: University of North Carolina Press, 1981.

Kibbey, Ann. *The Interpretation of Material Shapes in Puritanism: A Study of Rhetoric, Prejudice, and Violence*. New York: Cambridge University Press, 1986.

Kitch, Sally L. *Chaste Liberation: Celibacy and Female Cultural Status*. Urbana: University of Illinois Press, 1989.

Lacan, Jacques. *Feminine Sexuality*. Ed. Jacqueline Rose and Juliet Mitchell. Trans. Jacqueline Rose. New York: Norton, 1985.

————. "Seminar on 'The Purloined Letter.'" *Yale French Studies* 48 (1972): 38–72.

LaPrade, Candis A. "Pens in the Hand of God: The Spiritual Autobiographies of Jarena Lee, Zilpha Elaw, and Rebecca Cox Jackson." Diss., University of North Carolina, 1994.

Leyda, Jay. *The Years and Hours of Emily Dickinson*. New Haven: Yale University Press, 1960.

Lowance, Mason I., Jr. *The Language of Canaan: Metaphor and Symbol in New England from the Puritans to the Transcendentalists*. Cambridge: Harvard University Press, 1980.

Lyford, James O., ed. *History of Concord, New Hampshire*. Vol. I. Concord: Rumford Press, 1903.

MacCannell, Dean. *The Tourist: A New Theory of the Leisure Class*. New York: Schocken Books, 1976.

MacCormack, Carol. "Nature, Culture and Gender: A Critique." *Nature, Culture and Gender*. Carol MacCormack and Marilyn Strathern. Cambridge: Cambridge University Press, 1980. 1–24.

Mack, Phyllis. *Visionary Women: Ecstatic Prophecy in Seventeenth-Century England*. Berkeley: University of California Press, 1992.

MacLean, John P. *A Bibliography of Shaker Literature*. Columbus, OH: Fred J. Heer, 1905.

Madden, Etta. "Reading, Writing, and the Race of Mother Figures: Shakers Rebecca Cox Jackson and Alonzo Giles Hollister." *A Mighty Baptism: Race, Gender, and the Creation of American Protestantism*. Ed. Susan Juster and Lisa MacFarlane. Ithaca, NY: Cornell University Press, 1996. 210–34.

————. "Resurrecting Life through Rhetorical Ritual: A Buried Value of the Puritan Funeral Sermon." *Early American Literature* 26 (1991): 232–50.

Marini, Stephen A. *Radical Sects of Revolutionary New England.* Cambridge, MA: Harvard University Press, 1982.

Matarese, Susan, and Paul Salmon. "Assessing Psychopathology in Communal Societies." *Communal Societies* (1995): 25–54.

McCully, Susan. "Oh I Love Mother, I Love Her Power: Shaker Spirit Possession and the Performance of Desire." *Theatre Survey* 35 (May 1994): 88–99.

McKay, Nellie. "Nineteenth Century Black Women's Spiritual Autobiographies: Religious Faith and Self-Empowerment." *Interpreting Women's Lives: Feminist Theory and Personal Narratives.* Bloomington: Indiana University Press, 1989. 139–54.

McKinstry, E. Richard, comp. *The Edward Deming Andrews Memorial Shaker Collection.* New York: Garland Publishing, 1987.

McLoughlin, William G. *Isaac Backus and the American Pietistic Tradition.* Boston: Little, Brown and Company, 1967.

Mercadante, Linda A. *Gender, Doctrine, and God: The Shakers and Contemporary Theology.* Nashville: Abingdon Press, 1990.

Miller, Perry. *The New England Mind: From Colony to Province.* Cambridge: Harvard University Press, 1953.

Mitford, Jessica. *The American Way of Death.* New York: Simon and Schuster, 1963.

Morley, John. *Death, Heaven and the Victorians.* Pittsburgh: University of Pittsburgh Press, 1971.

Morse, Flo. *The Shakers and the World's People.* Hanover, NH: University Press of New England, 1987.

Muller, Charles R., and Timothy D. Rieman. *The Shaker Chair.* Canal Winchester, OH: Canal Press, 1984.

Murray, John E. "Determinants of Membership Levels and Duration in a Shaker Commune, 1780–1880." *Journal for the Scientific Study of Religion* 34 (1995): 35–48.

———. "Human Capital in Religious Communes: Literacy and Selection of Nineteenth Century Shakers." *Explorations in Economic History* 32 (1995): 217–35.

Namias, June. *White Captives: Gender and Ethnicity on the American Frontier.* Chapel Hill: University of North Carolina Press, 1993.

Neal, Julia. *By Their Fruits: The Story of Shakerism in South Union Kentucky.* Chapel Hill: University of North Carolina Press, 1947.

Newkirk, Thomas, and Patricia McLure. *Listening In: Children Talk about Books (& Other Things).* Portsmouth, NH: Heinemann, 1992.

Niemtzow, Annette. "The Problematic of Self in Autobiography: The Example of the Slave Narrative." *The Art of the Slave Narrative: Original Essays in Criticism and Theory.* Ed. John Sekora and Darwin Turner. Macomb, IL: Western Illinois University Press, 1982. 96–109.

Nissenbaum, Stephen. *Sex, Diet, and Debility in Jacksonian America.* Westport, CT: Greenwood Press, 1980.

Olson, Kathryn M. "The Role of Dissociation in Redeeming Knowledge Claims: Nineteenth-Century Shakers Epistemological Resistance to Decline." *Philosophy and Rhetoric* 28 (1995): 45–68.

Ong, Walter J. *Orality and Literacy: The Technologizing of the Word.* New York: Methuen, 1982.

———."The Writer's Audience Is Always a Fiction." *PMLA* 90 (January 1975): 9–21.

Orsi, Robert A. "'He Keeps Me Going': Women's Devotion to Saint Jude Thaddeus and the Dialectics of Gender in American Catholicism, 1929–1965." *Belief in History: Innovative Approaches to European and American Religion.* Ed. Thomas Kselman. South Bend, IN: University of Notre Dame Press. 137–69.

Ortner, Sherry B. "Is Female to Male as Nature Is to Culture?" Ed. Michelle Zimbalist
    Rosaldo and Louise Lamphere. In *Woman, Culture and Society*. Stanford, CA: Stanford
    University Press, 1974, 667–87.
Ortner, Sherry B., and Harriet Whitehead, eds. *Sexual Meanings: The Cultural Construction
    of Gender and Sexuality*. Cambridge: Cambridge University Press, 1981.
Pagels, Elaine. *Adam, Eve, and the Serpent*. New York: Random House, 1988.
––––––. *The Gnostic Gospels*. New York: Random House, 1979.
Patterson, Daniel W. *The Shaker Spiritual*. Princeton, NJ: Princeton University Press, 1979.
Pike, Martha V., and Janice Gray Armstrong, eds. *A Time to Mourn: Expressions of Grief
    in Nineteenth Century America*. Stony Brook, NY: The Museums at Stony Brook,
    1980.
Porter, Dennis. *Haunted Journeys: Desire and Transgression in European Travel Writing*.
    Princeton: Princeton University Press, 1991.
Proctor-Smith, Marjorie. "'Who Do You Say That I Am?' Mother Ann as Christ." *Locating
    the Shakers: Cultural Origins and Legacies of an American Religious Movement*. Ed.
    Mick Gidley. Exeter: University of Exeter Press, 1990. 91–93.
––––––. *Women in Shaker Community and Worship: A Feminist Analysis of the Uses of
    Religious Symbolism*. Lewiston, NY: Edwin Mellen Press, 1985.
Promey, Sally M. *Spiritual Spectacles: Vision and Image in Mid-nineteenth-century
    Shakerism*. Bloomington: Indiana University Press, 1993.
Ramazani, Jahan. "'Daddy, I Have Had to Kill You': Plath, Rage, and the Modern Elegy."
    PMLA 108 (Oct. 1993): 1142–56.
Reynolds, David S. *Beneath the American Renaissance: The Subversive Imagination in the
    Age of Emerson and Melville*. Cambridge, MA: Harvard University Press, 1988.
Richmond, Mary L., comp. *Shaker Literature: A Bibliography*. 2 Vols. Hanover, NH:
    University Press of New England, 1977.
Rotundo, Barbara. "Crossing the Dark River: Shaker Funerals and Cemeteries." *Communal
    Societies* 7 (1987): 36–46.
Sacks, Peter. *The English Elegy: Studies in the Genre from Spenser to Yeats*. Baltimore:
    Johns Hopkins University Press, 1985.
St. Armand, Barton Levi. *Emily Dickinson and Her Culture: The Soul's Society*. New York:
    Cambridge University Press, 1984.
St. George, Robert. "'Heated' Speech and Literacy in Seventeenth-Century New England."
    Publications of the Colonial Society of Massachusetts. 63 (1984): 275–322.
Sanchez-Eppler, Karen. "Bodily Bonds: The Intersecting Rhetorics of Feminism and
    Abolition." *The Culture of Sentiment: Race, Gender and Sentimentality in Nineteenth
    Century America*. Ed. Shirley Samuels. Oxford: Oxford University Press, 1992.
Sasson, Diane. "A 19th Century Case Study; Alonzo Giles Hollister (1830–1911)." *Shaker
    Quarterly* 17 (Winter 1989): 154–72; 188–93.
––––––. "Individual Experience, Community Control, and Gender: The Harvard Shaker
    Community during the Era of Manifestations." *Communal Societies* 13 (1993): 45–70.
––––––. *The Shaker Spiritual Narrative*. Knoxville: University of Tennessee Press, 1983.
Schenck, Celeste M. "Feminism and Deconstruction: Reconstructing the Elegy." *Tulsa
    Studies in Women's Literature* 5 (Spring 1986): 13–27.
Scribner, Sylvia, and Michael Cole. *The Psychology of Literacy*. Cambridge, MA: Harvard
    University Press, 1981.
Sears, John F. *Sacred Places: American Tourist Attractions in the Nineteenth Century*. New
    York: Oxford University Press, 1989.
Shaw, Peter. *American Patriots and the Rituals of Revolution*. Cambridge, MA: Harvard
    University Press, 1981.

Simonds, Wendy, and Barbara Katz Rothman. *Centuries of Solace: Expressions of Maternal Grief in Popular Literature*. Philadelphia: Temple University Press, 1992.

Smith, David E. *John Bunyan in America*. Bloomington: Indiana University Press, 1966.

Smith, Valerie. *Self-Discovery and Authority in Afro-American Narrative*. Cambridge, MA: Harvard University Press, 1987.

Smith-Rosenberg, Carroll. "Discourses of Sexuality and Subjectivity: The New Woman, 1870–1936." *Hidden from History: Reclaiming the Gay and Lesbian Past*. Ed. Martin Bauml Duberman, Martha Vicinus, and George Chauncey, Jr. New York: New American Library, 1989. 264–80.

Spufford, Margaret. *Small Books and Pleasant Histories: Popular Fiction and Its Readership in Seventeenth-Century England*. Cambridge: Cambridge University Press, 1981.

Stannard, David E., ed. *Death in America*. University of Pennsylvania Press, 1975.

Stein, Stephen J., ed. *Letters from a Young Shaker: William S. Byrd at Pleasant Hill*. Lexington: University of Kentucky Press, 1985.

———. *The Shaker Experience in America: A History of the United Society of Believers*. New Haven: Yale University Press, 1992.

Stepto, Robert B. *From behind the Veil*. Urbana: University of Illinois Press, 1979.

———. "Narration, Authentication, and Authorial Control in Frederick Douglass's *Narrative of 1845*." *Afro-American Literature: The Reconstruction of Instruction*. Ed. Dexter Fisher and Robert Stepto. New York: MLA, 1979. 178–91.

Swain, Thomas. "The Evolving Expressions of the Religious and Theological Experiences of a Community: A Comparative Study of the Shaker Testimonies Concerning the Sayings of Mother Ann Lee; An Exploration of the Development from Oral Traditions to Written Forms as Preserved in Four Documents." *Shaker Quarterly* 12 (Spring 1972): 3–31; (Summer 1972): 43–67.

Taylor, Frank G. "An Analysis of Shaker Education: The Life and Death of an Alternative Educational System, 1774–1950." Diss., University of Connecticut, 1976.

Thurman, Suzanne. "The Order of Nature, the Order of Grace: Community Formation, Female Status, and Relations with the World in the Shaker Villages of Harvard and Shirley, Massachusetts, 1781–1875." Diss., Indiana University, 1994.

Tompkins, Jane. *Sensational Designs: The Cultural Work of American Fiction, 1790–1860*. New York: Oxford University Press, 1985.

Toulouse, Teresa. *The Art of Prophesying: New England Sermons and the Shaping of Belief*. Athens: University of Georgia Press, 1987.

Turner, Victor. *The Ritual Process: Structure and Anti-Structure*. 1969. Ithaca, NY: Cornell University Press, 1989.

Ulrich, Laurel Thatcher. *Good Wives: Image and Reality in the Lives of Women in Northern New England, 1650–1750*. New York: Oxford University Press, 1980.

———. "'Vertuous Women Found': New England Ministerial Literature, 1668–1735." *American Quarterly* 28 (1976): 20–40.

Urry, John. *The Tourist Gaze: Leisure and Travel in Contemporary Societies*. London: Sage Publications, 1990.

Van Sant, Ann Jessie. *Eighteenth-Century Sensibility and the Novel: The Senses in Social Context*. Cambridge: Cambridge University Press, 1993.

Vygotsky, L. S. *Mind in Society: The Development of Higher Psychological Processes*. Ed. Michael Cole et al. Cambridge, MA: Harvard University Press, 1978.

Walker, Alice. "Gifts of Power: The Writings of Rebecca Jackson." *In Search of Our Mothers' Gardens*. New York: Harcourt-Brace, 1983. 71–82.

Welter, Barbara. "The Cult of True Womanhood, 1820–1840." *American Quarterly* 18 (1966): 151–74.

Wergland, Glendyne R. "Lust, 'A Snare of Satan to Beguile the Soul': New Light on Shaker Celibacy." *Communal Societies* 15 (1995): 1–23.

Williams, Richard E. *Called and Chosen: The Story of Mother Rebecca Jackson and the Philadelphia Shakers*. Metuchen, NJ: Scarecrow, 1981.

Woolf, Cynthia Griffin. *Emily Dickinson*. New York: Knopf, 1986.

Yellin, Jean Fagan. "Texts and Contexts of Harriet Jacobs' Incidents in the Life of a Slave Girl: Written by Herself." *The Slave's Narrative*. Ed. Charles T. Davis and Henry Louis Gates, Jr. New York: Oxford University Press, 1985. 262–78.

Ziff, Larzer. *Writing in the New Nation: Prose, Print, and Politics in the Early United States*. New Haven: Yale University Press, 1991.

Index

Acton, Mary, 149
African-Americans, 104. *See also* Jackson, Rebecca Cox; Race
African Methodist Episcopal (AME) church, 12, 97, 100
Alcott, Louisa May, 76
Allen, Catherine, 122 n.24
American Indians, missionary work among, 67
Andrews, Edward Deming, 46, 168
Andrews, William L., 97
Androgyny, in Shaker theology, 38, 44–45, 72
Antinomian Controversy (1637), 64
Apostates, writings of, 11, 12, 16, 18–19, 23, 26, 40, 41, 48, 61, 80–82, 90, 135
Arts, and sciences, 21, 23, 24. *See also* Literary genres
Asceticism, 42
Ashbridge, Elizabeth, 89, 92 n.16
Ashfield, Massachusetts, 36

Backus, Isaac, 36
Backus, Margot Gayle, 139
Bacon, Nancy, 147
Bahktin, M. M., 60
Barthes, Roland, 8
Bassard, Katherine Clay, 97, 98, 108
Bates, Issachar, 57
Bates, Paulina, and Rebecca Cox Jackson, 98, 101–103, 108, 111

Bauman, Richard, 66, 78, 79
Baym, Nina, 75, 142
Beck, Clement, 19–20, 26
Beck, John, 130
Beedee, Hannah, 21
Believers. *See* Shakers
Bible: read by Shakers, 21; authority of, for Jackson, 100. *See also* Scripture; Scripture references
Bishop, Job, 128, 130–133
Bishop, Mercy, 37, 38
Bishop, Rufus, 71–72
Blinn, Henry C., 26, 125, 135, 136, 151
Bodies (human): images of, in Concise Statement..., 45; and Millennial Laws, 34, 45, 46; mortification of, 43; and performative metaphor (nakedness), 78–82; in resurrection theology, 38–39, 128, 139; Shaker views about, 5, 8, 17, 18, 28, 128–133; and spirituality, 45, 165; as uninscribed texts, 36–51, 59, 66–68, 78–82
Bodily codes: and discernment, 35–37, 96, 99, 106; and doctrine, 51, 56 n.33, 60; nakedness, 78–82; reading of, 40, 42, 46–47, 78–82; ritual of, and Shaker literacies, 51, 71–92
Boone, Joseph Allen, 75, 90
Braxton, Joanne, 97
Brewer, Priscilla, 126, 162
Briggs, Nicholas, 11, 12, 23, 26, 48, 135

attitudes to, 165–166; and Shaker literatures, 8, 13, 58–59; and unified dichotomies, 44–45, 49, 55 n.27; varieties of, in *Obituary Journal,* 126. *See also* Gifts

Spiritual literacies, 33–51. *See also* Literacy/Literacies

Stein, Stephen J., 13, 46–47, 50, 57, 126, 162

Stewart, Philemon, 24, 98, 101, 103

Stickney, Asenath , 145, 146, 149

Stone, Barton W., 57, 61–62, 69 n.7

Stowe, Harriet Beecher, 76, 153

Suffering: of Ann Lee, 85–86, 106; of Rebecca Cox Jackson, 106

Suicide, among Shakers, 151–153

Swain, Thomas, 72–73

Symbiosis, of body and spirit, 45

Symbols: grave markers, 128; and imagination, 96

Taylor, Amos, 79

Taylor, Frank, 22, 29 n.3

Taylor, Leila, *Shakerism: Its Meaning and Message,* 2, 7, 12, 27, 28, 161–168

Testimonies Concerning the Character and Ministry of Mother Ann Lee ..., (1816), 6, 17, 33, 34–35, 39, 42, 50, 51, 71–92, 108; (1827), 14

Textual analysis. *See* Literary analysis

Thayer, Cornelius, 78

Theology. *See* Doctrine(s)

Tiffany, Mary, 37

Tompkins, Jane, 13, 75

Travel, 118–119, 123 n.33

Tucker, Micajah, 131

Turtle Creek, Ohio, 57

Twain, Mark, 26–27, 32 n.28, 128

Union Village, Ohio, community, 11, 22

United Society of Believers in Christ's Second Appearing. *See* Shakers

Van Sant, Ann Jessie, 75

Violence: and nakedness, 81–82; and persecution, 87–89

Visions/Dreams: by Ann Lee, 36, 53 n.8; of deceased spirits, 122 n. 23; and discernment, 35–37, 99–100, 103–113; millennial, 36, 53 n.8; by Rebecca Cox

Jackson, 97, 101, 103–113; as uninscribed texts, 36, 98–103; of violence, 110–112. *See also* Imagery

Vygotsky, Lev, 101

Walker, Alice, 97

Walton, Hattie, 117

Wardley, John and Jane, 69 n.14

Warner, Susan, 99, 103

Watervliet, New York, community, 21, 37, 95, 97–98, 110–112, 116, 137

Weber, Max, 46

Webster, Daniel, 145

Webster, Noah, anti-fiction campaign, 15

Wells, Seth Young, 9 n.1, 15, 21, 71–72, 165; "Letter to the Elders, Deacons ... at Watervliet," 22; "Remarks on Learning and the Use of Books," 22

Wesley, Charles, 38

Western Reserve Historical Society Shaker Collection, 123 n.27

Wheaton, Noah, 80

Whitaker, James, 11, 17, 43

Whitcher, Benjamin, 131

Whitcher, John, 130–131, 152

Whitcher, Mary, 148

Whitcher, Susan, 150

White, Anna, *Shakerism: Meaning and Message,* 2, 7, 12, 27, 28, 161–168

Whitefield, George, 38, 53 n.13

Whitney, Abram, 114

Whitson, Robley, 5

Whittaker, James, 72

Wiles, Elijah, 130

Wilson, Delmer, 168

Wilson, Mary, 148

Wilson, S. F., 152

Winkley, Francis, 129–130, 145, 148

Wisdom's Valley. *See* Watervliet, New York

Women. *See* Femininity

Works and authors read by Shakers: *Agriculture Improved* (Norton), 26; *An American Reader,* 26; *Arithmetic* (Jackson), 21; Bible, 21; *Boston Weekly Journal,* 12; Brett Harte, 26; *Easy Lessons,* 21; *Grammar,* (Ingersoll), 21; Harriet Beecher Stowe, 153; Henry Wordsworth Longfellow, 153; *Life Illustrated,* 26, 135; *Life of*

About the Author

ETTA M. MADDEN is Assistant Professor of English at Southwest Missouri State University. She teaches courses in early American literature, from the age of European exploration to the Civil War, as well as courses on autobiographies, essays, and other prose nonfiction. Her interest in literature and culture has centered on religious writing and is beginning to encompass the literature of science.

ISBN 0-313-30303-7

90000>

EAN

9 780313 303036

HARDCOVER BAR CODE